JOURNEY
TO
THE NORTH OF INDIA

JOURNEY
TO
THE NORTH OF INDIA,

OVERLAND FROM ENGLAND,

THROUGH RUSSIA, PERSIA, AND AFFGHAUNISTAUN.

BY
LIEUT. ARTHUR CONOLLY.

IN TWO VOLUMES.

VOL. II

SECOND EDITION, REVISED

GYAN

Published by

Gyan Publishing House
5, Ansari Road
Daryaganj, New Delhi-110002
Phone: 011-47034999, 9811692060
E-mail: books@gyanbooks.com

Distribution Network
gyanbooks.com
India, USA, Canada, UK, Australia, France

ISBN : 978-81-212-3656-0 (Set)
ISBN : 978-81-212-4888-4 (HB)
First Published, 1838

2nd Impression 2020

Printed at: Gyan Press, Delhi.

Journey to The North of India
Author: Lieut Arthur Conolly

JOURNEY

TO

THE NORTH OF INDIA,

OVERLAND FROM ENGLAND,

THROUGH RUSSIA, PERSIA, AND AFFGHAUNISTAUN.

BY LIEUT. ARTHUR CONOLLY.

IN TWO VOLUMES.

VOL. II.

SECOND EDITION, REVISED.

LONDON:

RICHARD BENTLEY, NEW BURLINGTON STREET,

Publisher in Ordinary to Her Majesty.

1838.

AFFGHAUN NATIONAL DANCE

CONTENTS

OF

THE SECOND VOLUME.

CHAPTER I.

CHAPTER II.

CHAPTER III.

CHAPTER IV.

CHAPTER V.

CHAPTER VI.

CHAPTER VII.

CHAPTER VIII.

CHAPTER IX.

CHAPTER X.

CHAPTER XI.

NARRATIVE

OF AN

OVERLAND JOURNEY

TO THE

NORTH OF INDIA.

CHAPTER I.

Heraut and its environs—Climate—Divisions of the province—Agricultural produce—Government assessments and general receipts—Commerce—Political condition of Affghaunistaun—Character and prospects of Shah Kamraun.

HERAUT is a well-fortified town, three quarters of a mile square, comprising four thousand dwelling-houses, twelve hundred shops, seventeen caravanseras, and twenty baths, besides many mosques, and fine public reservoirs of water. It contains about forty-five thousand* inhabitants, the majority of

* When we first inquired about the population of Heraut, the inhabitants told us that there were twelve thousand houses within the walls; but our host, who was the calenter of the city, said that only four thousand "*house doors*" were registered in the Shah's books. At the high computation of ten persons to each house, we have only forty thousand souls, but one entrance may lead to more than one domicile,

whom are Sheahs; and there may be one thousand Hindoos settled there, and forty families of Jews. The outside wall is thickly built upon a solid mound formed by the earth of a wet ditch, which, filled by springs within itself, goes entirely round the city. There are five gates, defended each by a small outwork, and on the north side is a strong citadel, also surrounded by a wet ditch, which overlooks the town.

The interior of Heraut is divided into quarters, by four long bazaars covered with arched brick, which meet in a small domed quadrangle in the centre of the city. The town itself is, I should imagine, one of the dirtiest in the world. Many of the small streets, which branch from the main ones, are built over, and form low dark tunnels, containing every offensive thing. No drains having been contrived to carry off the rain which falls within the walls, it collects and stagnates in ponds which are dug in different parts of the city. The residents cast out the refuse of their houses into the streets, and dead cats and dogs are commonly seen lying upon heaps of the vilest filth. In a street which we were obliged to

and I think that, considering this, and taking into account the inmates of the citadel and palace, those who reside in seventeen large caravanseras, and in some of the shops, the residents may altogether be rated at the round number of forty-five thousand. Captain Christie estimated the population of Heraut at one hundred thousand souls: either I conceive that officer was misled by the statements of the inhabitants, or he took into account some quarters outside the walls, which were destroyed when the city was besieged by the Candahar Sirdars, I think in 1824.

pass through to get at the bazaar, lay for many days a dead horse, surrounded by bloated dogs, and poisoning the neighbourhood with its unwholesome effluvia. More could be said about the bestiality of the citizens, but as it is not a choice theme, I will not enlarge upon it. "*Rusm ust,*"—"It is the custom," was the only apology I heard even from those who admitted the evil: my wonder was how they could live, but, as the Aukhoond-zadeh observed, "the climate is fine, and if dirt killed people, where would the Affghauns be!" Candahar is quite as dirty a place, and Caubul, the "city of a hundred thousand gardens," is said to be little better.

But though the city of Heraut is as I have described it, without the walls all is beauty. The town is situated at four miles distance from hills on the north, and twelve from those which run south of it. The space between the hills is one beautiful extent of little fortified villages, gardens, vineyards, and corn-fields, and this rich scene is lightened by many small streams of shining water, which cut the plain in all directions. A dam is thrown across the Heri-rood, and its waters, being turned into many canals, are so conducted over the vale of Heraut that every part of it is watered. Varieties of the most delicious fruits are grown in the valley, and they are sold cheaper even than at Meshed; the necessaries of life are plentiful and cheap, and the bread and water of Heraut are a proverb for their excellence. I really never in England even tasted more delicious water than that of the Herirood: it is "as clear as tears," and, the natives say, only equalled by the waters of Cashmere, which make those who drink them beautiful.

The Baugh-e Shah, or the king's garden, was formerly one of the wonders of Heraut, but its parterres have been neglected, and "its palaces lie desolate;" a beautiful avenue of fir-trees, a mile in length, extended from its entrance to near the city wall, but when we were at Heraut, the Shah, in a spirit of barbarous economy, was felling some of the trees for the purpose of repairing his palace. A mile to the north of the city are the remains of what anciently was the wall of Heri, and not far from it is a pile of magnificent ruins,—the "Moosullah," or place of worship, built by a pious king of the house of Timour, to receive the remains of the Imaum Reza: when, at the death of the saint, the victorious disputants for his body took and buried it at Meshed, this edifice was neglected and left to ruin. The buildings were commenced on a grander scale than those at Meshed, as may be seen by the foundations of such parts as were not completed, and great must have been the cost of erecting what now stands. An "Iwan," built so high that the eye is strained in looking up to it, fronts a court one hundred paces square, the cloistered sides of which are embellished with beautiful designs of flowers, &c. set in mosaic work of white quartz and coloured enamel tile. From the square you enter a large circular hall of great height, covered with a fine dome, and this leads into another apartment of the same shape, but of smaller proportions. This is one part; it would be difficult to describe the rest, for it was not uniformly completed: there are the remains of twenty minarets, among many buildings of designs at once chaste and costly, the pillars and arches of which are broken into a mass of irregular and beautiful ruin. We ascended by one hundred and forty steps to the top of the highest minaret, and thence looked down upon the city and the rich gardens and vineyards round and beyond it; a scene so varied and beautiful, that I can fancy nothing like it, except, perhaps, in Italy. The cultivators of this "happy valley" enumerate, if I remember right, seventeen different sorts of grapes which they grow;—the marble and the raisin grape, that which is translucent and without seeds, the golden grape of Cas-vine, and the small red grape of Budduckshan, with other temptingly-named varieties of this delicious fruit. The vines are planted in trenches, and trained over a sloping bank of earth, on which they are suffered to ripen, a method which I conceive would answer only in a very dry atmosphere.

The climate of this country is said to be salubrious; the heat is excessive for two months in summer, and in winter much snow falls. The year before our coming to Heraut, the cholera morbus had swept away many thousand persons from the city and the provinces round; but this is a scourge which seems to visit all climes. The smallpox, I imagine, occasionally makes sad havoc among the people of this country; they hardly know the practice of vaccination, and are so dirty that any contagious disease must spread rapidly among them. On the 24th of September the thermometer stood at 85° (in the shade at the hottest time of the day): between that date and the 6th of October it fell gradually to 65°, and on the four last days of our stay at Heraut, the mercury stood at 70°. The nights were very cold, and winter was evidently fast approaching.

In the province of Heraut there are eight belooks, or pergunnahs, into which are divided the lands in the valley, chiefly watered by eight large canals from the river, and four small velaits or counties. We were able to obtain the following registered account of the villages, water, ploughs, assessment, and *teool* lands, which I have every reason to believe a correct one.

" *Teool* " is jagheer; land held free, or on condition of military service, as the greater part of Affghaunistan is, or rather was, under the royal government, for the rebel sirdars have in a great measure resumed the crown grants. The produce is calculated from the number of ploughs that are rated against the villages of each district, for every plough is averaged to turn up land for three khurwars of seed. The soil of Heraut returns at a medium calculation tenfold, and at this rate the produce is estimated; *i. e.* for every plough three khurwars of seed, and ten times the quantity of the seed for the gross produce.

The eight belooks are named—Injeel, Aulinjaun, Oodvan-o-Teezan, Khiabaun, Subbukkur, Ghoori-vaun-o-Pushtaun, Goozara, and Kumberrauk; and in these districts are 446 villages, eight large canals, which feed innumerable smaller ones, 123 canauts,* and 2288 ploughs. The gross produce of wheat and barley in the eight belooks, by the above calculation, amounts to more than 68,600 khurwars, or measures of one hundred maunds:† of these, 28,000 are assigned to the crown, and the rest to the cultivators, except a tithe which is set apart for seed.

The velaits, or counties, are—Oubeh, Koorkh, Shaffbaun, and Ghourian. Our accounts gave to the three first—eighty-three villages, 103 canauts and 648 ploughs, or a produce of 19,440 khurwars, of which 5700 were assigned to the crown. We could obtain no statement of the produce of Ghourian, further than that the Shah received 500 khurwars, and granted the rest in teool; but as it is the finest of the velaits, its produce may well be estimated at 10,000 Tabreez khurwars. Formerly the country of Ghourian sent in much money and grain, but of late years it has suffered from the inroads of the Toorkmuns, and there has been a great falling

* Artificial water-courses.

† Khur-bar, or war, an ass-load. The khurwar of Heraut is one-fourth larger than the standard one of Tabreez; our statements are according to the latter measure.

off in the duties which were once levied upon the passing trade. When we were at Heraut, the government of Ghourian was held by a brother of sirdar Yar Mohummud Khan, protected by whom, it was said, he generally gave a very Flemish account of his receipts.

The above estimates give a total of about 98,000 khurwars of wheat and barley. So much of the land being teool, the produce can only be guessed at, but I should conceive it to be greater than above calculated, because Kamraun has frequently laid extra taxes of grain upon the cultivators, and as they do not appear in the first instance to get their just share, they could not well otherwise have met his demands. The lands were considered to be under-assessed, and, as far as we could judge from the information we received, very irregularly: of the crown share, eight-ninths were stated to be given in teool. The population of the province must now be great, and were this fertile country settled, and equitably governed, there would scarcely be bounds to the produce.

Kamraun's money receipts from the city of Heraut and its vicinity were rated at 20,288 Heraut tomauns. An Heraut tomaun is divided into twenty reals (or rupees), thirteen of which make one tomaun of Irâk; so that we have 32,968 Irâk tomauns, or 21,429*l.* 4*s.*

This money was collected by assessments on the eight belooks, on the many gardens and vineyards, and on city lands; from several Elaut tribes (or portions of them) tributary to Heraut; from the customs ($2\frac{1}{2}$ per cent. upon every thing, whether money or goods,) and from the mint (said to yield a good profit.) Part was realized by many vexatious duties imposed upon nearly every thing marketed in the city, few articles being allowed to be sold without the Shah's stamp upon them; the law extended even to butcher's meat, and any one who transgressed it rendered himself liable to a fine and a beating. The strangest item in the account was the sum of a lac of Heraut rupees, said to be the rent from the police; so that our visiter, Meerza Agha, had to make a profit upon this sum,—by charging the inhabitants for the protection of his night-watch, by taxing wine and gambling-houses, and levying penalties upon every sort of immorality, real or pretended, he not being likely to want evidence of any offence that he might choose to affix upon a person able to pay a fine. In bad seasons, he was obliged to stretch a point or two to make up his rent, sure of support from the Shah; and the monarch sometimes made him his instrument for performing an act of violence with a show of justice. Not long before our arrival, they had carried into execution the following ingenious scheme for plundering a very respectable and wealthy merchant who had come to the city. As he was too prudent a person to give the authorities any just cause of offence, Meerza Agha gave a dancing-girl money to make her way into the man's house at night and create a disturbance; he took care to be in the way, and when the noise commenced, entered the house with a party of myrmidons, and took the stranger prisoner, for acting immorally and making an uproar; nor was the man released until he had paid a very heavy fine. In the lock-up house in the bazaar there were generally one or two offenders, sentenced to punishment on a certain day, who continually shouted out entreaties to the passers-by to contribute a trifle towards the sum required for their release, and they often obtained it.

With regard to trade, the merchants declared that Kamraun's exactions were scarcely proportioned to their means of meeting them, and that they were for the most part ruined; assertions in which there was evidently much truth. "If we but knew," they said, "the actual sum that he would extort from us yearly, we would make up our minds to pay it, or to go and live elsewhere; but in addition to the regular heavy duties, we are constantly called upon for extra contributions." The sum of 20,288 Heraut tomauns was the nominal amount to be collected as above stated, but the people said that his Majesty had not failed one year to exact fully as much more upon some pretence or other. In the accounts which were shown to us, there was no mention whatever made of the districts of Furrah, Subzaur, and Ghore; neither were the money receipts from the smaller places given. These governments are held by the Shah's sons, or by favoured sirdars, who doubtless do not account very strictly for their collections either in money or grain. The province of

Furrah, we learned, is almost entirely teool, and, as I before observed, the capabilities of a country thus disposed of are not easily ascertained: however, though many items were wanting on the records, the total annual money income was stated in a sum amounting to *Irâk* tomauns 137,305, or 89,248*l.* 5*s.*

In my account of the trade at Meshed, I mentioned the articles that are exported from Heraut. Silk is obtainable in the neighbourhood, but not in sufficient quantity for export. Many lamb and sheep skins are made up into caps and cloaks in the city, and returned into the country round from which they were brought. There were, if I remember right, more than one hundred and fifty shoemakers' shops in the city, but they were unable to supply the demands from the province, and many camel-loads of ready-made slippers were brought from Candahar, where they are manufactured in great quantities. The leather comes from Hindoostan.

The lead-mines in the vicinity of Heraut are reported to be rich, but they are scarcely worked. The carpets of Heraut, so famed for softness and for the brilliance and permanency of their colours, truly deserve their repute: they are made of all sizes, and at any price, from ten to one thousand rupees; but carpets of any size and value are now seldom ordered, and the trade has altogether declined of late years. The best pieces that we saw appeared to me to equal the Turkey carpets, and considering their texture and beauty, to bear a moderate price; but I fear that the expense of the land carriage would prevent our receiving many of them in Hindoostan, in barter for the goods which the Affghauns yearly take from us.

During our stay at Heraut, we obtained the following sketch of the political state of Affghaunistaun, which I give here, as I imagine that the condition of that country has not been materially altered since the period at which I wrote.

Shah Kamraun's actual rule extends westward to a little beyond Rosanuck, and for about two hundred and twenty-four miles on the road to Candahar. The Belooches care so little for his authority, that they come from the south and infest this road; and northward, it may be a question whether his influence extends to the Moorghaub river.

Sheer-dil and Poor-dil Khans are dead; and the province of Candahar is now held by three younger brothers of the rebel family,—Cohun-dil, Raheem-dil, and Meher-dil Khans, men who are only notorious for their bad qualities. They have pursued a narrow line of policy, making no provision for the future; for they have exerted themselves to put down the old nobles, and have set over the people men of low birth and indifferent character, whose enormities they connive at, in order that they may have interests in common. Their thought is to sustain themselves by military force, and they keep in regular pay six thousand unmatched horsemen (all

Ghilgies, for they will not entertain a Doorraunee), who are let loose upon the people. We were assured that, in spring, to lessen the expense of their military establishment, they would march to some part of their county and let their troopers forage for themselves, provided the unhappy peasants could not pay them to go elsewhere. They have ruined trade by their exactions, and all people within their sway, groaning under every species of oppression, look anxiously for Kamraun, or for any one to relieve them.

In bright contrast to these is Dost Mohummud Khan, now the eldest of the family, who governs at Caubul. Albeit not formerly of very good character, he is now widely famed for the excellence of his rule; and the inhabitants of Caubul, chiefly Taujicks, would probably be sorry to see him supplanted. He is said to command the services of eighteen thousand regularly-paid horse, and he has a dozen guns. Dost Mohummud Khan has followed a liberal line of policy, endeavouring to conciliate the nobles and all classes of the people; he enlists Doorraunees, and has brought under subjection the disaffected Ghilgies within his district. He affects the strictest forms of the Soonnee creed, while he is most tolerant to the many Sheahs of Caubul. Of late years, by all accounts, he has been ambitious of the character of a saint, pretending to have celestial visions. In one of these he declared the arch-impostor himself appeared to him, and reproved him for the immorality of his countrymen; upon which he ordered all women of bad character to marry or to leave Caubul, and forbad the introduction of any intoxicating drug into the city. Though the policy of Dost Mohummud Khan has evidently been to endeavour to prepare the way for the introduction of another line of kings, he probably doubts whether the Suddozye interest will not again prevail, and it seemed to be thought that he would not object to compound for his treason by helping Shah Shoojah to the throne. His feud with Kamraun (though unauthorized by Doorraunee law, which professes to consider the life of a Suddozye sacred) is bitter, and could with difficulty be quenched.

Ameer Mohummud Khan, another brother, who rules at Ghuzni, bears a fair character. His troops are included in those of Dost Mohummud Khan. There are some other brothers at Jellallabad, who have eight hundred or a thousand horse. Peshawar is held by Sooltan Mohummud, Peer Mohummud, and Syud Mohummud Khans, also brothers of the family; but the inhabitants of the latter place, having suffered from the visitation of the Sikhs, must be desirous to see the end of a power, which, while it is strong enough to oppress them, is not able to protect them from foreign enemies.

Kamraun is now a well aged man; he has ten male children, the eldest of whom, a fine young man of three or four and twenty, is named Jehangire. The two next in age are named Syf-ool Moolk and

Saadut-ool Moolk; the seven others are not yet grown up.

Of Shah Kamraun's character there is not much to be said in praise. Even his enemies give him credit for courage and natural talent, but he is avaricious, cruel, and debauched. When I say that he has been guilty of breaking his solemnly pledged oath, I need not add a word more against his private character:—as a king, he has behaved unwisely and ill, for he has ruined trade by heavy imposts, and no man living within the influence of his authority dares avow himself possessed of wealth.

The following anecdote, which was related to me by several different inhabitants of Heraut, will enable the reader to appreciate the character of the heir to the Affghaun monarchy. A merchant of the Bukhteeauree tribe gave a Hindoo banker the sum of eighteen hundred golden ducats for a bill of exchange upon Caubul. This he covered with cloth to make it look like a charm, and hung it about his neck, hoping thus to convey it safely to Caubul. Somehow or other Kamraun learned what he had done, and sent two or three men to take the pretended charm from him. They accost e their victim by asking him for a pinch of snuff, and when he replied that he had none, they abused him for being without so necessary an article; then swore they believed he had snuff but would not give away a pinch, engaged him in a quarrel, scuffled with him, and tore the charm from his neck. They next went to the Hindoo banker, and returning him his draft, forced him to refund the cash, which there is no doubt they duly paid to their royal employer. The Bukhteeauree petitioned the Shah, who, affecting to take pity upon him, ordered that he should be paid a real a day from the royal treasury. This pension was discontinued after a week, and the man was ordered to receive, in lieu of it, a daily portion of bread from the royal oven. Even this dole was denied the man after a short time, and he long remained as a beggar at the palace gate, hoping that part even of his money might be restored, "but he received not a black farthing, and returned to his own country."

On his first coming to Heraut, Kamraun thought it good policy to be liberal to the peasantry of the province, but when, after a few years, he saw the rebels in settled possession of the country which had been so foolishly ceded to them, he became desponding and morose, and rigid in exacting from every one the dues of that royalty, the name of which only remained to him.

Kamraun was always of a gloomy disposition; a circumstance not to be wondered at, considering that at an early age he was initiated into scenes of stratagem and bloodshed, and taught to sacrifice the best feelings of humanity to the interests of ambition. Morality of any sort was not likely to be studied to much purpose in such a school, and Kamraun is now a slave towine and the harem. We learned that his majesty would at times deliberately set about making himself drunk; not for love of drinking, for he could get no liquor except vile arrack, or thin sour wine made by the Jews, but solely to raise his spirits, which would sometimes be excited to perfect phrensy. No one, it was said, but the Attar Bâshee dared attend on the king while he was in "the horrors;" and, during the days of illness which succeeded such debauches, unlucky did that person deem himself whose affairs brought him under the royal cognizance. At all times the people of Heraut seemed to labour under considerable fear of his majesty, and the only man who appeared always merry and at ease was Shemshooddeen Khan, whose sister, report said, influenced the disposition of her royal consort as she would, by the fascination of her beauty.

But notwithstanding all Kamraun's faults, the people would be glad to see him restored to the throne; the interests of the Suddozye tribe, and of all the old Doorraunee families, are connected with his, and the Affghauns generally, have in every way suffered so much from the consequences of the revolution, that they would hail the resumption of the royal authority, whether by Kamraun or by any other man of the family. Whether or not Kamraun will realize their wishes is a question. Constant reverses of fortune, caused generally by the faithlessness of those whom he trusted, seem to have unsettled the decision of his character; for of late years he has frequently summoned his friends, and made demonstrations of marching to recover Candahar, and then, when the time for action came, suddenly deferred the project. His subjects, after two or three false alarms, decided that the Shah's object in thus acting was, that he might have pretence for imposing extraordinary taxes upon them; but though this is a consideration which his majesty doubtless on no occasion lost sight of, it is probable that he really entertained the designs which he professed, but that he wanted nerve to prosecute them, when he came to reflect upon the chance of his losing the only retreat that fortune had left him. The consequences of such indecision may be fatal to the existence of the Affghauns as an independent nation; for the Persians will assuredly press eastward, and if they expel the nominal king of the Affghauns from Heraut, what is to prevent them from subjugating the rebel states into which the Doorraunee kingdom has been divided? More impossible events have happened than the extension of the Persian empire from the Arras to the Indus.

CHAPTER II.

Personal narrative during sojourn at Heraut—Pecuniary difficulties—Moollâ Ismael and the Jews at Heraut—Arabic copy of the scriptures—Suggestions regarding the extension of Christian and other knowledge among Mohummudans.

We continued to receive every civility from our host: through him it was intimated to me, that Shah Kamraun had been pleased graciously to accept the letter which I had forwarded, and that I should be received at audience, and presented with a robe of honour; but as the Shah was bestowing such distinctions upon those whom he wished to engage in his projected attempt upon Candahar, I feared lest I should be represented as an ambassador extraordinary from the British Government, and so, with many protestations of my sense of the great honour proposed to be conferred upon me, I declined it, on the ground of my being a mere traveller, not possessed of an offering for the king, unprovided even with apparel suitable to the occasion of a presentation, and added that, having had the honour to forward the sincere expressions of my chief's consideration, I would pray for his majesty, and proceed on my journey as soon as opportunity served and he permitted.

This answer was not taken in ill part, and subsequently, some indirect communications were made to me through the same channel, the purport of which was, profession of Shah Kamraun's immense esteem for the British, and hope that if he succeeded in recovering his kingdom, lasting friendship would be established between the two nations. The commercial advantages which could accrue to the English from the restoration of order in Affghaunistaun were adverted to, and our friend would have touched upon the political relations which should exist between the Affghauns and the English, as regarded the Franceese and the Oroos, but here he fairly bothered himself, and appeared to be relieved when I assured him that we had no great dread of the attack of either nation. I was much pressed to say if I came in any way as an agent of the British Government, but I answered that I was a mere traveller, and could say nothing in the name of my masters, though, I added, every Englishman knew that his rulers wished to see the Affghauns united and happy, and to be friends with them, (witness their embassy to Shah Shoojah, the shelter which that monarch had found in the British provinces, and the great encouragement given to Affghauns trading to India), that, Inshallah! affairs would turn out for the best, &c. Apparently these answers were sufficient, for the only subsequent communication that I received was, an inquiry whether I possessed, or could prepare, a liquor which would make his Majesty drunk at once.

Abbas Khan was said to enjoy much of the Khan's favour, and I believe he did, for Kamraun felt that he could better depend upon his foreign servants than upon many of the lords of his own country, since the former could exercise no influence among the Doorraunee tribes. The favour of monarchs may sometimes be so great as to be burdensome, and perhaps our host thought so one evening, when he returned home quite exhausted from the effect of the Shah's graciousness to him. He had engaged to come over to our house, but sent an excuse by his servant, who told us the reason, with many interjectional remarks upon the greatness of the Shah's *sheffakut* for his master.

The Khan was out riding, about three miles from the city, when he met Shah Kamraun on his return from hunting. He dismounted to do reverence, and the Shah was pleased to honour him with a call to the fortunate stirrup, and to ask what horse he was riding. The Khan took occasion to state that it was a colt of the Coord chief's best breed, which he had brought from Meshed, in the hope that it might be deemed worthy the regard of the royal eye; upon which the Shah was graciously pleased to notify his approval of the Khan's dutifulness, and then, moving on towards the city, still in conversation with the Khan, he allowed him to run at his bridle all the way, discoursing with him about one thing or other, a degree of *mihir baunee** which was seldom shown to any one, and for which the Khan was bound to be grateful, though it sent him to bed.

Shemshoodeen Khan, the king's favourite, expressed himself civilly towards us, and told me to come and see him in the citadel, when he would show me the king's horses. I appointed a day to go, but the evening before it, the Khan was ordered out suddenly in command of one thousand horse, to check a large body of Toorkmuns said to be in the neighbourhood, so I missed the opportunity of seeing the interior of the citadel. We were told that Kamraun had a large stud of good horses, seven or eight of which were famous for their pedigree and for their performances. These fine animals were trained to a a quick amble, a pace which enables horses to perform long marches with ease both to themselves and to their riders, and which certainly might be well adopted by the hussars of European armies. At a rough guess, formed from what I have heard of the marches of troops in these countries, I should say that their pace on a forced march is a fourth quicker than ours, a circumstance worthy of consideration.

Kamraun, while we were at Heraut, used to ride out twice a week far into the country to hawk or hunt: he would start early in the morning with a dozen attendants, and seldom return till past sunset,

* Affability.

riding in the course of the day from fifty to sixty miles. There was one horse in his stable, which, though old, was still watched with great care. It had been bred by the chief of an Hazaureh tribe, and was so famous, that when Kamraun sent to demand the animal, the clan protested against their chief's giving it up,—for with these mountaineers, as with those of our country, "the laird's honour is Dugald's," and fearing lest the prince should endeavour to possess himself of their famed steed by force, they kept guard round the tent in which it was stabled. Kamraun's desire to obtain the horse was not lessened by this tribute to its value, but he craftily pretended to have lost his fancy, and some time after invited the chief to a conference at Heraut. When the Hazaureh Khan arrived, he was seized and confined, and a strong party were immediately sent to his country to possess themselves of the horse; the relations of the chief, fearing lest Kamraun should injure him, did not resist the party sent, and the steed was brought off. When Kamraun had seen the animal in his stable, he released its owner, with expressions of regret that his unwillingness to oblige his prince should have led to his inconvenience. We ventured to ask a man who was relating this anecdote, whether the act did not come under the head of oppression.—"No doubt," was the answer. "Zoolm bood; it was oppression; but the horse was a rare horse, and the Shahzadeh could not have gotten it any other way."

On the 12th we made a party, with our host's brother and the Aukhoondzadeh, to visit the shrine of Khojeh Abdoollah Ansarree, a Soonnee saint and philanthropist of great celebrity, who lies buried in a garden on the hills which are to the north of the city. The morning was lovely, and my companions, having plenty of pipes to keep them in spirits, exerted themselves to be witty, so we rode in the greatest possible harmony to the village of Gauzer Gau. Here we picketed our horses under a fine tree, and proceeded to the gate of the garden, on either side of which was a small mosque, kept by attendant servants of the shrine, who desired us to enter and say a mass, and to leave as much money as we were anxious should be given in charity. We deposited our slippers here, and then passed into a walled garden, the trees of which shaded several tombs of white marble, built over the dust of the descendants of Timour-lung. At the end of the garden, under a low spreading tree, was the grave of the saint, covered by a large stuccoed mound of conical shape, and headed by a pillar of white marble, on which were sculptured choice Arabic sentences. The shape of the pillar was very elegant; but, unfortunately, when the Cujjers came to Heraut they cracked it, in their desire to dishonour the grave of a saint of a sect opposed to their own. All our party were Sheahs, so that if they did not consider the act a very meritorious one, they in no way found fault with it, and as they entertained no great idea of the sanctity of the place, I was enabled to indulge my curiosity without constraint. About the tomb were many rags, left there by votaries who had bad husbands, or who were childless, &c., and several rams' horns, which, I could not learn why, are brought to all holy places. Near the head of the tomb was a withered tree, stuck full of nails, which had been driven in by persons afflicted with toothache;—a certain cure. It is odd that just such a conceit appears to have prevailed formerly in our own country, for in an old English book, among other quaint notices, is written the following recipe for relief from that distressing malady: "To cure the toothache—Take a new nail, and make the gum bleed with it, and then drive it into an oak. This did cure Sir William Neal's son, a very stout gentleman, when he was almost mad with pain, and had a mind to have pistoled himself."

The shrine is well endowed, a Motwullee and thirty attendants being retained to perform the duties of reading the Korân and keeping the garden in order; and they, and numberless cats, lounge about and sleep, and profit by the visiters. Khojeh Abdoollah Ansarree extended his philanthropy to the brute species, and was very fond of cats, of which I should think not fewer than a hundred are kept in honour of his memory; not that the shrine is put to much expense, for the townspeople continually make picnic parties, to enjoy the *sail* (prospect) from these hills, and what they do not eat, they leave for the cats and beggars.

Timour-lung's descendants constructed summer palaces on this hill, made other gardens, and basins of water; but these only remain as evidences of a grandeur which has passed away. We wandered among the ruins and over the hill, enjoying varied prospects of the beautiful valley below us, and then sat down to dine under a shady tree. Our host had munificently kabaubed a sheep, and our cloth was besides spread with bread and cheese, curds, grapes, and pistachio-nuts; our beverage was clear and sparkling water from the rill, and the repast was seasoned with the best humour and Persian wit. While we feasted we were surrounded by cats, who watched and fought for morsels thrown to them, and two or three old beggars shared with them the fragments of our repast. The glow of an autumn sun, which had bathed the whole valley in a flood of light, was fading into the gray of evening when we mounted our horses to return home: the moon rose almost as soon as the sun had set; by its light we visited other gardens on our way to the city, which we reached when its inhabitants were at rest, and retired to our couches in that pleasant state of weariness which closes a day happily spent.

Our residence at this beautiful place would have been delightful, had we not been exposed to the many evils attendant on poverty. The money which we had obtained at Meshed, only sufficed to pay our debts there; Gholam Reza, the Yezd merchant, would not advance a sous more; and "a commander of ten" of Kamraun's horse, who, with great show of goodnature, had forced a loan of fifteen gold ducats upon the Syud during the march, having acquired considerable doubts of our solvency, in consequence of the kotwâl's unprofitable visit, used to walk up daily to know if we meant to pay him when his cash became due, and never would leave us until we had propitiated him with a cup of tea. The Yezd merchant also pressed us unfairly for his money; for alarmed at the place he had come to, he wished to depart with all speed, and seeing us unmoved by his insinuations that there was small chance of our messenger's escaping the dangers of the road from Tehraun, even if he had been despatched thence with money, he set a host of relations upon us, who scrupled not to hint that they considered us little short of swindlers. One of his uncles, a most ill-favoured old man, would sit *dhurna* in our room the whole morning, occasionally asking gruffly how and when we meant to pay his nephew; and when answered that the term of payment had not arrived, he would endeavour to make himself as unpleasant as possible, by calling for water to drink, and then almost putting our servant upon his oath that I had not touched the vessel in which it was brought, taking the opportunity of saying something sarcastic under pretence of apology.

If at Meshed money was with difficulty to be got, at Heraut it was a still scarcer commodity: merchants were alarmed at a demand for ten tomauns, and shook their heads at the mention of a bill on Persia or Hindoostân. We had pawned every thing that would be taken in pledge, no news of our messenger came, winter was approaching, and our prospects were altogether so gloomy that we did not like to think upon them.

Not many days after our arrival, we had been visited by one Moollâ Ismael, a worthy old Jew, who having lost a fortune in the troubles of the country, subsisted as best he could. Five years back, he said, two Feringees, now Sirdars in Runjeet Sing's service, had lodged with him, and therefore he had called upon us to offer his services in any way. When told our wants, he confessed that our chance of being relieved from them was small; but he said that as men sometimes did enter into desperate speculations, Inshallah, one of that class would be found, and he commenced searching for this rara avis,—the "*Oonka*" of Meerza Mousa's ornithology,— with a zeal for which we could never feel less than grateful.

Moollâ Ismael was the richest of the Jews at Heraut, and he said that he had nothing. He gained his livelihood in the bazaar, as a dellal or broker, being patronised by the merchants, in consequence of his generous conduct some years before, in enduring much ill-treatment rather than confess a knowledge of certain goods which had been confided to his care. The contrast between this man's fidelity and his mendacity was striking: he was so virtuous as to suffer torture rather than betray his trust; but, at the same time, he did not scruple to swear by solemn oaths to the Hâkim's officers, that he knew nothing about the merchandise which they desired to seize, although he had it concealed in his own cellar.

His brethren, the old Jew said, did not now number forty houses in Heraut: long and constant ill-treatment had reduced their numbers and beggared them; but, clinging firmly to the hope of their fathers, they patiently eked out a living as best they could, knowing that whenever they might remove, it would be but to exchange one oppression for another.

> Tribes of the wandering foot and weary breast,
> How shall ye flee away, and be at rest?

I sat with Moollâ Ismael one afternoon during the Feast of Tabernacles, in a small tent made of boughs and chintz cloths, which he had set up in the court of his house: every now and then a party of lads would come to the court door, and shout out the master's name, in order that they might make sport of him, "Ho Moollâ Ismael! why have you become a tent-abider?"—"Because, lord of my life, it is commanded."—"It is not written in the book, you old dog!" would be the retort, and then would generally follow a chorus of contemptuous laughter, or a volley of curses and abuse. The old man felt their taunts, but dared not reply to them, so he comforted himself with an expression which, as he spoke it was full of pathos—"Well! it is but for a time, and Ullah has willed it; we are scorned and injured, but God will remember our sufferings. When the Lord bringeth back the captivity of his people, Jacob shall rejoice, and Israel shall be glad."

Our friend had a less scriptural way of comforting himself, and to judge by his frequent inebriety, he found it necessary to counteract the effects of much sorrow. When he came to us of an evening, he was usually attended by a friend who watched his steps, and sometimes he would in the day-time show signs of having taken his "morning;" but when he had any real business on hand, he would take an oath against strong drink, as an Irishman does against whiskey. I must add also, that on sabbath and holy days, Moollâ Ismael most scrupulously abstained from drinking; indeed he was so particular about observing his religious ordinances to the very letter, that he would not strike a light after Friday's sun had set. Drunkenness is a vice which I imagine is very prevalent among the Jews, and professed Christians, whose societies are scattered over the land of the Crescent; those whom I had opportunities of seeing, appeared to think it proper to drink, because the Mohummudans did not; but I could not observe that they made it a duty to differ from their enemies upon many other points of conscience.

In order to procure us a little temporary relief, Moollâ Ismael introduced us to a person who advanced a few ducats upon the pledge of our watches and pistols,—an old moollâ, whose conscience would not allow him to take usury, and who therefore charged us for the risk of keeping the articles in his house; a distinction which he begged might be appreciated. These men have the easiest modes imaginable of evading the spirit of their religious ordinances, as I observed, rather to my astonishment, in a case in which Hadjee Moollâ Ramazaun took a part.

The Caubul merchant, whom I mentioned as having made great affectation of poverty on leaving Meshed, seeing how much we were in want, came to us privately, and telling us that a kafilah was about to set out for Caubul by the direct road through the mountainous country of the Sheah Hazaurehs, proposed that we should accompany him this way, a journey of fifteen or sixteen days; to enable us to quit Heraut, he offered to obtain for me three hundred ducats, if I would engage to pay him double that sum at Caubul, where he said he thought I might find merchants who would accept my bill on India. Our prospects were so very uncertain, and our situation was so unpleasant, that I inclined to accept his offer, usurious as it was, and we adjourned to Hadjee Moollâ Ramazaun's house to talk the matter over. The Hadjee was appointed broker; so, sending for two or three of his relations to witness the transaction, he ordered an old shawl to be brought, and first pretending to sell it to the Caubul merchant, he said to me—"You agree to give A'Mo'mud Bauker six hundred ducats when you reach Caubul, for this shawl, and other articles to be furnished by him to you;—and you engage not to quit Caubul until A'Mo'mud Bauker permits you; even, added the last-named person, though you should have to borrow twelve hundred ducats to pay me my six hundred. I demurred about agreeing to this strange compact, for I had not made up my mind to accept such hard terms, and all Agha Mohummud Bauker's dealings savoured so much of duplicity, that I felt averse to putting myself in his power; some instances of his conduct at this conference determined me not to trust him, so I signified my resolve to await intelligence from Tehraun. Hadjee Moollâ Ramazaun rather approved of the determination, but the circumstance of his superintending such a transaction showed the laxity of his sect's moral system; for all who knew him declared that a better or more conscientious man than their Moojteheid, would with difficulty be found in the country.

Hadjee Moollâ Ramazaun had lately received from Tehraun the present of an Arabic copy of our scriptures. One day that we were seated with him in the house of his son-in-law the Aukhoond-zadeh, he produced the book, and made such remarks upon different passages, as showed that he had interested himself in the perusal of it. In the course of his comments he here and there threw out objections, and I, essaying to answer them, presently found myself engaged in a religious discussion, a circumstance which I began to regret, as I was not sufficiently versed in scholastic language to argue in proper terms, and though both the Hadjee and Moollâ Mohummud laid it down as a rule, that we were to dispute upon neutral ground, we soon fell back, each on our own, and whenever I made a stand against any very dogmatical proposition, the Aukhoond-zâdeh would press me with—"But what says Al-Korân? what is written in the book?" upon which, uttering a solemn and guttural Arabic quotation, he would pour out such a torrent of words in paraphrase of it, as for the moment to overpower me, and then, smoothing his beard, and running over his beads, he would sigh and roll his eyes, and gravely ejaculate, "Ullah Ho Acber!" as if he wondered how it was possible for a man to hold such heterodox opinions. This is a master-stroke with the logicians of these countries, and when a discussion between two doctors waxes warm, each disputant keeps his voice up to the proper pitch, to guard against his flank being turned by the well-known manœuvre; so it may be imagined what a noise they make.

Mohummudan divines argue, as indeed do most other people, more or less, not to establish the rights of a question, but to get the better of their opponents, and an infidel will in vain talk to them about *petitio principii* and prejudiced opinions: Al-Korân is their *point d'appui*, and they will successfully rally upon it when backed by an assembly of "the faithful." There is but one remedy for this,—spread of knowledge among the people; except indeed we fight them with their own weapons, as recommended by "St. Louis" in his advice to the Sieur de Joinville—never to waste words on an infidel, as all that a Christian could do in an obstinate case, was to thrust his sword into the unbeliever's belly as far as it would go.

I am sure the bulk of the Mohummudans in this country do not believe that the Feringees have any real religion. They hear, from their friends who visit India, that we eat abomination, and are never seen to pray; and they care not to inquire more about us. "Kaufir'und!" is their exclamation, "they are infidels!" and it is a matter of indifference to them how many shades there may be between all those whom they include under the denomination, between the Jew and the Christian, the Guebre and the Hindoo!" It is therefore greatly to be desired, that such translations of our Scripture as may invite their study, should be sent among these people, in order, first, to satisfy them that we have a religion; and secondly, that they may know what our religion is; in order that they may learn to respect us, which they do not now, and gradually to regard us with kindlier feelings; for until they do, we shall in vain attempt to propagate the gospel among them.

Hadjee Moollâ Ramazaun praised the talent and labour of those who had made the translation sent him, though he said that, of course, with regard to idiom and cadence, it was far from being what it ought to be; but I must not omit to add, that he approved of a literal version. I make a point of mentioning the latter opinion, because I myself entertain a contrary one, formed in a great measure on the judgment of my acute and unprejudiced travelling companion. It certainly may not be amiss, for the sake of critical reference, to have a word for word translation of our sacred writ in Arabic,—which is to most Mohummudans, what Latin is to the various Christians of Europe,—but although a few men like our friend the Moojteheid, might betake themselves to the dry study of a work literally written, the generality would not, and therefore I conceive that we should use a more attractive style when rendering our Bible into the other tongues of Asia, even if we do not prepare a second, more popular, version for those to whom Arabic is yet a living language. The interest and prejudice of those crafty doctors "the pillars of Islam," would induce them to exhibit only the errors, or what they would argue to be such, in writings which threaten the very base of the temple that they uphold; so, to prevent their being unjustly biassed, we should give the people at large every inducement to read for themselves; and in order to this, we should not only translate from the original, so as to preserve the similarity of idiom which runs through all Eastern languages, but not insist upon a strictly literal rendering, when, fully preserving the sense, we can express a sentence more beautifully. Judge from the Persians, who though indeed too prone, like the nation with whom they are so often compared, to sacrifice soberness to jest and sophism, are not only naturally intelligent, but very fond of inquiry and reasoning. Except the Arabs, no people are more susceptible of the beauties and sublimities of language, more fond of dwelling upon them, but they will not read what is written in a hard style. It is in their easy, harmonious, and widely-diffused tongue, that we should begin to labour earnestly for the extension in Asia of all knowledge and truth, and I consider that much facility for this great undertaking is offered to us in their country. In order, for instance, to obtain a good translation of the Old Testament, we might get the assistance of Persian Jews. The descendants of Israel who live in Irân, retain their own language, and some of their moollâs not only acquire a classical knowledge of Persian, but become skilled in Arabic, which is so nearly related to Hebrew, and one of these would have a heart in the work, which no Mohummudan assistant well can. Perhaps, too, partial aid might be got from the most learned of the Armenian Christians settled in Persia.

During the Mohurrum at Meshed, the lecturers read from an Arabic work passages which appeared greatly to affect the multitude. The book is attributed to Hossein's son, Ali Awsut, and is entitled

"Sahifa Sajjadea," the book of the Adorer, a name by which Ali Awsut was designated, or Sahifa Kamila, the full or perfect book. It is written much in the style of the Psalms of David, consisting of lamentations for sin, adoration of God, and entreaties for his mercy, and doubtless many idioms and expressions might be adopted from it, and from similar works, to suit a translation of our psalmist's verses.

The Arabian impostor borrowed so much from our Scripture, to interweave with the forgeries which he palmed upon his superstitiously ignorant countrymen, that a Mohummudan now thinks he convicts a Christian by his very Testaments; for he recognises in them much that corresponds with his own traditions, and he has been taught to believe that we have indeed portions of the revealed writings, but that all such parts of our sacred history as do not agree with his, are corruptions, which were made by Jews and Christians for their own wicked purposes. Now the Korân can no more bear an impartial comparison with the Jewish Testament, than the licentious tenets that it inculcates can stand before the purity and charity of gospel precepts; the very harmony of the prophecies which bind the parts of the old revelation together, would induce candid Mohummudan examiners to give a verdict in its favour, and then must follow their right acceptation of the Saviour whom the Jews deny, for, as argued by Sir William Jones, they are already a sort of heterodox Christians, devoutly believing, as they do, in the immaculate conception, divine character, greatest miracles, and ascension, of "*Huzrut Esau!*"—the Lord Jesus!

It is plainly, therefore, desirable that we should court every means likely to lead Mohummudans in general to compare their scriptures with ours. But more than this, it is necessary that we should impart to them as much of the knowledge now current in the enlightened world, as will enable them to set about the comparison fairly. There has already been excited, among the Persians in particular, a bold spirit of religious doubt and inquiry, but this now generally loses itself in a scoffing and loose infidelity, dignified with the title of Sooffeeism,* because these people neither know the true principles by which to discern and prove truth, nor possess a well-based and highly-raised standard of morality. We should sup-

* Sooffee—signifying pure—was originally a term for certain ardent devotees, who while professing respect for the established religion of Islâm, departed widely from its creed and institutions, and aspired to something like that holy abstraction, and spiritual absorption into the divine essence, of which Hindoo mystics dream. The liberty of this vague faith soon degenerated into licence among many of the sects who adopted the appellation, and all grades of its numerous followers are banned by the sober and orthodox Mooselmaun. The title comprehends religious and poetical enthusiasts, abstrusely speculative philosophers, ("falsely so called,") and practical epicureans; one reading figuratively, and referring to the delights of a future world, a theme of wine, harmony, or love, which another construes and applies in its literal and gross sense; and nowadays the title is claimed by many a would-be "esprit fort," who can do no more than repeat a few sceptical commonplaces, and quote Hâfiz, or Moollâ Roomee, for his liberal indulgence in the goblet, music, and sensuality.

ply all their wants, and first, from our stores of historical fact and inductive learning, compile for them works calculated to prepare the way for religious discussion. At present there is no common ground for debate between us.*

Much care and tact will be required for the preparation of the latter books. Our long-bearded pupils must be addressed as men, even where it may be necessary to teach them as children, and he who would instruct them, should not only be thoroughly master of the subjects to be discussed, but acquainted also with the extent, and particular form, of their literary attainments. Our modern primers of learning carry a look of insult to the conceit of wisdom in which they have been accustomed to hug themselves, and they take disgust at medicine which would cure their ignorance were it only disguised. They must be approached in their own style, and humoured to their least points of taste. Even in the "getting up" of books which they might accept as far as matter is concerned, we offend their prejudices. They dislike stiff print: we persist however in sending them this, on indifferent-looking, narrow-cut paper, when through the aid of lithography, we might give them multiplied pages scarcely to be distinguished from

* Part of this paragraph having been quoted in reviews, I would remark that the editor of my Journal, mistaking "enlightened world" for enlightened word, slightly altered my text to suit his reading. I have now endeavoured to make my meaning clearer, and put all my suggestions on this important subject in one place.—Note to second Edition.

those of their exquisitely-penned, broad-margined, glazed and gilded manuscripts; and we excite their very indignation with the common covers in which we bind sheets containing matter which we profess to hold sacred, when, with a little moulding and gilding, we might impress them with a handsome and oriental appearance. Books of the latter fashion would be more expensive than those now published; true, but it would be better to distribute half a dozen copies of a sort that would be valued and probably read, than half a hundred of a kind which we see at once thrown aside as unsightly by the majority of those to whom they are given. Just let the experiment be tried. We possess, in Henry Martyn's version, a good copy of the New Testament in Persian: lithograph from this, in the best style, just the Sermon on the Mount,* and send it to Persia for circulation. All would receive this "Sahifa Kamila," and many would read it, who might not be induced to undertake the perusal of the whole Testament. Few of those who revere our Saviour's name, could sincerely study this portion of His revelation without desiring to have the rest, and for such the complete volume might be forwarded in the same style, with any such literary treatises as might be prepared, calculated to stimulate inquiry and establish sound knowledge.

* Of late years there has been a special demand for the Sermon on the Mount among the *Sikhs*. It has been printed separately, and is largely given away to members of this sect, who annually visit the great Hurdwar fair.

CHAPTER III.

Kamraun's projects on Candahar—Account of roads between Heraut and Caubul—Hindoo merchants at Heraut—Holy family of Pisheen—Syud Muheen Shah—The Author generously relieved by him—Departure from Heraut, and march under his escort to Girishk on the Helmund.

On the 14th of October, Shah Kamraun publicly announced his determination of marching upon Candahar. The wealthiest Hindoos took flight upon the first intimation, but Meerza Agha was immediately set to work upon the purses of those who remained in the city. A tax in money and grain was laid upon all the villages round; guns and marching equipage were put in order; influential Khans were presented with robes of honour, and sent to raise the clans on the road, and the Sirdar Yar Mohummud Khan was formally invested with the title of "Vuzeer of Affghaunistaun." Many of the townspeople seemed to think that this was only one of Kamraun's excuses for raising money; but when he expended some of it in fitting out tents, their doubts were shaken. Little as Kamraun was liked by the Herautees, they seemed all to wish that he really would attempt the recovery of his kingdom; for, bad ruler as he was, he was a very

Noorshewân in comparison with the rebel Sirdars of Candahar, and therefore there was hope that the people would rise to assist him. In the restoration of order, merchants saw a prospect of the roads being again open to trade, "and at least," shrewdly observed a townsman to me, "if the Shah fixes his presence at Candahar we shall be gainers, for now he is but in name a king, while this poor city of Heraut is alone made to pay for all the appendages of royalty.

Although the Shah had announced his determination to march upon Candahar, no time was fixed for his setting out, so we indulged a hope that we might still receive a remittance from the westward time enough to let us travel on under convoy of his majesty's army to Candahar, and witness his struggle for the kingdom. Our host said it was probable that the royal force would not move until the winter had set in, when not only would Heraut be secure from the attack of troops which might at other seasons be sent through the Sheah Hazaureh country from Caubul, but Dost Mohummud Khan would be unable to march to the assistance of his brothers at Candahar. The first road, from Heraut to Caubul, eastward through the country by the Sheah Hazaurehs, is described as very difficult, leading continually over high and steep mountains. During the favourable months, occasional parties of travellers go by this route, and we know that it has been travelled by armies of horse, but guns cannot be drawn over the steeps. Early in winter the passage is shut, and it remains so till near the end of spring. Those who have seen the places over which the horsemen of Persia and Affghaunistaun ride, will not suppose this road to be an easy one, from hearing that a mounted army has marched it, and I question whether it could at any season be taken, except by the lightest troops of an European army. One old moollâ, who had just come from Caubul this way, when applied to for information regarding the road, could scarcely do any thing but groan at the very recollection of his journey. The mountains, he said, were for the most part so steep, that there was no riding down, much less up them; his horse had died upon the way, and he knew not how it was that he had not died too; and "Lord of my soul," he added, "it is not alone the labour that a man has to encounter, but his very life is in danger, from the commencement to the end of this cursed journey. God knows I have suffered abuse enough for being of the true faith, but when I got among men who I thought would honour me for being of that which they profess, I was cursed and called Soonnee! *Lâ hoûl-e wo lâ koovut-e illâ billâ-hil âlee-yil âzeem!** That such men should bring a reproach on us by calling themselves Sheahs!"

It appears that the inhabitants of this mountainous

* There is no repentance (for sins), there is no power (to act right), except by the aid of the Allglorious and Almighty God!—a common Mohummudan ejaculation.

tract are as fanatical as wild: they abominate the Affghauns, and are very suspicious of the few who travel through their country as professed followers of Ali; besides which, they like to make infidels of strangers, in order to confiscate their effects according to law. There are two or three Sheah guides only who can safely convey travellers by this road, and they do not travel often backwards and forwards in the course of the year. Our friend the Aukhoondzadeh told us that he once travelled a little way into this country, and took with him a bundle of shrouds, on which sentences of the Korân were stamped; these procured him the best treatment wherever he went, and a profit to boot, for the Sheahs conceive it of great import that their remains be wrapped in such holy cloths.

The great road from Heraut to Candahar is open the year round, but that between the latter place and Caubul is shut in the middle of winter; or at least it is considered dangerous to travel it, and many instances are related of persons having perished in attempting the journey at this season. There is risk of being lost in the deep snow-drifts; and, between Ghuzni and Caubul especially, they say winds blow which are sharp enough to "cut the life out of a man."

Moollâ Ismael endeavoured to persuade some Hindoo merchants to assist us, but they one and all refused. About a thousand of these idolaters, it is calculated, reside in the city: they have private houses, and some of them dwell in a large brick caravansera which they possess in the main street. A few keep shops in the bazaar, the others are engaged in agency and general traffic, the extent of which is known only to themselves; but the greater number of them are reputed rich, and they should be so, for nothing, one would imagine, but the certainty of considerable gain, could induce men of so wary yet indolent a race, to give up their friends and country, and to come through so much danger and hardship to a land where they are despised, denied the exercise of many of those religious observances upon which they set so much store, and continually brought in contact with what to them is defilement. Neither the climate, nor the decent fashions of the country, would allow of their dressing in the loose costume of Hindoostân; so they case their spare bodies in tight-fitting vests and pantaloons, and crown their painted heads with small stiff caps. No dress could well be less becoming to men of their figure and complexion, and many of them might sit for pictures of meanness and famine.

The chance of enormous profit sometimes tempts these men to try what they call "a *wind* speculation," and my friend Karaumut Ali took it into his head that he should be able to talk some of them over with his Indian tongue; he therefore put on his best abba one afternoon, and set out for their caravansera. Our household tried several "fâlls," which they declared spoke propitiously; and the Syud, at the particular request of his *protegé*, stepped across the threshold with his most fortunate leg, and walked away confidently. We awaited his return with much hope, for our servant had dreamed that he saw a cossid arrive from Tehraun with a bag of money, and we had each "a sort of impression" (grounded, as such feelings usually are, upon our hopes), that the Syud would succeed in the object of his errand: we were however grievously disappointed; our friend returned at dark quite crest-fallen, and addressing no other words to us than "Neh shood!"—"a failure!"—threw himself at length upon his carpet, and studied the ceiling for some time in gloomy silence, when he began to ease his spirits by consigning the idolaters, and the fathers of the idolaters, from the remotest generation, to every thing bad, and by taxing his wit for abuse to bestow upon them. The last exercise had a happy effect upon his temper, for he was so pleased with the point of some of his sarcasms, that he got on good terms with himself again, and forgot the worst part of his anger; then, over a game of chess, he gave me an amusing description of his interviews with a round of little dried old men, the heads of the mercantile establishments, who each heard his story with the utmost patience, on the chance of there being a word of profit in it, and then quietly answered that our affair was not in their way of business.

I had after this an offer of assistance, but it was

such a one as I could not accept. The Dahbâshee of the Shah's guard walked up one morning, and when he had sippêd his tea, and asked if we had yet received any money, assured me that his heart bled for me, that he had been afflicting himself with thoughts upon my lonely situation in a strange country, and that perhaps he could enable me to continue my journey, if I approved of a plan which he had conceived. A friend of his, he said, was about to take an investment of assafœtida to Mooltân; but if I would engage to pay this man the sum which he expected to realize by the trip, he would lend me his money, and take me directly through the mountains into the Punjâb. This looked well, but on coming to inquire into his friend's expected profits, I found that he had calculated them at the rate of about nine hundred per cent., so that I at once declined the proposal. The Dahbâshee urged me more than once to think upon his plan, saying that the winter would soon shut the roads to India; but a suspicion crossed my mind that he had been sent to find out how much money I could command in Hindoostân, and this made me decline the offer in more decided terms. We were however at last relieved from our difficulties, and in a manner which I have pride in mentioning, as it shows how fair a character my countrymen have acquired abroad: I am moreover happy to have an opportunity of making known the man to whom I am so especially indebted.

Moollâ Ismael, as a last chance, applied to some

Syuds of Pisheen, a large family of the Prophet's descendants, who live in the valley of Pisheen, three marches south of Candahar. These men are supposed by the superstitious Affghauns to inherit the power of healing diseases, charming the elements, and putting spells upon gunpowder, &c., and of blessing or cursing their neighbours with sure effect; consequently, their persons and their property are respected by the most lawless tribes, and they are enabled to carry on trade (which they are nearly all engaged in) when less gifted persons could not.

Moollâ Ismael brought some of these merchants to our house, one of whom said that he would give me indigo for a bill upon India, if his partner, who had lately returned from that country, did not object; and on the morrow he brought this person, who after a little conversation, pronounced me to be a *bonâ fide* Englishman, and one whose word might be relied upon. It was a great satisfaction to hear him run over the names of Mr. Elphinstone, Sir John Malcolm, and other gentlemen known for the high office they held in India. Mr. Elphinstone had given his brother's son a handful of money for answering a few questions; Mr. Cole of Mysore had bought a horse from him; Hunter Sahib, of Mutchleebunder, had given him a rifle; we were a most excellent tribe, who never gave our words falsely, and, please God, he would take my debts upon his head and shoulders, and convey me safely to Hindoostân. Money he said he possessed not, having just completed the

SYUD MTHEEN SHAH.

purchase of thirty horses for the Indian market, but Inshallah! his word was good for any sum, and he would be our security.

Syud Muheen Shah, for it is time that I should mention his name, is a Peer Khaneh, or elder, of the Pisheen Syuds: he had come to Heraut to recover a debt, and was about to return immediately home, to march his horses to India, when his partner told him of a foreigner's being in the city in distress, and brought him to see us. Having engaged to serve us, he would listen to none of his friends remonstrances, but calling upon our creditors, struck hands with them for our debts, and sought for one who would give us money on the best terms.

We found many who would accept our friend's bond, but they would only give us merchandise for it. Still we determined to proceed on our journey at any sacrifice, and so, after spending a few days in useless attempts to procure cash, I gave a promissory bill to the amount of nine hundred and ten ducats, or four thousand five hundred Bengal rupees, for a bale of Cashmere shawls; these we sold in the bazaar for about one thousand nine hundred rupees, with which we paid our debts: Syud Muheen became security for me, and we prepared to journey on to India under his escort.

We need lose no time, our new friend said, in waiting to see what course Shah Kamraun would pursue, but start at once, in confidence that he would be fully able to get us through any troublesome parties who might have risen to disturb the road between Heraut and Canhahar, on the rumour of approaching hostilities. We felt bound to receive his advice as law, and therefore sent to beg the Shah's congé, which was graciously given us.

From the good Aukhoond-zadeh we parted with much regret, for he had been a real friend to us; but, as he expressed in a Persian verse,

> "Friends must part! for a time—and for ever!
> It was my heart's wish ever to be near you.
> But what can a man do against the decrees of fate?"

Since our arrival at Heraut, we had received increased marks of Moollâ Mohummud's kindness and attention, not the worst of which were,—sundry delicacies of food, prepared by the doubtless fair hands of the lights of his harem, which would find their way to our house in unostentatious little dishes, about the hour of evening meal; now, as a parting gift, our good friend brought several articles of men's dress, beautifully worked with most spider-like embroidery, by the same fingers which had ministered to our other senses. We accepted each a token, and forcing upon him in return as large a mark of our gratitude as we could spare, took a very affectionate adieu, receiving his farewell benediction outside the city gate.

We had nothing to offer Abbas Khan but our unfeigned thanks for his hospitality; it was, however, signified to me by one of his confidants, that the Khan would like a pair of pistols to be sent him from Hindoostân, so, at leave-taking, I begged he would allow me to send a brace, as a sign of our having reached India: his farewell speech was as kind as his preceding conduct, and our parting words expressed a hope that he would not forget us, but that he would keep fresh the meadow of friendship, by a continual stream of letters bearing assurances of his health and prosperity.

It was on the 19th of October that we rode from Heraut, under the escort of Syud Muheen Shah, and a dozen other travellers, chiefly Syuds of Pisheen. Four miles from the city we crossed the Herirood by a long bridge of brick called Pool-e Moulaun, which gives a name to the river. So much of the water had been drawn off above, that the stream here was inconsiderable, but it was swift, and clear as a diamond. Twelve miles to the southward of the city, we entered a break in the hills, through which a hard and tolerably good road took us ten miles to Meer Daoud, an old caravansera, where we slept from midnight till four the next morning.

20th.—Twenty-three miles south, to Meer Ullah, an old caravansera. Eleven miles on the way was the ruined caravansera of Shah Beg, where there is always a small stream of clear water. Our road was good, between low rocky hills running on our course, and for the last three miles we had a rill of water with us. We halted until four in the afternoon, when as we were about to continue our journey, one of the party called out that a party of horsemen were coming in pursuit of us. "Oh! *zoe di womrah!*" exclaimed Syud Muheen Shah, "death to your son! but you have spoken the truth, and my house is ruined;" and looking up the road, we saw, at no great distance, three horsemen who were urging their jaded steeds towards us, and by cries and gestures desiring us to await them. They proved to be troopers of the Shah's guard, but our fears that they had been sent to bring us back, were relieved when we heard them in loud altercation with a lad of our party, who it appeared was also a trooper in the Shah's army, but who, not liking the service, had taken French leave, and was retiring in disgust to his home. The horsemen had been sent by the Sirdar to bring him back, but he put himself under the Syuds' protection, and, drawing his sword, declared he would cut down the first man who attempted to lay hands upon him. A sword was unsheathed by one of the other party, and there appeared probability of a fight; but the Syuds interfered, saying that the young man was travelling under their protection, and could not be taken away by force: after a little angry discussion, they decided that the youth should give his sword as a present to those who had been sent in pursuit of him, and the latter were bound, on penalty of "the curse of the Syuds of Pisheen," to say, on their return to the Sirdar, that they had been unable to overtake the deserter.

We rode for six miles to a small brook called "Rood-e Guz," which we followed for six miles more, till it was lost in the "Rood-e Adruscund," a full stream of the clearest water, said to come twenty fursukhs through hills from the east, and to fall into the Furrah-rood, near "Kullah Laush." A body of men who lay on the bank of the stream, challenged us sharply as we were about to cross it; but when they understood who headed our party, they came forward peaceably to request a blessing, and to ask the news from Heraut.

Eight miles from this stream, we passed the ruins of a building called Ziarut-e Khojeh Oureh, where there was water. A mile beyond this point, a road went off to the town of Subzaur. We rode on till eleven at night, when the moon going down, we halted in the plain to sleep: thieves had followed us, and although watch was kept, a man succeeded in creeping up unperceived in the dark, and snatching a carpet-bag from under the head of a Candahar moollâ who was travelling with us, he made off with it. We were awakened by the cries of the moollâ, who said that his bag contained his best clothes, three rupees, and a Korân; and many were the lamentations that he made for the loss of the latter. At the first alarm the whole party had started to their feet and handled their arms, but it was too dark to pursue the robbers, since we could scarcely see each other where we stood; so Munheen Shah adopted another course, and stilling the moollâ's lamentations, shouted to the thieves in Pushtoo, threatening them with a curse for robbing Syuds of Pisheen.

After much calling, he was answered by one or two

voices afar off, the owners of which, being encouraged by fair promises, came to parley in the distance. "Ho!" called out our friend, "listen to my words; I am Syud Muheen Shah, and we are Syuds of Pisheen; restore the things you have taken, or"— and here followed an enumeration of the dire consequences of offending such holy men, murrain among sheep, and the swelling of camels' bellies, with sickness, and bad luck of every kind, to themselves and those belonging to them. "You are not Pisheen Syuds," was shouted in answer.—"'Tis an oath, that we are."—"It's a lie, you are not all Syuds."— "No matter, I, Inshallah, am Syud Muheen Shah, Peerkhaneh, of Shadeezye; keep the money and clothes, but return the Korân, or it will bring a curse upon you and yours."—"Good!" shouted a voice, which after a short silence added, "it is under the single fir-tree in front of you; come and take it. Two of our party went forward with their swords drawn, and found the book as described; but the rogues had torn the cover off, and they were deaf to all calls for further restitution.

The next morning early we rode twelve miles to Kullah kooshk-e Jamburan, a small fort situate in a fertile plain twenty miles in breadth, enclosed by hills, which on the east break into a valley running from it. Close to Kullah Kooshk is a stream of delicious water, and many other forts (that is, from ten to forty houses, enclosed by a weak mud-wall,) extend over the plain of Jamburan to the town of Subzaur, which is just seen under a hill in the distance, bearing about sixteen miles south-west by west.

Subzaur is a town of one thousand houses: the governor resides there in a good fort, and exercises sway over a district in which there are one hundred small Kullahs or fortified villages, all of which are within moderate distance of the town. A son of Kamraun's ruled there when we passed. News of the Shah's coming had gone before us, and much interest had been excited by the report: all seemed to think that the restoration of the Suddozyes would better the state of the country, but the majority doubted Kamraun's quitting Heraut. "I hope," said one of the party, who had seated themselves near us to discuss the question, "that if Kamraun does come, he will come in the apricot season, for my father has a garden, large as from here to the river, and he takes twopence a head from as many as like to eat therein." Many owners of gardens near cities in this country, are accustomed to charge a certain sum to visiters, who are allowed to enter and eat fruit *à discrétion:* the Persians, who must invent a joke upon every thing, declare that at Caubul the eaters of fruit are weighed on entering and on coming out of the gardens, and charged for the difference; and they tell how that a certain wag put stones in his pocket, which he threw away in the garden, so that when he had eaten his fill of fruit, and was weighed on coming out, he was found lighter than when he had gone in,—a problem which long puzzled the wise men of "the city of a hundred thousand gardens."

Quitting Jamburan on the afternoon of the 21st, we rode till midnight, about twenty-eight miles. After twelve miles we entered hills again, but the road, though stony, was good for fourteen miles, when it became uneven and bad. Eight miles on the way was a spot called Gundutsau, where were two wells of good water: at Jansau, as many miles beyond, was a small rill, and again three miles further on there was a spring. We slept on the road till six o'clock the next morning, and then marched nine miles and a half, by a hilly bad road, to the foot of the high hill Kharuck, a peak in a range which runs W. S. W. by E. N. E., bordering the Furrah-rood valley. We rested under the shade of khunjuk (mastich) trees, by a tiny stream of deliciously cold water; and having brought food for ourselves and horses from the last station, we were content to be without visiters in our retreat. Our course in this march was indirect, but Kharuck peak bore about thirty-five miles south-east of our last stage. At three in the afternoon we continued our journey, and riding for an hour to the summit of a not very high cotul, looked down upon a fine plain bounded by a nearly parallel range, through which flowed the Furrah-rood. Across this valley we rode sixteen miles to "Dowlutabad," a ruined mud fort, close to the river, in which were reflected the many lights of two large Noorzye khails encamped upon the bank.*

* A road turns off three miles before Kharuck, which passes to the

25th.—This morning we halted, and from the near khails obtained provisions for ourselves and cattle, in barter for kerchiefs of coarse but gay-patterned chintz, tinsel ornaments, needles, &c., which our guide had brought with him for the purpose. For six needles we got bread for as many persons, and for a few tinsel rings, chopped straw for our horses; provision that some less provident men of our party with difficulty obtained for two common reals; so little does money circulate among this unsophisticated people. There was however a Hindoo resident among them, who was by no means ignorant of its value, as we shortly afterwards found, when we had to deal with him for corn. This miserable creature actually resided here alone, cut off from his kindred, and exposed to every sort of indignity, for the sake of making a little money. When it was told that we were Syuds of Pisheen, the superstitious shepherds brought their sick to be cured. Syud Muheen, as the elder of his sect, laid hands upon the diseased persons, muttering a few words, and bidding them expect relief; in return for the service, he received a fowl, all that the Syuds of Pisheen allow themselves to accept. The patients had evidently great faith in Syud Muheen, and I am sure that he thought himself possessed of the virtue for which they gave him credit; imagina-

right of the cotul, through, not over, the hills, and then crosses the plain to Dowlutabad. There is a halting place on this road called Aub-e Koreish.

tion goes a great way in such cases, and no doubt people are often cured by having their minds relieved. I was amused to observe our friend's manner towards me, when he first began to give out his blessings, for he had seen enough of my countrymen to suspect that I might not suppose him gifted to the extent that his own people did, and he felt uneasy at not knowing what I thought of the matter. I of course did not hurt his feelings by acknowledging that I was sceptical, and saw that I had lightened his mind greatly by congratulating him on his good fortune in being born to so much virtue, for he commenced a detail of cases in which his benedictions or curses had taken effect, telling me, among other anecdotes, that on one occasion in Sinde, when a man refused food to a small party which he headed, he had cursed his camels, and that they nearly all died within three months. A servant of his, who heard us conversing, anxious that no doubts should remain upon my mind, called to me when we dismounted, and baring his arm, showed me a slight scar near his elbow; "This," said he, "was done when I was a lad; we had a fight with the Cawkers, and they thought to beat us, but Syud Muheen's father put a spell on their powder, and the ball which cut my elbow did not strike me harder than a stone from the hand would have done."

One would think that their battles with the Sikhs had cured the Affghauns of the latter conceit, but they still hold to it: in a company of Persian and Affghaun gentlemen at Heraut, a Khan of the latter nation was very curious about the European system of warfare, and, being told that we took most care to have an efficient artillery, he said good-naturedly, but with rather a scornful laugh,—"Artillery! What would you do with your artillery against us? Inshallah, we shall be invading Hindoostân some of these days, and then our Syuds shall make your powder turn to water, while our horse will gallop in upon you and cut you down at your guns."—"And if you do come," I replied, "as enemies, Inshallah! we'll make roast meat of you all!"—a retort which was received with the greatest good-humour by the whole company.

Furrah-rood valley runs down sixty miles to Kullah Laush: half way is Furrah, a town of two thousand houses, near the river, and built under a single hill, which is in the centre of the valley. There are three hundred small forts in the province; the land is fertile, and much grain is cultivated, as the shepherds for many miles round are supplied with it hence; but nearly all the land is teool, the province, we learned, being bound to furnish three thousand horse to Shah Kamraun. Shumshooddeen Khan, whom we met at Heraut, had been appointed governor: we were told that he received annually from the district twelve thousand Heraut rupees, and three thousand khurwars of grain. The Furrah-rood was at its lowest when we forded it,—a quick clear stream, fifty yards across, flowing through the valley in a broad bed of soft pebbles. In spring this is a wide and deep river, and there is always sufficient water in it for much cultivation.

From Dowlutabad we rode thirty-one miles to Largebur Kahreeze. After twelve miles across the valley, we entered hills, but our road through them was level and good all the way: twenty-two miles on the road was Checkau, a spring of good water, and near to it was a small fort. At Largebur Kahreeze there was plenty of good water; we put up in some pomegranate gardens, and procured bread and corn from a neighbouring khail of Noorzyes.

25th, afternoon.—Twenty-eight miles to Gunneemurgh. Our road was stony and bad, and lay close between high hills. Four miles or so on the way, at a spot called Caravancasee, were two or three small canauts of water, which the Noorzyes of a neighbouring khail had turned upon land cultivated with cotton and melons. The tribes in the neighbourhood have a bad name; a month before we passed, they had nearly killed a Syud, by pelting him with stones to induce him to abandon his property, at which he stood guard with his matchlock, and Kamraun, as a summary punishment, had ordered the country round to be chuppaoed. Syud Muheen Shah could not contain his indignation when relating the circumstance. "Not," said he, "that he was one of *us*; but if *any* Syud is to be thus with impunity injured, there is an end of our religion. But Inshallah Taullah," was added, in the spirit of that religion, "they will make a clean harry of the rascals this time."

On a former occasion, when a Sirdar was sent to punish these people, a man robbed him as he was riding at the head of a party of soldiers. In parts the road is very narrow, between low sloping hills, on which grow thick bushes, so that although a man may run up them, a rider cannot follow him, and a thief, starting from behind a bush as the Sirdar rode by, snatched a shawl turban from his head, and was over the hill out of sight before the chief had well recovered from his astonishment. To judge by the many good stories related of their feats, the Affghauns are all expert thieves, and, like the Spartans of old, only know shame in detection; that is, in being detected before they have accomplished their robbery, for afterwards, it is a very good joke with them.

Fourteen miles on the road was a spot called Toot-e-Gussermau, said to be the half-distance point between Heraut and Candahar; it was night when we passed, but we remarked the lights of many khails, and were told that there was much good water there. The old city of Ghore was said to lie about thirty-five miles north of this point. Ghore is now a ruinous ill-inhabited town, the capital of a petty province, governed by one of Shah Kamraun's sons, who has his residence there. At midnight we reached Gunneemurgh, a small open space between low hills, where was the spring of a clear rill.

Though it was so late in the year, our night marches were pleasant: being well clothed, we felt the air rather bracing than unpleasantly cold, and as we had all become intimate, we rode socially along in the bright moonlight, chatting with each other, or joking aloud, whilst occasionally one of the party would shout out a wild Pushtoo song. Plain food, with plenty of exercise and continual change of scene, kept us in health, and when we halted to rest, we needed but to lay our heads to the ground to be immediately asleep. Syud Muheen Shah and I had become great friends, and our affection for each other was strengthened by our mutual liking for tea: we generally took the first watch, and cooked a kettle-ful which we drank sociably while the others were sleeping around us, he telling me anecdotes of the different tribes of his wild countrymen.

In describing their pastoral life, he would draw a most Arcadian picture of the pleasant spring meetings in the hills of Toba, where the water was like running diamonds, the plentiful fresh verdure as a carpet of emeralds, and the air like the odour of musk; the last simile certainly, and most probably the two others, borrowed from the poem of Youssoof and Zuleikha, a well-thumbed copy of which my friend used invariably to produce from his saddle-bag when he had leisure to con it over by daylight.

The shepherds of Toba, he said, would at this blithe season pitch their camps together, and entertain each other, for joy of the increase which the new year brought them, feasting on lamb and fresh curds, and all the varieties which their wives made with milk; hunting with hawks and greyhounds during the day, or perhaps following a wolf or a hyena to his lair, and tying him there; while at night, they would sit out late in social parties, conversing and telling stories, dancing the *Attun* in a a ring, and singing their common songs, or the odes of their poet Rehmaun. Or he would relate how among some of the Cawker clans the manners were so free, that at evening men and women would meet unreservedly, join hands in circles, and together dance the intoxicating Attun, when haply, among the young men, two rivals for the smile of a girl would exchange angry words, and go aside to draw swords upon each other in the moonlight. And this would lead him to an anecdote of gallantry in fight, such as that displayed by Tor Khan, Kharoot, who, when the small band with whom he fought was defeated by the men of the Nawaub of Dèra, disdained to fly from their numbers, but standing his ground, called out and challenged any "man of heart" to meet him in single combat; then, seeing that no one dared to cross swords with him, strode up to a cannon, and, throwing it over by the strength of his arms, struck his sword deep into the carriage, and stood there defenceless, taunting his foes till a ball struck him mortally, when he fell, but with his face towards those whom he had defied, that it might not be said that Tor Khan retreated a foot from an enemy.

I have great pleasure in recollecting this journey;—there was something very exciting in our vagabond life, every day showing much that was novel and interesting; above all, there was connected with it a feeling of independence, which gave an elasticity to the spirits, and tinged every thing *couleur de rose*,—which made the very air taste fresher than elsewhere, the sky seem clearer, and the stars shine larger and more bright. With a friend with whom to exchange thoughts, I know not many ways in which a man could spend part of his life more pleasantly; but a friend is indispensable, for in sickness or danger, or anxiety of any sort, it is disheartening to have no one to look to for sympathy and advice, and, often as it has been quoted, I must for its truth re-echo the sentiment of Marmontel,—" Il est triste de voir une belle campagne, sans pouvoir dire à quelqu'un, voila une belle campagne!"

At Gunneemurgh we were visited by some Atchickzyes of a near khail, who sold us flour and corn. And here our friend was waited upon by a young man of good family, who had ridden to the road from some distance, in order to gain intelligence of the Shah's plans. He was mounted on a very beautiful mare, which he had received as a present from Kamraun, and it need hardly be added that he was a zealous royalist. He told Syud Muheen that he had forty men ready to put foot in stirrup, and said sanguinely, that, Inshallah, the whole country would be up for the Suddozyes as soon as they showed that they were determined to march against the rebels. After a little conversation, he rose and humbly asked a blessing from Syud Muheen; receiving which, he mounted his beautiful steed and rode away home.

From Gunneemurgh we made a march of more than forty miles to Washeer. We started two hours after noon, and were on the saddle until one at night, travelling in considerable fear of the Belooches, who frequently come in parties upon running camels, and wait near the road for travellers. Since the dethronement of Shah Zemaun, the weakness of the ever-changing government has permitted these savages to make their inroads with impunity, and they have become a terror to the merchants who travel within their reach; for not content with robbing those whom they meet, they seldom spare their lives, perhaps on account of their superstition, that they may come under the law which makes a dead man's goods lawful plunder.

On their marauding expeditions, these Belooches ride fleet camels, two on each beast; they are generally well armed with matchlocks and swords, and, provided with a certain number of days' food, they lie in wait at some distance from the road, keeping a look-out for travellers. The Affghauns, to give a strong idea of their ferocity, call them *Adum-khoor*,—eaters of men, and describe them as demoniacal looking fellows, who appearing of a sudden from some ambush, trot up *en masse* with wild yells to within a short distance of their prey, when they spread, and, without listening to parley, proceed diligently to kill as many as they can, and having collected their spoil, trot home again on their *baadees*, or camels of the wind. Now and then they spare a remarkably useful-looking man to carry him off into slavery, but he had better be killed, for he can never hope to escape, and indeed they do *leur possible* to deaden his wish to return to his kindred, by disfiguring him so that he would be ashamed to be seen at home; cutting his ears off, destroying the roots of his hair and beard, &c.

When a kafilah is attacked, all who can, run away; those whose fate obliges them to stand their ground, do it with the courage which distinguishes the *Pooshtooneh*,* and sell their lives dearly; nay, I heard of a young Affghaun Syud, who being left with a few others on foot with their camels, defended himself with such gallant success, after escaping many shots which were fired at him, that the superstitious robbers thought him specially protected, and neither offered further to hurt him, nor to seize two camels which he separated from the file as his own, and shouted out as they were leaving him and his

* The name the Affghauns call themselves by.

murdered friends,—"Your blessing, O Syud, goes with us, Inshallah!"

Scarcely credible journeys are performed by the running camels of this country. I am afraid to assert positively how far these animals can run in the course of twenty-four hours, because the natives exaggerate their performances very much, and when you cannot believe the whole of a story, it is difficult to decide how much of it you are to believe; but I do not think I shall greatly err in saying that, at a push, a good baadee can be trotted one hundred miles in a full day and night.

Mais revenons à nos moutons.—Syud Muheen Shah led us in so many directions, to avoid places where he thought an enemy might be, that at the end of the stage I could not precisely recollect how we had come; but the general direction of the road from Gunneemurgh is east south-east, and the direct distance is, I should think, little short of forty miles. After the first four miles, we got out of the hills, upon a level stony plain, and went in the direction of a single high mountain, called Koh-e-doosd, or thieves' mount, because the Beloochees set watchers upon it to look out for kafilahs: far in the distance across the plain, we could see a line of hills, behind which the nearest tribes were said to range.

Three miles from the hills of Gunneemurgh we crossed the Brahim-jooe, or Ibrahim-jooe river, a little water flowing south in the broad bed, which is filled in spring. A fursukh or so up the stream is

Kullah Suffeid, a small fort inhabited, Syud Muheen told us, by a set of Atchickzyes, who were as bad as Belooches, and in his endeavour to steer well between this Scylla and Charybdis, he made so many turns, that he must have added two or three miles to the march. His advice to us was, if the enemy comes, do not spare your horses, but keep close to me, and never look behind you. I should not omit to mention, as a trait of this man's generosity, that he insisted upon my changing horses with him, that I might have a better chance of escape in case flight should be necessary, saying that he perhaps might save his life, but that if I lost mine, and he survived, his good name would be gone for ever. We had been drilled into being alarmed, and rode together in silence at a brisk walk, the very horses seeming to share our feelings.

Nineteen miles from the Brahim-jooe river we came to the broad bed of the Kash-rood, in which there was not much water. This was considered the point of greatest danger, for in the bed of the stream grows much high grass, concealed by which, the robbers and their camels lie until travellers pass. "Now, for your lives, not a word," said Muheen Shah; "these fellows have ears like hares;" and we scarcely drew breath until we had crossed. Our *nusseeb* was good, not a living creature moved in the grass, and when we had ridden a little distance, our guide stroked his beard and muttered a short thanksgiving for danger past, not forgetting to add an encomium upon his own particular *bukht*, upon which we slackened our pace, and let loose our tongues again.

I am not quite sure that our worthy leader did not make as much as possible of the danger, in order to heighten our esteem for that *bukht* of which he made such frequent and honourable mention; but at all events, his great apparent anxiety, and his grave injunctions, had kept us so long quiet, that all felt glad when the restraint was taken off, and fifteen minutes afterwards we could hardly have been known for the same party, as we straggled on carelessly, talking and joking freely about the enemy whom we had just been treating with so much respect.

Each person had a story to tell about the wild Belooches: one was, that Hadjee Syud somebody had been among them, and seen that they had made bags for their grain, &c. with cashmere shawls, which they had plundered from a kafilah; the dogs! how should they know the value of a shawl! The burden of the second anecdote was, how Syud somebody else, having been robbed of several camel-loads of sugar, had bethought him of a clever mode of at once revenging himself and doing a public service. On reaching Heraut, said the story, he mixed up strong poison in a quantity of sugar, which he packed on two camels, and himself mounted on a fleet horse, took to the road again. Several times did he pass the dangerous places without meeting the enemy, because he wanted to meet them; but at last they came, and he fled away, leaving his camels in their hands. Thinking, doubtless, to enjoy such another treat as they or their brethren had before done, the robbers paid their hearty respects to the sugar, as those who have seen the fondness of Asiatics for sweets can fancy, and so dreadful was the consequent mortality among them, that the Syud's most vengeful hopes were realized, and it is a standard rule among the Belooche marauders of the present generation, to partake of no edible thing that may fall into their hands. I rememher no more of the anecdotes told at this time, for I was latterly so fatigued as twice to fall from my horse from sheer sleepiness: considering our pace for the greater part of the way, I do not think that we could have ridden much less than fifty miles; we were all completely knocked up when we reached our stage, and slept under some trees till the sun was near the meridian the next day.

At Washeer were four little mud forts, plenty of water, and some large fields prepared for cultivation. The gates of the fort were closed, and the owners were encamped outside the walls in felt tents. We visited one khail, at the risk of being devoured by a troop of savage dogs, which singled me out, as if they suspected what my unguarded English exclamations might have betrayed when they fastened on the skirt of my long robe; my good genius appeared in the guise of a wrinkled old woman, who quietly laying down her distaff, rose, and with little apparent exertion lifted up a large stone, which she threw among the dogs as a token of her disapprobation, and then politely told me in Pushtoo that I was welcome. The tents were of wretched construction, and the people seemed poor. Both men and women were working at small frames, weaving coarse cotton cloths. I looked in vain for beauty on the scarcely veiled gipsy countenances of the women; perhaps had the faces of the youngest been cleaned, charms might have been brought out, like the beauties of a neglected picture.

Kamraun's rule ended here. The men crowded anxiously around to hear the news from Heraut, some loudly expressing their hope that the Shah would come. "God rouse his manhood!" was the expression of a man built like a Hercules, who had stood leaning on a staff listening to the conversation. "Does he think we have no swords?—The Suddozyes have become women! How many times has Kamraun talked of coming and disappointed us!"—"Whatever Ullah wills happens,"—answered our friend warily; for as we approached Candahar, both he and his fellow Syuds were careful not to commit themselves by expressions which might be repeated to their disadvantage, and they referred every thing to *nusseeb o kismut*, fate and fortune. If it was Kamraun's fate and fortune he would recover the throne, and if it was the Sirdars' fate and fortune, they would prevent him;—decisions which sounded like oracles from the mouths of men deemed inspired.

26th.—Thirty-four miles and a half to Lur. At the third and fifth miles on the road were villages, where there was much excellent water and some cotton-fields. After eight miles, we came to the villages of Possaud and Namzaud, near to which was an old boundary pillar called Yaiklung. Here a road goes off to Candahar, through the rich country of Zemeendawir, but no one may travel to the capital otherwise than *viâ* Girishk, on penalty of forfeiting his beast and any goods that it may be laden with, because customs are levied at the latter place.

Lur is a small mud fort in the plain. Quitting Washeer, we travelled thirty miles or so through low hills to Kullah Dooshauk, the station at which travellers usually halt: hence on to Candahar the country is plain, of a light sandy soil, which, when irrigated, is very productive. The hills which run irregularly over the country between Heraut and this place, are high and bare, and chiefly composed of mixed reddish and black rock, streaked, and apparently containing much ore. I picked up two specimens to carry to India with me, but unfortunately lost one of them. I am not sure that it was not stolen from me by some one who conceived that I had discovered in it matter for making gold; for on what other account a person should trouble himself to pick up stones, a native of the East cannot conceive, and if he is not sure who a stranger is, he sets him down for a spy or an alchemist. The second specimen of rock was pronounced by a learned geologist of Calcutta to belong to the formation called Greywacke slate. These hills contain mineral springs, the water of some of which was described to be cold in the daytime and warm at night. Twelve miles from Heraut are some famous springs, from bathing in which, it is said, persons afflicted with cutaneous disorders experience much benefit.

Our next march was to Girishk, on the Helmund; a distance of about thirty-two miles. Eleven miles on the road was the strong little fort of Saadut, about which much land had been cultivated by means of Kahreeze water. This fort was built by Vuzeer Futteh Khan for his mother, a lady much renowned for courage and goodness, who held a petty court here while she lived: the Affghauns speak of her by the name "The Mother." On the road we met a large kafilah of camels, laden with indigo, the merchants of which came anxiously to us to learn whether Kamraun had moved out of Heraut, as if his army was on the road, they would not venture forward with their merchandise; they told us that the Candahar Sirdars were out with their troops, fighting against some of the Sheah Hazaurehs.

At Girishk we halted near a large and strong fort, lately built by the Baurickzye Sirdars, and below a gravelly hill, on which is buried one Syud Daoud, a Soonnee saint of note, who in time of yore rode upon a wall, and cut a passage through the Helmund for somebody's army. Under the fort were a few wretched huts, inhabited by persons who supplied us with food and corn.

The banks of the river Helmund are about a thousand yards apart: the right bank is low and sandy, but the left rocky and high: the stream, then at its lowest, was distant from the fort about two miles and a half; where we forded it the water was stirrup-deep, and flowed smoothly, but with force, in a clear stream of three hundred and fifty yards width.

The rise of the Helmund commences in winter, much rain falling at that season: the stream is swelled to great depth and breadth in spring, when the snows melt, and on the quantity of snow which falls in the mountains during winter, depends its fulness and rapidity. So much snow fell during the cold season of 1829, and winter broke up so suddenly, that very early in the next spring a great torrent came down from the mountains, which at night swept away some entire khails from under the very walls of the fort, and flooded the whole country on the right bank of the river.

Ameer Ali, our Meshed acquaintance of rascally memory, crossed the Helmund at Girishk, in spring, when it was at its height. There were two large crazy boats, of the art of governing which the watermen were quite ignorant, and on board one of them got some forty souls and half a dozen horses: when they loosed, all repeated a fateheh, "Ushudoo Un, La Illah Il Illah!" and away they went down the current for three miles, the boatmen hallooing and straining to work to the side, and the most timorous of the passengers making all sorts of vows in case they should safely touch shore again. At last they got out of the current, struck happily against the bank with a shock which threw them atop of each other, and were then quietly towed up stream again opposite to their starting-point.

In summer the water of the Helmund is so clear, that you are liable to be deceived about its depth. Two months or so prior to our coming, the Sirdars had lost their best gun, in consequence of the drivers mistaking the depth of water at a part they attempted to ford, and men were still engaged in the endeavour to get it out. The banks of the river are yet marked by villages and cultivation, but the oppressions of the rebel governors have made the view very different from what it was, for so late as in the days of Zemaun Shah, the Helmund was said to flow through a garden.

CHAPTER IV.

Journey on across the rivers Helmund and Turnuk to Ghoondee Munsoor Khan—Halt—Author's severe illness—Keramut Ali's visit to Candahar—Remarks upon the government and country—Descriptions of Affghaun character and manners—Continuation of journey over the Khojeh Amraun mountains, and across the river Lora, to Syud Muheen Shah's home in the valley of Pisheen.

We arrived at Girishk late at night, and were detained the next day, and until the night of the second, by two officers of the customs, a Mooselmaun and a Hindoo, who, whatever was the difference of their religious creeds, held the same opinions on the point of honesty. The first day one of them was absent, so no business could be done, much to Syud Muheen's vexation, for he said that a kafilah was to leave Heraut the day after us, with which would travel some persons whom it was prudent to avoid.

The next morning early we saw about two hundred horsemen ride in: as soon as Muheen Shah had reconnoitred them, he bade me observe one young man, that I might avoid him. "He wished to travel with me," said my friend, "but, knowing him to be a meddling fellow, I told him I was not going to start for four days; now, if he sees you with me, he will suspect something, and if the Sirdars hear of you, it is all up with us; there is not such a dog in the world: but I must humour him, so you go and stay in 'The Mother's' garden, below there, till I come to you." I accordingly went, and lay "perdue" all day, in a fine garden made by the mother of Futteh Khan.

In the evening came my friend in good spirits, to say that he had quite blinded his acquaintance, pretending to have left the city suddenly, for fear that Kamraun was going to exact something from him. "I knew," said the Shah,* "that he wished to marry into my father-in-law's family at Caubul, so I pretended to favour his suit, hinting that if he left the matter to me, I would arrange it; so now we are fast friends, and whatever he sees or hears, he will say nothing." Further, my friend told me, that he had arranged matters so that our departure would be connived at that evening.

The duty of three and a half golden ducats is levied upon every horse at Girishk, besides six and a half more at Candahar, and the contents of all loads should be examined and declared at the first place. Syud Muheen Shah, thinking that it might not be so well to submit some little knick-knacks that we had

* The title of "Shah," I should have observed, is given in these countries to men esteemed holy.

to the view of the officers, and also that it was prudent not to let our arrival be known at Candahar, bribed the Hindoo and his colleague to let us pass unsearched and unregistered. To his countryman he gave a little money and many promises of blessings, and to the Hindoo a sum in hard cash, the only thing that would move him: we were desired to load and steal away without bustle, lest the other travellers should observe our departure, and afterwards inform against us, accordingly, about eight o'clock, we quietly left our ground. The Hindoo agent stood upon a small bridge to see us fairly off, and warn us to secrecy, doubtless congratulating himself upon this roguery; but had he known who I was, he would not have been so easily satisfied.

"That is a work well done," said Muheen Shah, when we were *en route* again. He is a deep fellow, that dog of an idolater, but, Inshallah! I have been too much for him." I did not feel myself called upon to object to my friend's lies and illegal acts, for I saw that they were the coin of the country, and that there was no getting on without them. My morality, I fear, had suffered a little from contact with these people, for I remember seeing so much reason in Syud Muheen's apology for his contrivances, that I did not attempt to gainsay it. "When I am among honest men," said he, "I defy any one to say that an action or a word of mine is crooked; but what would my honesty avail me among such rogues as these?"

A man who was going to his home over the water, offered to show us the ford for a trifle, and under his guidance we crossed at a point about three miles and a half below the fort. In the centre of the stream, a pony belonging to a Syud of our party lost footing, and fell with a load of silks; so when we reached the opposite bank, it was decided to remain there till morning, and the wetted cloths were laid out to dry in the wind. It was a sad misfortune to the proprietor, but, as it had happened, I did not regret the accident, since it gave me an opportunity of seeing this noble river to advantage by daylight from the high bank. I asked our guide how much water there was in spring. "As much as it pleased God to send," was his reply; a fair specimen of the answers you may expect when seeking information in these countries. This pious man, seeing the silks laid out to dry, extorted some money from their owner, by threatening to go and inform against him for smuggling; and just as he was about to depart with what he had thus obtained, he profited by a second temptation of the same sort; for hearing loud shouts from the river, he went down to the ford, and caught a person in the middle of it, who proved also to be charged with smuggled goods. It was the unlucky Candahar moollâ, who had been robbed of his Korân the night we slept in the plain near Jamburan. I have seldom seen a more ludicrous figure than this man presented when he toiled up the bank, with one hand holding a bundle on his head, and with the other grasping the tail of a half-drowned little pony, which pulled him along. He paid the guide his hush-money in kind, protesting that he had no cash, and then, sitting down by the fire, he declared his conviction that he was under a course of visitations for some bygone sin, for that no undertaking now prospered with him. He had, it appeared, gone back on the Heraut road, and then made a great circuit to arrive at the ford, which he reached a little after us, then, attempting to cross where he had seen our torches, he had ridden his pony into deep water, and felt himself compelled to halloo for assistance. He did not even get sympathy, for the party were too much engaged with their own losses to think of his; therefore with another sigh at his evil fate, he sought the only worldly refuge that a man has in sorrow—sleep.

The next morning we rode, in the teeth of a cutting wind, thirty-one miles to Khoosh-nakhood, where we found several "khails"* pitched about some large pomegranate gardens. We remained here two hours, and then marched on fifteen miles more to Houz-e Muddut Khan, a reservoir of water near which we halted to sleep. I got little; for the fatigue of so long a ride, added to the injurious effects of marching alternately in the heat of the

* "Khail" is the Affghaun name for an open village or encampment.

sun and the cold night-air, had made me ill, and I suffered a very common misery, in lying restless, while ten others were snoring around me.

At sunrise the next morning we rose to conclude our journey, and after travelling along the road together for a little distance, parted company; our companions following the high road to Candahar, which they said lay directly east, about seven forsukhs distant, and Syud Muheen taking us across country to Ghoondee Munsoor Khan, a point said to be about sixteen miles south of the city. Our cross-road took us by many villages, the fine lands of which were well watered and industriously cultivated. Twelve miles on the road we forded the Urghandaub, still a quick stream, although so much of its water had been drawn off above, for the cultivation of fields which marked its course from a great distance.

Three miles before Ghoondee Munsoor Khan (or Munsoor Khan's mound), we crossed the river Turnuk, a shallow stream between high banks of crumbling sandy earth, and an hour after noon we reached a small kullah, lately built by Syud Muheen Shah, in which one of his wives, and his brother-in-law's family were residing. Muheen Shah and I had ridden on ahead with one of his men: I missed the latter at the river Turnuk, and guessed that he had been sent on to notify our approach, when I saw my friend washing and combing out his beard, and making a few alterations in his dress.

At a little distance from the fort, Syud Muheen was met by his brother-in-law and two or three relations, a brace of household slaves, and the other male domestics of the family, who received him with much ceremony, and led the way into the interior, where the same forms of welcome were repeated. "*She raughlé! she juree!—be khiree!—Salaumatee!—she juree! be khiree Salaumatee! be juree! be khiree!*" &c. "You are welcome! you are opportunely come, happily, and in good season, you are welcome, you are happily come, you are welcome," &c., terms all of nearly the same signification, which are exchanged with much gravity several times, by all Affghauns who meet after a few days of separation.

Syud Muheen and his brother-in-law met upon terms of equality, and hugged each other "à l'Affghaun," by pressing shoulder to shoulder; but the lowest menial in the house offered his respectful welcome, and was kindly answered by the master; nor were the complimentary inquiries restricted to the person of Muheen Shah, for the state of his attendant followers was also asked after, through their master; he with the utmost gravity turning to each man to inquire how he felt himself. "Lulloo, you are well? Muttoo? Anzul?"—and Lulloo, Muttoo, and Anzul, nodding their heads in the affirmative, and ejaculating each "Shookr Ullah,"* he felt himself at liberty to answer for their respective healths. The manner in which all this was

* Thank God.

done was amusing to a stranger, but as an instance of national manners, it spoke well for the people, and it called to mind the history we read of the "good old times" in our own country, when masters treated their servants more as if they conceived them to be fashioned out of the same clay, and the latter repaid the courtesy with affection tempered by respect.

Our friend had talked much to me on the road about his second wife, and I expected to see him make at once for the "underoon," to be welcomed by her; but etiquette would not allow him to betray a desire to see his lady, until he had sat a due time with the males of the family;—in such superior estimation are men held in these barbarous countries! As we rode along in the morning, we had been considering the merits of our respective countrywomen, and my friend, I thought, had displayed a very gallant feeling for the sex in general; I therefore took the liberty of asking him why he did not hasten to salute his wife. "What! before my brother-in-law?" was the answer, "that would never do." Now the man professed to be very fond of his wife, and I know did not care a rush for his brother-in-law, for he cautioned me against too intimate an acquaintance with him. "He is my relation," were his words, "'tis true, and under obligations to me; but though his tongue is smooth, his heart is not better than any body else's, so do not trust him with many of your secrets."

This relation, Syud Syfooddeen, (or the sword of religion,) called "for short" Syud Syfoo, made a great dinner for us, and we sat down to it in the evening, more than twenty persons of all degrees. The host was, I imagine, very much the man that Muheen Shah described him, except that he was a fanatic, and any thing but smooth-tongued when discussing religious topics. On seeing Karaumut Ali and his protegé, he guessed that they were Sheahs, and set himself to work to prove them; but he met his match in Karaumut Ali, who was too well versed in the tenets of the Soonnees to be taken unawares, and he led the prayers, and traced his descent from the best branch of the orthodox Syuds, with a self-possession that quite baffled his inquisitor, who, still unconvinced, changed his battery, and began to heap maledictions upon the sect of Ali, —sentiments which my friend echoed with perfect *sang froid*, and which his *protegé* assented to for safety's sake. I pitied the latter, knowing that his feelings would be much hurt; but he made himself some amends afterwards, for when we retired to rest, and he had laid himself snugly under his coverlid, he spent half an hour in muttering the bitterest curses on the three first Caliphs, and on all who might follow them, without reserve, and doubtless went to sleep with a mind much relieved.

Once upon the subject of religion, Syud Syfoo would not let it rest, and next he attacked me, by asking if my countrymen did not eat hogs. Seeing the company look very much disgusted, I shook my head, in the hope that they would not believe in the possibility of such a thing; but here I reckoned without my host, for Syud Syfoo had been at Bombay, and hastened to insist upon it that he had seen a hog being prepared for the food of the Feringee soldiers; "they had him in a tub," he explained; "they had cut his throat from ear to ear, and were shaving him with hot water." The credit of my nation was at stake, and in such a case veracity would have been a fault; so I boldly corrected him, by saying that we had indeed a low caste of men who partook of swine's flesh, but that no *ashroff*—no *gentleman* among us ate pig; and Syud Muheen cleverly nodding assent to this, and adding that I was a gentleman of the first order, and an altogether clean person, who did not even drink wine, I more than recovered the ground which I had lost.

I felt truly glad when the assembly broke up, for I was very ill, and the next morning found that I had got the jaundice, and to boot, what the French are pleased to call "*une bonne fièvre.*" My first act was to send for a barber, but when he came he would not bleed me, because it was Friday; so I took at a venture a large dose of calomel, and abstained from food. During the nine days that we remained here, I was confined to my bed, and more than once thought that I should die; for I could not shake off the fever which was daily reducing my strength, and those who professed to understand the other malady, said that if my colour did not shortly change for the better, it would go hard with me. So many recipes were offered, that had I used half of them I might have died of another disease. One of them I remember was—a breast of roast mutton;—a remedy which one of Syud Syfoo's dependents assured me had brought him round when he was very bad indeed with the same complaint. Syud Muheen Shah thinks that he was the means of curing me, by advising the decoction of a bitter herb to be drawn up the nose, so as to produce a discharge from the head,—the usual mode of treating the jaundice among the Affghauns; but I was so very ill, that I cannot ascribe my cure to any medicine, and should be sorry to omit expressing my gratitude to that Providence which preserved me in this as in every other chance of my journey.

The route by which we came from Heraut to Candahar has not, I believe, been travelled by any other European. It is reputed to be the most difficult, because the most hilly, of three roads, but a little labour would make it an easy one. The Dilarâm, or usual kafilah road, was taken many years ago by Mr. Foster, and there is no reason to suppose that its state has been materially altered since the period at which that traveller wrote.* The third road is said to be similar to the Dilarâm one.

During our journey, we met very few of the in-

* Two distinguished officers now commanding the forces of Maharajah Runjeet Sing,—Generals Allard and Ventura,—travelled through Persia and Affghaunistaun to the Panjaub some years ago, but they, unfortunately, published no account of their journey.

habitants of the country, and were able to form but an imperfect notion of the extent of population: in the daytime we scarcely saw any body, but at night lights would shine out all round us, from distant khails or sheepfolds. Near some of the usual halting-places are found khails, from which travellers obtain flour or bread, and grain for their horses; but the body of the people, divided into small pastoral societies, wander with their flocks in the broad valleys away from the road. Still, however, judging from the barren appearance of the country, and from the circumstance of so little of it being cultivated, and also from the general result of our inquiries, I should say that the country between Heraut and Candahar is but scantily populated.

Though the appearance of the land was bare (we viewed it the end of autumn), so bare, indeed, that an English farmer would probably deem it impossible to feed sheep upon it, the flocks that we saw seemed to thrive upon the short and scanty herbage which it produced. The soil is in most places such as might be profitably tilled where there is water, though it is not generally used otherwise than as pasture-land, distinct parts of the country being set apart for cultivation, such as the neighbourhoods of Furrah, Subzaur, Ghore, &c., to which the people repair at proper seasons to cultivate grain, and then return to the care of their flocks again. We occasionally saw spots cultivated with cotton, but except in the vicinity of towns, I conceive that this plant is grown more for private use in the khails than for sale. The Affghauns are all for a *far niente* life, and, dwelling under rude felt tents, they are content to live poorly, so that they may live idly and independently. They are clothed coarsely; gaily when they can afford it, but always dirtily, and their fare is very simple. The common food of the Affghauns is kooroot, hard pressed salted curds, which are scraped and boiled up with butter, and eaten with unleavened bread. They never tire of this food, and it is amusing to see the eagerness with which a party will get round a bowl, break their bread into it, and then thrust their huge fingers into the mess. I have heard a man who had been eating little else all his life, exclaim with a sigh of sincerity after licking his fingers—"Hei kooroot! by heaven, it is a good thing, kooroot!"

It is chiefly in spring that the nomade Affghauns allow themselves the luxury of flesh; they roast or make broth of it, not having palates for the delicacies which are eaten in cities. At a feast, the master waits upon his guests, sees that their dishes are filled, and encourages them to eat, handing choice bits to the most favoured persons. Words are not wasted during the meal, the company addressing themselves to the food set before them, with a gravity becoming the grand occupation of life, and when they have qualified their meat with a hearty draught of water, and washed their hands, the eldest man of the company prays for a blessing upon the host, to which the rest say "Aumeen!—God bless him, and increase his store, Inshallah!"

From Heraut to Largebur Kahreeze, the people who inhabit the country through which our road lay are of the Noorzye tribe; between the latter place and Gunneemurgh, the country is chiefly occupied by Atchikzyes; and then again on to Girishk, you meet Noorzyes. They are fine-looking men, tall and stout, with clear brown complexions, black hair and eyes, and brilliantly white teeth, and wear an appearance of great manliness and good humour. Sometimes a man descrying our party from afar, would make for a point in the road, and there await us, to see who we were and learn the news, or to beg a blessing from the Syuds of Pisheen. Our patron, Muheen Shah, appeared to be known by every body, and when his (I may call them) adorers ran eagerly to his stirrup for a benediction, he patted them affectionately on the head, with "God prosper you brother, and give you increase!" and such other expressions as were suited to their circumstances.

All sorts of accidents and desires were submitted to the consideration of the Shah, and he prescribed for the different cases with much tact. "God increase your store!" said he to a petitioner for his blessing;—"Inshallah! God is gracious," was the answer, "but our two camels have been sick ever since spring, and Jandaud lies up there sick with the shaking fever; do something for us!"—"Shé, shé, good, good! we will say a 'fâteheh,' for Jandaud."—

"Ho! Syud Moortesa! Syud Daoud! a fâteheh for Jandaud Khan!"—and getting their horses together, they held up their palms while Muheen Shah muttered a prayer, reverentially stroking their beards when he had finished it. "And the camels?" asked the suitor. "Keep a good heart! I swear to you that I lost my best camel not two weeks ago! it was fated! nusseeb kismut!—but never despond; Ullah kureem deh! Ullah is merciful! it will be well, Inshallah!" and with such homely consolation he comforted and dismissed his follower, who remained on the road-side after we had ridden on, to supplicate all blessings upon so good a man.

From meeting so few people between Heraut and Candahar, I was induced to ask our friends whence Shah Kamraun expected to get his partisans. In the different khails of the road, I was told, were many horses, and as friends to the royal cause would muster from all quarters, far and near, there would be no great difficulty in getting together a volunteer levy of four or five thousand cavalry. The statement was probably correct, for during the last civil war in Affghaunistaun, large bodies of irregular horse were frequently collected on short notice. Every man is a soldier according to the fashion of the times; he has a sword, if not a gun, and if he does not himself own a horse, he can borrow one. It is easy to raise an army in this country, the difficulty is to keep it together; for if their wants are not provided for, the soldiers soon betake themselves to their homes, and frequently, when experiencing the best treatment, mere caprice will induce some of them to desert their standard and go over to the opposite party.

While I lay sick at Syud Muheen Shah's house, my friend Karaumut Ali went to the city: on his return he gave me the following, I am sure, correct description of it:

"The city of Candahar is a third larger than Heraut. In shape it is a parallelogram, three thousand six hundred ordinary paces long, by eighteen hundred broad, and its length is north and south. The city is enclosed by a bastioned mud wall, on the ramparts of which three men can walk abreast, and a ditch, lately made by the Sirdars, encompasses the entire extent of this. The depth of the ditch was about nine feet; it was partly dry, and in parts retained pools of water, which had run through the city into it. Water is conveyed into the town from a little distance by three canals; this supply might be cut off, but there are many wells inside. In the south quarter of the town is a citadel of no great consequence; the city is nowhere commanded, but it is not on the whole a place of strength."

Provisions, my friend said, were very plentiful and cheap, two broad and well supplied bazaars, according to his description, running across the city at right angles to each other, and meeting in the centre of it under a small domed square. The Syud was lodged in a house with half-a-dozen Affghauns, at whose dirtiness he expressed much disgust; and, to describe the city, he said, "You know what Heraut is! well then, imagine (if you can) a town and a people some degrees more filthy:—Tooff!—I spit upon the beards of such beasts: I shall never be clean again!"

The city of Candahar being a third larger than Heraut, its population, if my calculation regarding the latter city be correct, may be rated at sixty thousand souls. We could not procure accounts of the produce of the country, but were told that the Sirdars had resumed all the lands which had been held in *teool* under the royal government, and that they exacted as much as they could from the cultivators. By taxes, and by oppressing all classes of people, they were said to collect annually one hundred thousand gold ducats, which are equal to about £50,000.

The climate of Candahar is not so good as that of the country about Heraut, for in summer the heat is much greater, and in winter more rain than snow falls: but still the place is esteemed healthy. As in Persia, the inhabitants of Affghaunistaun can easily change their climate. In summer many of the Candaharees make a journey of two or three days to the hills of Toba, where it is always deliciously cool.

The finest fruits and vegetables are grown in the neighbourhood of Candahar: among the fruits, the pomegranates are especially esteemed. Were this city the seat of a just government, it would be the centre of a large circle of rich cultivation. The soil is good, and water abundant, and though the cultivators were oppressed by the rebel Sirdars, still it was apparent from the cheapness of grain at Candahar that much was raised. We required no stronger proof of the Sirdars' misrule, than the circumstance of Shah Kamraun being desired. He certainly was no Noorshewân, yet we met few who, on being told that he was coming, did not express a hope that he would bestir himself, and add a prayer for his success against the *zaalim** usurpers.

On the last day of the Syud's stay at Candahar, he saw the Sirdars ride into the city. They had lost some men in battle with the Sheah Hazaurehs, and hastily made peace with them, on hearing that the Shah was about to march from Heraut. He described them as "portly, richly dressed, but vulgar-looking men, who rode their horses stiffly in order to appear consequential."—Their troops were all called in, couriers were sent to Caubul, as well as to their partisans in the country round, and orders were given to put their artillery (six or eight good guns) into the best state. It was moreover said that instructions had been issued to prevent any traders from proceeding with their merchandise to Heraut, lest Kamraun should seize them, and by thus enriching himself be better able to prosecute the war. A similar order, we heard, was about to be issued by Kamraun, when

* Tyrannical.

we were on the point of leaving Heraut;—a sad instance of the opinion that the belligerent powers entertained of each other, and a very satire on the fortune of princes.

On the same day the Syud was singularly accosted in the bazaar of Candahar by an Affghaun, who would insist upon it that my friend was an European, and lately arrived from Bokhara. He only got rid of the fellow by treating him as though he thought him crazy, and indeed it argued great want of sense in the man to take a person of my friend's complexion for a Feringee. It was evident that the Indian who had endeavoured to rob us at Heraut, had visited Candahar, and reported our intended coming, and that the man who accosted the Syud, had been imperfectly informed of the story regarding us. When Muheen Shah was told of the circumstance, he urged the expediency of continuing our journey, and an old Doorraunee nobleman, whose kullah was close to Syud Muheen's, (Munsoor Khan of honourable fame,) being told in confidence of my being there, advised my making no longer stay than necessary, lest the Sirdars should hear of my arrival, and cause me to be detained or ill-treated.

There could be little reason to doubt the sincerity of Munsoor Khan's advice, for his own brother had been murdered by the rebel chiefs, in violation of their pledged word, and he himself had suffered many indignities at their hands. Infirm and impoverished, the old noble maintained his loyalty, and spurning their offers of favour as the price of blood, in the midst of adversity, preserved that true dignity of which the worst fortune cannot deprive an honest man.

Munsoor Khan, if my recollection serves me aright, was the nobleman selected by Zemaun Shah as his ambassador to the court of Persia, and very worthily, it is said, did he discharge his office. We heard frequent mention of his name, and it was always coupled with terms of regard; nor do I remember any trait of the Affghaun character which struck me more pleasingly, than the devoted fidelity with which the Khan's vassals seemed to cling to their master in his adversity.

Men such as the younger brothers of Futteh Khan, who possessing neither principle nor talent, found themselves suddenly raised to great power which they had no certainty of retaining, were not likely to look much beyond their immediate interests; and, accordingly, we see that they employed every means to enrich themselves, at the expense of those who had been thrown into their power. Such conduct, they were probably able to foresee, could only lead to a strong reaction of feeling in favour of the royal family, and therefore they sought to crush those influential men who were disposed to restore the Suddozye dynasty; but though by murder and rapine they removed some, and weakened others of the chiefs whom they feared, among the nobility generally they met with a spirit of hereditary pride and deep-rooted attachment to old institutions, which resolutely opposed itself to their usurpation; and instances of devoted fealty to the Suddozye family are recorded of Doorraunee chiefs, which call to mind the unflinching and generous loyalty of those gallant gentlemen of our own nation, who engaging in the long unfortunate cause of the Stuarts, sacrificed their lives and fortunes rather than acknowledge the authority of those whom they considered usurpers of their place.

Among the many names thus distinguished, I remember hearing that of Munsoor Khan's brother above alluded to, Mucksood Khan, who, well known as a loyal and influential nobleman, was marked out for destruction by the Candahar Sirdars, but who, the soul of honour himself, believed the rebels when they swore not to injure him, and trusting himself in their hands, was basely plundered and deprived of life by them. And of old Munsoor Khan himself, who when carried before the Sirdars, and told that he should be tortured if he did not declare his wealth, answered them by scornfully asking how much malice they could wreak upon his limbs, crippled as they were by wounds and age, and told them that he had expended his riches, as became a nobleman, on his soldiers, and in relieving the needy; then remembering his brother, the old Khan raised himself, and fearlessly upbraided the usurpers with their cruel treachery, and told them that they were a curse on the land, whom God would soon remove, and follow with his vengeance for their wickedness;—and they were awed, and dared not hurt him, but, affecting to laugh scornfully, let him go, because, as they said, he was the old soldier Munsoor Khan,—that is, privileged.

On the eve of our departure, when Muheen Shah came to my bed to propose continuing our journey on the morrow, I felt far from equal to the undertaking; but he expressed himself so anxiously, that I agreed to attempt it. There was reason in what my friend urged,—that as I had made some stay at Heraut avowedly an Englishman, the Sirdars, if they heard of my living *incog.* at his house, would fancy that my journey was in some way connected with the king's affairs. "And do not fancy," added he, in a low tone, "that your being here can long remain a secret; there is Syud Syfoo, my own brother-in-law, if no one else would, I do not know that he would not inform against me, if he thought it would serve his interests to do so. Sahib! you do not know my countrymen; on such an occasion I would not trust my own brother."

In order to give his relative an interest in my welfare, Syud Muheen bought a horse from him, for which he engaged to pay on his return from Hindoostân. "He knows now," argued the Shah, "that our nusseebs are bound together, so for his own sake he will be careful not to injure us: he must not, however, see that I doubt him, or have any complaint against him, (though I have, as I will tell you another time;)—we will talk him fair now, but when I get to Pisheen, see if I do not play him a trick. Inshallah! I can throw dust into a man's eyes as well as another."

Syud Syfoo, it was frequently made evident by his manner, could not get the better of his prejudice against my companions: he had assured himself that the Persian and the Lahoree were Sheahs, for they went about the Soonnee forms in so slovenly a manner, that I could have detected them myself; and though he could never catch Karaumut Ali tripping, he took it for granted that he was of the heretical sect also: moreover, the man was a hypocrite as well as a bigot; he felt that my friend saw into his character, and hated him for his acuteness. For me "the sword of religion" latterly affected the warmest regard, and when I took leave of him, he prayed that I might become a Mohummudan. I did not believe that his wish had even sincerity to recommend it, and we had so many times come to the conclusion that he was an arrant rascal, that I did not feel in the least degree obliged to him; but, politician as I had become, I thanked him for his consideration, and bade him adieu as though he had been one of the best men in the world.

We marched from Ghoondee Munsoor Khan on the 10th of November; our own party, two Syuds of Pisheen (the one a friend, and the other a follower of Muheen Shah), and a Khanehzâd, or home-bred slave, half negro half Affghaun, who called our host master. We had given two of our horses and some money for three camels, which carried our baggage and the Lahoree. Muheen Shah lent one of his horses to Karaumut Ali, and mounted me upon a Chahargoosht, or four-eared* Bokhara pony, a stout shaggy animal, not unlike a a bear, which had been trained to a quick and easy amble. We made a short march of sixteen miles to the Dooree river, in the bed of which there was much good water. Five miles on the road was the brook Arghestaun, the water of which is famed for its excellence. Ahmud Shah Doorraunee, we were assured, would drink no other when he was at Candahar, and by his orders it had been weighed in a scale with other waters, and proved to be far lighter than any of them.

11th.—Thirty-one miles to Kullah Futoollah. After three miles, we got upon the road coming from Candahar, near to Lylee Mujnoon, a high rock, under which there is a spring of water. Some account for the name of this rock, by asserting, that "that ornament of frantic lovers, the heart-consumed, anguish-pierced Mujnoon," threw himself from its peak, in order to convince the father of "the Empress in the dominion of loveliness, Lylee, the heart-ravisher," that he was really in love. They assert that he fell upon his legs, and that where he lighted the spring gushed; but there are others again, who,

* So called, because the animal's ears are usually slit in two.

presuming on their college education, treat the story as an idle tradition, and go so far as even to doubt whether Mujnoon was ever in this part of the country. There, however, as our friend's friend acutely remarked, stands the rock, and at its foot the spring, and a man may believe just as much or as little of the tale as he feels inclined to.

Kullah Fut, or Put-oollah (for the Affghauns generally use *p* for *f*), is a mud fort, situated in a broad bare valley, four miles beyond a narrow line of hills, called Gautee, which run nearly parallel with the range of Khojeh Amraun. The Noorzyes who inhabited the fort, Muheen Shah warned us as we were riding up, were a set of great Namrauds (Anglicè blackguards), whom it would be well to have nothing to say to; and his words were shortly verified, for a man of the crowd which assembled round us to hear the news and sell necessaries, began to quarrel with him about the price of something. Words ran very high till our friend, finding that his opponent's voice was the loudest, and that as a stranger he was fighting at disadvantage, turned to the crowd, and holding up his hands, exclaimed, "Very well! very well! I say not a word more! but please God, you will see some accident befall that man before eight days. Only wait eight days! Inshallah Taullah! the curse of Syud Muheen Shah will not go to the wind. Inshallah Taullah!" and then he turned away, muttering, and looking as black as possible.

This very much altered the state of affairs, for

these men well knew the name of our patron, though they had not till then been acquainted with his person, and they sought to pacify him. The quarreller attempted to keep up his high tone, but he presently slunk away on seeing the turn that the matter had taken. Muheen Shah for a time indignantly refused to listen to those who now crowded round him, with endeavours to appease his anger. He wore the appearance of a deeply injured person, and would only answer their apologies by quietly repeating, "No, no; say nothing! say nothing! only wait eight days." At last the offender was brought between two of his friends to ask pardon, and when he had humbly cried "*Toba*" (peccavi), Muheen Shah suffered himself to be entreated, and took off the anathema, gravely congratulating the man upon his timely submission, and warning him not to trust his tongue again in a dispute with a Syud of Shadeezye.

We here witnessed another instance of these people's credulity. A woman with a swollen arm came in the evening to Muheen Shah to be cured, when he spat upon the limb, and muttered something, ordering her to remain quiet and do no work. The next morning the woman came with a plate of raisins as a thanks-offering to our friend, saying that the swelling was reduced, and that she felt much better. Muheen Shah magnanimously refused to accept the raisins, but he took all the credit of the cure, and the woman went away blessing him.

We could not fail to observe that there was a considerable portion of cunning mixed up with the Shah's superstition, and I was sorry to remark it, for I felt so much obliged to the man, that I wished to consider him above the mean immoralities, a disposition for which I am now inclined to think all Asiatics imbibe with their mother's milk. I regretted the discovery also on a selfish principle, for if you happen to see one of your best friends impose upon another, it is difficult to exclude from your mind a lurking doubt of his perfect sincerity towards yourself. However a second, more powerfully selfish, feeling interfered to prevent our laying the first one too much to heart; we profited too well by our patron's conduct to feel beyond measure disgusted at it, and in all things relating to his treatment of us, he was, to use the praise of the Lahoree, not a man, but a Ferishtah, a very angel of a man.

12th.—As we were shivering round a fire in our poosteens, an hour before sunrise, an old graybeard, with a fresh, golden-pippin sort of complexion, came up and laughed at us for looking so cold. He told us that he was a native of the hills of Toba, where the snow lay for five months in the year, and where in summer the water was so cold, that you could not take a long draught of it. He was ninety years old, he said, and had lately married his third wife, and he talked as if there was no likelihood of his dying for the next fifty years.

From Kullah Putoollah we rode across the valley

twenty-four miles to Chokee, a small spring of good water, at the entrance of the Khojeh Amraun hills. After we had travelled six miles, Syud Muheen led us off the road some little distance, to show us an extraordinary excavation, called Bhoulee Khan-e-Aulum, or the Well of the Lord of the World. A passage some eight or ten feet broad, and two hundred paces in extent, was cut down through hard gravelly earth, to a circular chamber of, if I recollect right, about twenty-one feet diameter, which had been sunk perpendicularly, like a well, to a depth of perhaps one hundred feet below the surface. From this level a small well had been dug, in which there was water at the depth of thirty feet, and which we were told was often used by the shepherds, who, in different parts of this plain, have dug other wells from which to water their sheep.

Who Khan-e-Aulum was, it does not appear. Like the King of Bohemia, he is described as "a certain king," who was marching at the head of a large army; arriving at this spot very thirsty, and being unable to get any thing to drink, he ordered a halt, and commanded that water should be found while he slept; upon which the troops set to work, and laboured so strenuously, that a goblet of water was presented to "The Lord of the World" on his awakening. It was a valley of wonders, for we were shown a rocky hill in the distance, whence on a certain night every year would come the sound of sharp firing of musketry, and groans like those of dying men, sounds which, whatever they were, were not mortal.

Ten miles on the road from Kullah Putoollah, we crossed the dry bed of the Kudunny, which holds water only in winter and spring, and towards sunset we arrived at the foot of the Khojeh Amraun hills. We all felt inclined to halt at the spring, except Muheen Shah, who said that we must get on as far as possible that night, so as to pass a police station before light on the next day's march; and accordingly we rode on.

The Khojeh Amraun hills are a broad range, which rise gradually above each other to the main line. The first are very low, and the highest have no great altitude. From Chokee spring to the foot of the main range, a distance of about four miles, our road was on a gradual ascent, and it was bordered by many little dells, in which grew khunjuck trees and many shrubs. "In spring," said Muheen Shah's friend, "it is *Behisht* here (Paradise); the snow melts into clear rills, and a light cool air is always blowing, to bear to you the fragrance of a thousand odours from the shrubs and flowers which cover the hills." We were too weary to applaud this poetical description, having ridden without food all day; and Syud Muheen led on without the least regard to our fatigue. We crossed the highest ridge by a steep and narrow but short ascent, and then, descending leisurely two and a half or three miles, by a rocky and winding path, halted for the night at a spot where the road opened out between the rocks. We made a blazing fire of sticks, upon which we placed the trunk of a tree, and then, making a frugal meal of bread and water, betook ourselves to a comfortable slumber. The camels, which were up with us at Chokee, did not arrive till within an hour of midnight, so difficult was the path to them.

Very early the next morning, Muheen Shah made us march on, in order that we might escape particular notice at the dreaded station. It was six miles, by a broad good road, to the outlet of the hills, where, at a post called Chookee Shumshoo khan, we were stopped by a party of the Pisheen Hâkim's men, and ordered to pay duty upon our camel-loads. It was now sunrise, so that Muheen Shah's object in hurrying us on had been frustrated; but he knew what was to be done in such a case, therefore desiring me to wrap my poosteen about me, and sit apart, so as to let it appear that I was unwell, he set himself to make friends with the collectors of customs, and when he had said a fateheh for one, and spoken encouraging things to the others, he told them that he was in an extraordinary hurry, and begged that they would not detain his camels. The beasts, he protested, were only laden with pomegranates, which he was going to take to the Hakim at Quetta; the horse-merchants were anxiously waiting his arrival, as it was time they should be on the road to India, and he had much to do before starting, &c. My companions, he said, were return pilgrims, I a lad of Heraut, son to Syud somebody's friend, and very sick with the yellow complaint, as they might see; and to make a long story short, he gave them a bribe, and they let us pass.

Five miles to the right of this post, was visible the castle of the Hâkim of these trustworthy fellows, Abdoollah Khan Atchickzye; a man so notorious for his villany, that (according to the Shah's idea) there was no reason to entertain the slightest scruple of conscience for having cheated him.

Ten miles from the outlet of the hills, our road entered a jungle of tamarisk wood, which runs far up the Pisheen valley: through this we rode six miles to a river called Lora, which comes from Burshore, as stated by Mr. Elphinstone. The water of this stream was rather muddy, and lay in a deep bed of soft crumbling earth. We crossed where the water was about three feet deep, and rode four miles beyond, to Shâdeezye, the khail of the best families of the Syuds of Pisheen.

Our coming was observed when we were at some distance from the khail, and all the Syuds who happened to be at home came out to welcome us.

There were twenty or more men, and a crowd of fine children, who discontinued their sports when we dismounted from our horses, and stood in a body respectfully behind their elders.

Gravity being considered a great sign of wisdom in these countries, there was no lively expression of pleasure at the meeting, but much ceremonious salutation, solemn repetition of inquiries after healths, and hugging; which being duly over, Syud Muheen walked to a small enclosure, within which was the grave of his deceased elder brother, where he stood some time in prayer. After his devotion had been accomplished, he introduced us to his younger brother, and then led us to the court of his own residence, within which he pitched a small tent for our accommodation. I need scarcely add, that we received hospitable treatment as long as we remained here.

CHAPTER V.

Khojeh Amraun, Speen Taizhe, and Toba hills—Valley of Pisheen—Shorawuck and Shorarood—Inhabitants of Pisheen—History of the Shâdeezye, Hyderzye, and Kerbolah Syuds—Affghaun social life—Personal narrative during a sojourn at Pisheen.

THE range of hills named by Mr. Elphinstone Khojeh Amraun, or rather that portion of it which is visible from the valley of Pisheen, runs N.N.E. and S.S.W. We crossed it by what is termed the Kozhuck cotul, four miles to the left of which, viewed from Pisheen, is another similar pass, called Roghanee; and again, six miles to the left of Roghanee cotul, is the pass of Ghwozhe, which comes through, not over, the hills, and is passable by any thing.

This range has three names. Speen Taizhe, Khojeh Amraun, and Toba. The centre, or Khojeh Amraun division, extends from a point twelve miles to the right, or north-north-eastward, of Kozhuck cotul, to another point about twenty-eight miles to the left of it. The Speen Taizhe division runs to the south-south-westward of Khojeh Amraun, twenty-four miles, when the range ends in sand. Where the Khojeh Amraun division ends (twelve miles) on the right of Kozhuck cotul, the hills take the name of Toba, with which they run up a hundred and sixty miles, to Murgha in Bukhteeauree country. They first, according to my information, go through the country inhabited by the Noorzyes Ahmud Khan; but I confess that I am not certain about the course of these hills beyond Pisheen, as I do not know where either the Noorzyes Ahmud Khan or the Murgha Bukhteeaurees are seated. At best, a traveller across this country must feel much uncertainty in laying down chains of mountains from native report. The land is covered with irregular hills, to almost every peak or turn of which the people give a separate name, and it is only by learning that several parallel routes come to cotuls about the same line, that you may presume them to cut a connected range. When I was seeking information in Pisheen, I was entreated not to appear curious about the country, but to wait for Syud somebody, who would join us on the march, who knew all the hills in Khorassaun. This person (if there was such a person) did not join us, and it was not till after our arrival in Hindoostân, that I obtained the latter part of the information which has been given above.

Every body gave the same account of the climate of Toba. Between the long and severe winters which the inhabitants of these hills experience, they enjoy a very delicious climate: the tops of the hills are table-lands, which are greatly cultivated by means of the water which springs every where in abundance; one enthusiastic resident of this part of the country, in describing it said, that even if there was not water there, the very air would raise the crops.

The valley of Pisheen, or as it is sometimes called Pisheng, is formed by the Khojeh Amraun range, and another nearly parallel but scanty line called Ajrum, which divides it from the province of Shaul. The valley is thirty miles broad, and twice that distance in length, and apparently is high land between Burshore and Shorawuck, for at both of these places we heard great accounts of the cultivation, while the water of the river which runs down Pisheen, lies in so deep a bed, that it cannot well be raised for the purposes of agriculture.

Lora is the Pushtoo for river. The Pisheen lora, as stated by Mr. Elphinstone, has its rise at a spot called Tubbye, above Burshore, which is a small fertile tract at the head of the Pisheen valley. The stream has the name of Aub-e-Burshore during its course from Tubbye to the end of the district; there it receives the water of the Soorkaub, a stream of the same size, and flows on down the valley with the name of Lora, or, the river.

The khail of Shâdeezye is built on the bank of another lora, which rises at a place called Ser-e-aub, ten miles to the southward of the town of Quetta. It comes up to Hyderzye khail, then turning, flows down past Shâdeezye, four miles or so below which it joins the Pisheen lora, and the united streams flow on past Shorawuck and Shorarood, one hundred and twenty miles, into an aub-istaada, or lake, described as eight miles in circuit.

Shorawuck and Shorarood are two districts about twenty miles distant from each other, which, being well irrigated by the waters of the lora, are greatly cultivated with wheat, barley, and bajra, of which grain, of the last especially, many camel-loads are yearly exported to Kelaute-e Nusseer, Pisheen, &c. When the snow melts and runs from the mountains in spring, the loras, after their junction, form a deep and rapid stream. The lake which receives their waters appears to be on the border of the sandy desert; it decreases much in size during the hot months, but it is never dry. A young Syud, who told me that he had spent several days there shooting wild fowl with ball, said, "The lake is deep at flood (spring) time, but the sand drinks so much water, that a man does not know how much flows to it then, and at other times the cultivators draw the water off before it reaches the lake."

Pisheen is inhabited by Tor Tereens, by different families of Syuds, and a few Humsayehs, or naturalized strangers. Situated between the well-cultivated districts of Burshore and Shorawuck, the Pisheengees can be easily supplied with grain from either quarter; yet still the Tereens cultivate portions of the valley by means of canaut and rain water. Both they and the Syuds possess flocks of sheep, which thrive, as elsewhere, upon very little. Formerly the Syuds of Pisheen held the best part of the valley in free tenure, but the rebel Sirdars resumed all the crown grants, in spite of the remonstrances, nay threats, of the holy men, and the latter now occupy themselves rather with commerce than with agriculture.

The far-famed Syuds of Pisheen are divided into three classes: the Shâdeezye, Hyderzye, and Kerbolah-e. The Shâdeezyes call themselves the first, though I imagine the Hyderzyes make as much of themselves; but neither admit the Kerbolah-ees to any thing like an equality; for as the credit of their supernatural virtues is valuable, they are anxious to share it with as few as possible. The following account of these esteemed men was extracted by my friend Karaumut Ali from the Tuạrikh-e-khan Jehan-e. The Syud's own traditional account differs somewhat from it, but as neither is true, the discrepancy is of no great consequence.

Kyse, *Abd-ool Resheed,* or "the slave of the Deity," is looked up to by the Affghauns as the ancestor to whom they owe their conversion to Islâm; and they say that Mohummud, charmed with his zeal and gallantry in the cause, gave him the title of "Buthan-e Islam," or "the keel of the faith," whence is supposed to have been derived the word Puthan, the name by which Affghauns are designated in Hindoostân.

Fifth in generation from Kyse Abd-ool Resheed, descended Haroon. He was a fakeer, a poor devout man, who possessed one goat and one daughter, and subsisted chiefly upon what he got in the chase.

One day that Haroon was out hunting as usual, four Wullee Oollah (that is, friends of God, or holy men) having with them a lad, came to the tent. His daughter "was a girl of understanding, who had been well brought up," and she hastened to welcome the strangers in her father's name, baked a cake for their immediate refreshment, and killed the goat to dress it for their dinner. At even time Haroon returned from the chase, empty-handed and wearied, but he blessed his fortune when he found who had come under the shelter of his tent; he praised his daughter for her good conduct, then, forgetting his fatigue, set himself assiduously to wait upon his guests, washing their hands, and serving them at meat, &c. and at night, when they retired to rest, he gave them up his own covering.

The next morning, when the holy men were about to depart, Haroon frankly told them his circumstances; that there remained to him in the world but one thing,—his daughter; but he declared that rather than allow men of their character to leave his door without a present, he would give them that daughter, whom they might sell, or themselves retain as a slave.

Charmed with the good man's disinterestedness, the Wullee Oollah expressed their determination to reward him for it. His daughter, they said, they would marry to the lad who was with them, a youth of holy origin, by name Syud Doorjamaul, and they there made good their words. When they took leave of the young couple, they blessed them with all the virtues to which their descendants now lay claim, and they foretold that seven children should be the issue of the marriage, who should inherit their properties, and be widely known as the Saadzye (or posterity) of the Syud, and from a corruption of this word, or from shâdee, signifying marriage, the head khail of these descendants was named Shâdeezye.

The Syuds of Hyderzye khail derive their name from one Syud Hyder, who went out from the head quarters; therefore it is fair to suppose that they are as highly gifted as the generality of their connexions at Shâdeezye. I say the generality, because though Syud Doorjamaul's virtue is supposed to run more or less through all the family, it is judged to dwell with greatest potency in the persons of the elders, and the family in the direct line of descent claim the chief exercise of it.

The origin of the Kerbolah Syuds is thus described in the book from which the above information was extracted. When the Wullee Oollah were about to take leave of Haroon, they told him that under a certain tree, on a certain road, he would find a child, which had been there exposed to chance:* the

* This relates to a superstitious custom which prevails in parts of the East. Sometimes a parent whose child will not thrive, or who, perhaps, has lost several children successively, decides that an evil fate attends him, and fearing therefore the death of the infant, he exposes

foundling they said, was a Syud, and they directed Haroon to adopt and cherish it, and call its name Kerbolah; then, it is said, they predicted much good fortune to him and the child, and departed in a very mysterious manner.

The Shâdeezye Syuds affect not to be very sure about the last section of the above history, nor are they content with that part of it which relates to themselves in particular, for they contend that they can trace their descent from the martyr Hossein through Syud Doorjamaul, who, they say, was one of four brothers, Door-*jamaul, Door-jelaul, Door-kamaul, and Door-delail. Door-jelaul is the man widely known as Syud Jelaulooddeen Bokharee, who rose to fame at Bokhara, and afterwards settled in the city of Ooch, where he died and was buried. His genealogy is traced from Hossein; but, according to all that I can gather from some of the most esteemed Soonnee writers, he had only one brother, which is rather against the Pisheen Syud's claim.

It is very difficult to get at the truth of a story which is thought good enough to be adopted by several parties, for no one scruples to alter the circum-

it, in the hope that some more fortunate person will look upon and adopt it. I imagine that very few Mohummudans would hesitate to act the part of the good Samaritan to an infant thus cast out: we knew an old Indian Syud at Meshed who had adopted a foundling boy, and he complained that the father, seeing his son grown into a fine young man, had declared himself, and was continually endeavouring to recover his own flesh and blood.

* The word Door (Pearl) prefixed to the above names, is a favourite term of honour with the Affghauns.

stances of it to serve a special purpose or a prejudice, and what one knave writes, twenty fools copy. A Soonnee who traced his ancestry up to some Peer* or other, whom he wished to prove related to Syud Jelaulooddeen, showed me a clumsily devised Pooshtnameh,† which deduced the origin of the Syud from Hossein's son Ali Asghur, who was killed when he was but six months old; and when I happened to apply to an Indian Sheah Moollâ for information, he said, "All that I know about *that* Jelaulooddeen is, that on the eighth day of the month Mohurrum,‡ we give breakfasts, when before each person is placed a sweet milk cake, some radishes, ginger, onions, mint, cheese, sweetmeats, and a basin of mutton broth; then, as we eat, we invoke curses upon him, and his father, and his father's father, and upon all the dogs of the same faith who came before and after him; and upon all those who did follow, do follow, and will follow them: and to every curse that one invokes, the rest cry, '*Besh bad!* may it be worse than that! and be it upon him who echoes it not, or who feels sick at hearing it!'"

Ask a Sheah if Jelaulooddeen was not a Syud, he answers, "Yes, in the line of Jaffer the liar, to which hangs the following tale: When Huzrut Imaum-e-

* The head of a religious sect.

† Pedigree.

‡ The anniversary of the day on which Abbas, the brother of Ali, fell a martyr at Kerbolah. The Sheahs on this day give breakfasts, to commemorate his sufferings, and vent their spleen upon the sect who caused them.

Hussan Uskeree was at the death of his father declared Imaum, his younger brother Jaffer disputed the title with him; upon which it was agreed that they should seek a Hookum* at the shrine of Huzrut Ali. They went together to the tomb of the saint, and separately addressed the following salutation to him:—'*Ussalaamo Aleika Yah Ali Ibn-e Ubbee Taulib!*' Peace be upon you, O Ali the son of Aboo Taulib. To which a voice from the tomb answered—'*Wo Aleikoom Salaam Yah Imaum-e Hussan Uskeree!* And upon you be peace, O Imaum Hussan Uskeree!' This settled the question, and from that day Jaffer bore the name of "Kuzzaub," the liar. Soonnees name him Jaffer-e-Tuwwaub, Jaffer the penitent, and are not ashamed to trace their descent from him; but the Sheahs altogether deny his legitimacy, and when it does not suit them to allow a Syud's pedigree, they ingraft it upon Jaffer Kuzzaub's family tree.

However, the reputation of Syud Jelaulooddeen is too well established to be much shaken by such assaults, and as he belongs to the strongest party, the greater number of Mohummudans are bound to believe the following account of him.

The original name of Huzrut Syud Jelaulooddeen Bokharee, Ullah Sirrahoo,† was Syud Hossein. Jelaulooddeen signifies eminent in religion, and was the title given him on account of his excellence. In

* In this sense, a decision by oracle.

† The blessed Syud Jelaulooddeen of Bokhara; may God sanctify the place of his rest!

his youth, the Prophet (upon whom the highest blessing and the most perfect peace) appeared to him in a dream of the night, and commanded him to go to the King of Bokhara, who would give him a daughter in marriage.

In obedience to the fortunate mandate, the Syud took his excellent presence to Bokhara, and repairing to the gate of the Shah's palace, desired the parties to go and tell the King that the son of a Syud, whose name was Shah Hossein, and who had lately become a young man, had come to marry his daughter. The servants took in this plain message to the King, who fell into such anger at what he deemed his insolence, that he commanded the audacious stranger's head to be instantly taken off; but the Vuzeer, hinting that as the youth was the son of a Syud, such a summary act would not look well in the eyes of the people, suggested that the offender should be imprisoned, and had him sent to the royal cook-room, there to abide the Shah's pleasure.

It was determined by the King and his sage minister quietly to smother the audacious stranger, and when a quarter of the night was gone, they shut him up in a hot oven. The King then went to bed, but in his sleep the Prophet appeared to him with an angry countenance, and said, "O sinner, what presumption has possessed thee to shut up one of my descendants in an oven." The King, awakening in terror, on the instant,, with naked head and feet, repaired to the cook-room, and threw open the oven door, when he beheld Syud Hossein seated composedly inside, unscorched, and devoutly reading the Korân. Calling him forth, the King fell at his feet, and beseeched pardon for his great mistake, then leading the holy man to the royal apartment, he at once gave him a Princess for wife, and loaded him with honours. This is why the Syud is called Bokharee.

This being about one of the best stories going among the Soonnees, it is no wonder that the Pisheen Syuds should have endeavoured to identify themselves with it. They are illiterate men, who would have no objection to abide by any good tradition that served to raise them in their own conceit, and in the estimation of their superstitious countrymen. It is, however, but doing them justice to say, that they are to the full as great enthusiasts as cheats; that, the state of society considered, they do not make a bad use of their influence; and that, whether from consideration of their gentle blood, or from a necessary care of their conduct, they are far more respectable, and much better behaved men than their neighbours.

We remained eight days in Shâdeezye khail, and were kindly treated by all the people. Muheen Shah's friends, I believe, for the most part thought that, to use their style of expression, he had "ruined his house" by becoming surety for a stranger; but since he had embarked his fortune in such a venture, they felt themselves bound to put a good face upon the matter. When we left Ghoondoe Munsoor Khan, I could scarcely sit upon my horse; three days afterwards, such was the effect of change of air in this fine climate, I was suffering only from the weakness consequent upon my illness. Perhaps also I partly owed the amendment to the free use of the juice of fresh pomegranates, a sack of which fruit Muheen Shah had brought from Candahar. I mention the circumstance, because it gives me pleasure to note a trait of the kind attention which I throughout experienced from him.

At our friend's house I rapidly recovered strength, and amused myself by strolling about to observe the manners of this society. My great desire to ride up and down the valley, was opposed by Muheen Shah, who begged me not to go abroad, lest any of the horse-merchants assembled in Pisheen should report me to the Hakim, Abdoollah Khan, who would certainly detain us, and probably make his protection of me an excuse for ruining his family; so of course I did not press the point.

The khail of Shâdeezye consists of about one hundred and fifty families, whose houses are built in two villages, which are close to each other, and situated at a distance of two hundred yards from the crumbling bank of the lora. A few of the best residences are built with thick mud walls, covered with beams, but the greater number are mere huts. However they all seemed to live comfortably, and to take a very laudable care of each other. In Muheen

Shah's little court there was a house which he had given up to the family of a poor Syud, and he and the other heads of the khail gave the man grain, and such things as were necessary for his family—" for the sake of God, and that he might pray for them."

Our friend's residence consisted of a line of low rooms, which occupied one side of the court. There were no signs of riches in his establishment, but that was no better evidence of his condition than was his personal appearance. It is not politic for a man to exhibit his wealth in such a country, and Muheen Shah pointed out to me, in confidence, several excessively dirty fellows, who were reputed among themselves to be very well to do in the world.

The men were busily engaged during the day, some with their horses, which were picketed all round the khail, preparatory to being taken to India for sale, while others, or their male slaves, would take camels to the tamarisk wood, to bring in a store of fuel to last their families during the approaching cold season.

The females and their bondswomen were well busied in household labour; repairing to the river to fill water-skins, which they would bring back upon their heads, cooking food for the men entertained as grooms, and preparing needful things for their relatives' journey. Labour and exposure had, I fancy, made many of the women look older than they were, and less handsome than they otherwise might have been, but there were not wanting among them some sunburnt beauties, as I had opportunities of observing; for though their manners were very retiring and modest, living, as they were, like one separate family, they were not restrained by the rules which bind women who reside in cities, therefore instead of covering up their figures, and peeping through slips of bobbin-net, as the Persian women do, they wore plaids thrown loosely over their heads like the veils worn by Indian women, which but half-concealed their features, and frequently, when engaged in household occupations, they allowed their veils to fall upon their shoulders, so as to discover their heads. The hair was worn *à la Madonna*, and I remarked one very pretty girl, living near us, who had plaited hers where it was parted; a coiffure which I take the liberty of strongly recommending to the notice of ladies of all nations.

The apparel of the women was simple, consisting of a long chemise, which fell from the neck to the heels, trousers fitting tightly round the ankle, and the plaid or veil above described; and, like Scotchwomen, they appeared to feel *gênée* in shoes.

This leads me to the tale of Muheen Shah's grievances, which, when we were at his kullah near Candahar, he promised to tell me all about. On the road he had given me several hints that he had something in petto for Syud Syfoo, and when we had been a day or two at Shâdeezye, he unburdened his mind in a long conversation with me.

It appeared that, on some occasion when the khail

did not, he thought, pay sufficient respect to his opinion, he had paired off with Syud Syfoo, and, as he candidly confessed, made a fool of himself, by building, at joint expense, the kullah in which we had stayed at Ghoondee Munsoor Khan. However, as the money was burnt, he began to leave off thinking about it, but his chum soon gave him other trouble for his thoughts, by insisting upon the necessity of building this and that upon the joint account, and moreover teaching his wife to be dissatisfied because she had not fifty useless things which Syud Syfoo gave his own wives; but worst of all, when he returned this last time to his home, he found—that his spouse had forsaken the ways of the Pisheen Syudanees (I thought he was going to tell me that she had changed some material part of her faith). She had grown ashamed of the simple and modest habiliments which became the wife of a Syud of Pisheen, and arrayed herself splendidly in silk and satin *à la Persanne!*

This, he said, he could not overlook; he had given his lady a bit of his mind, and Inshallah Tallah! he had a *hoonur* (stratagem) which would astonish his brother-in-law. "This evening," concluded he, "you will see the chief Syuds come, in the name of all the khail, to make a formal request that I will send for my family to reside among them, as it is fitting the house of a peerkhaneh should. I will make a great favour of complying with their request, and then it will be known that I have listened to the desire of the khail. My 'House' will be sent for, as it were in their name, and then Syud Syfoo and his Persian women may make the most of the kullah."

In effect, at evening came a deputation of elders to wait upon Muheen Shah, as he had taught me to expect, and a long hour did they sit and argue with our friend, who met their words with loud Pushtoo orations, and, to judge from the tone of his voice, seemed quite opposed to their wishes. At last, however, he slackened, and allowed himself to be entreated; thanks and adulations were lavished upon him, and he gave a finish to the artifice, by putting on the air of a man who had sacrificed a private feeling to a deep sense of public duty.

The passion for intrigue appears to be inseparable from the character of an Asiatic. Throughout the eastern world it is the main spring of every action, affairs of state and the petty details of life being alike managed by it; and to such an extent is the feeling carried, that I really think I am justified in saying, that if a man were sure of gaining his point by going straight to it, he would risk the loss of it rather than not work it out by intrigue. A monarch who writes himself the Pole Star, the Grasper, the Asylum, the Father, and what not else of the world, and who is represented as powerful as Fate, exalted as the Pleiades, and dignified as Jupiter; the Sovereign of the age of the world; Ruler of the sea and land; who needs but nod his august head to cause those of a thousand of his too fortunate slaves to roll at his feet, has his brain full of plots and stratagems, the greater part of which are as unkingly as superfluous; and below him, from the prime minister to the peasant, affairs of the greatest moment and most trivial consequence must be directed by it; so assiduously do they heap intrigue upon intrigue, that they must sometimes be very much puzzled to know whether they are not plotting against themselves.

Muheen Shah and I had become so very intimate, that he did not scruple to tell me all his secrets. It is impossible that a man can live with the weight of an unshared grievance upon his breast, and my friend, perhaps feeling himself safer with me than with his own people, was glad of an opportunity of relieving his mind confidentially; at least he always appeared much lighter when he had said out his say. Nor did he, on other occasions, scruple to talk about domestic matters when he saw that they amused and interested me. Womanhood is a delicate topic to discourse upon with a Mohummudan, but Muheen Shah had received kindness at the hands of two or three ladies of gentlemen with whom he had dealt in the course of his professional wanderings in British India, and had seen much of the freedom of our life, therefore he was not in the least shocked or ashamed to answer me when I inquired about the customs of the females of his country. His "Asherut khanum," or Lady of delight—

> "The loved of all others, whose smile was the light
> That lit up his Harem, his beauteous and bright,"

was, he told me, at Caubul; a beautiful creature of thirteen (my friend was some eight-and-forty years old) whom he would really show me, English fashion, if ever I came to Caubul. Once set the Shah upon the theme of this love, and there was scarcely a possibility of diverting his thoughts; she was so beautiful and graceful,—I forget his extravagant similes,—so every thing that was perfection; and he loved her the more, that he had long wooed, and with difficulty won her; for her parents were of high rank, and though, of course, they esteemed him, they thought him not rich enough, or that they might marry her to some one of their own rank; and the mother made a difficulty about his having other wives; but at last they recollected that he was a Peerkhaneh of Shâdeezye, and all that, and overcame their scruples; and when at last every thing was settled, he so increased in fat, from very joy, that his clothes would scarcely contain him.

His first, rest her soul! had died some years ago, leaving him the pledge which he had shown me (a dirty little boy); perhaps he should take a fourth a year or two hence; why not? the Prophet, upon whom be peace, had four, and offspring were rare things; but still he did not know,—the one at Caubul was such a sweet creature! so sweet,—that were she to spit in the salt waves of the sea, they would become honey! And then the second one was a good girl at heart:—good when he was near at hand to keep her in order!

My friend's method of keeping a woman in order was a striking one. He had occasion one day, he related, to correct his wife, and he took up a bridle for the purpose. Unfortunately the iron bit which was at the end of it swang round and struck her on the side, and then he knew that she was really hurt, for she left off screaming, and lay down upon the ground and moaned. He was very sorry, very sorry indeed, for he never would have struck her to hurt her in such a manner, but he preserved his dignity, and walked away, and moreover he kept aloof from her for two days, when she came and assured him of her humble contrition, and promised not to offend again. "However," added the Shah, "I determined never to strike a woman again except with my hand,—never except with my hand,—and I am not sure now but that it is good not to strike a woman at all, for I have seen your countrymen's beebees in India, and they are not beaten;—but then again, your women have understanding, and do not make fools of themselves."

I took the liberty of asking my friend what fault his wife had committed. "I will tell you," said he. "One day I observed that she wore something hung from her neck, and told her to show it to me: she refused till I became angry, and when she did take it off and show it, I saw that it was a charm, which she had procured from some one or other, in order to keep me at home. I ordered her to take some water and rub the ink off the paper, but she not only would not obey me, but refused to give it to me even, keeping it fast closed in her hand; so I took up the bridle and threatened her, but still she kept it, saying that I should not travel, but remain at home! What could I do?"—"Do!" exclaimed I, with an indignation which quite astonished the Shah, "why it was an instance of great affection for you; she wished to retain you near her!"—"Oh! yes," said he, "that is all very well, but if I were not to travel, I wonder who would provide for the house, and what would become of the *Alika Malika*.*

I hope that any lady who may chance to read this will not think my friend a monster, otherwise I shall regret having made public details of a connubial fracas which he confided to me in the honest simplicity of his heart. By nature, the Shah was one of the most tender-hearted of men, but the prejudices in which he had been educated, made him think that a strong demonstration of authority was necessary to maintain the discipline of his house. The worst part of his deed was, by his own telling, accidental, for he only had recourse to the bridle as a last resource, when all his condescending requests had failed; and the ungallant ideas which prompted him to the use of it, were derived from too high an opinion of his sex; an error naturally to be entertained by a man whose religion teaches him that he is equal to four women.

Neither would I have it inferred from the anecdote

* The children. *Alika* is the Pushtoo for children; *Malika* is a word added for sound's sake, as if we were to say children pildren.

that the Affghauns ill-treat their women ; on the contrary, they are both proud and fond of them. Those who dwell in the country have such confidence in their women, that if they absent themselves from their homes, they leave their wives in charge of their establishments ; and a married woman may without a shadow of scandal entertain a traveller who happens to arrive at her husband's tent during his absence ; for by these, as by most other nomade people, a stranger would be thought to slight the inmates of a tent which he passed to take rest in another.

The Affghauns have a proverb upon the goodness of their women, for it is a saying with them, "Go to Hind for riches, and for pleasure to Cashmere ; but come to Khorassaun for a wife :" and the women themselves, I think I may say, are as well satisfied with their husbands, and with their condition generally, as any women in the world. With regard to the law which authorizes their husbands to beat them, the Prophet (on whom be peace!) made it, so they can have nothing to object to the institution, much as they may dislike coming under its exercise : it was only framed for cases of emergency, therefore when a man enforces it *ad libitum*, he breaks the law, and there is nothing to prevent any man, Christian or Mohummudan, from beating his wife, if he chooses to do it on such terms.

The free manner in which the Affghauns live in their pastoral societies, not to say that they are a poetically-disposed people, causes them to be less strangers than are most other Mohummudans to the romance of love, and they indulge in it when, as young men, they woo their brides; for they have a custom called Naumzaud bâzee, which nearly answers to the old Scottish one of trysting;—the lover being privately admitted to interviews with his mistress, and allowed to court her under the eye of her mother; the male relatives of the lady, if the suitor is a proper man, not being so impertinent as to know any thing about the matter; and two or three months, if not a longer period, are thus pleasantly passed before the marriage. But they profess the strictest morality, and so heinous a crime do they consider adultery, that they generally take the law into their own hands, and punish the offenders with death. A murderer may obtain the refuge which an adulterer cannot, for the law in the one case leaves vengeance to the nearest of kin, while in the other it imperatively dictates the punishment; and I was assured that even had the members of a khail given shelter to a guilty pair, they would not withhold them from an injured party who might come solemnly to demand them. In illustration of their feeling on this point, a late instance of stern principle was related to me in the case of a man whose sister fled to him one evening, pursued by her infuriated husband with a drawn sword. She gained his tent, and, ignorant of her offence, he prepared to defend her at all hazards, but when the injured husband solemnly swore that he had convicted her of adultery, the man became deaf to the pleadings of his sister, and put her forth to her husband, who with one blow of his sword struck her lifeless.

The boys of the khail were, to use a school term, "splendid fellows;" handsome, fresh-coloured lads, who were ready for any sport: we struck up an immense friendship with them, and generally had a large circle of them round our fire at evening. The second night after our arrival, a party of these wags, by means of burnt cork, wool beards, and their fathers' clothes, metamorphosed themselves into figures of the patriarchs of Pisheen, and came ceremoniously to welcome us to their valley. The mummery was got up much in the style of that which is acted by Neptune and his Tritons, when unlucky landsmen cross the line for the first time, and it ended in like manner,—in our paying tribute to the lords of the soil, and receiving the assurance of their friendship and protection.

We gave them a sheep which they were to kill and kabaub for themselves, and they were so pleased with the gift, that they presently returned with their heads full of an amusement for us. They said that somebody's donkey had died, and that where it had been carried out across the river, the print of a hyena's feet had been marked; that the beast would surely come again, and that, if we would ask Syud Muheen to ask Syud Daoud to come, we would go out hunting the next day.

Syud Daoud was a dark young man of perhaps twenty-five years of age, who was quoted by the boys of the khail as the Nimrod of the age: he happened to look in upon us at this time, in the hope of sharing in the contents of our tea-kettle, and, after a little opposition on the part of Muheen Shah, we arranged a hunting-party for the morrow. We set out about sunrise; a dozen of us on horseback, as many more men on foot, and all the lads of the khail, with some fifteen greyhounds and sheep-dogs. Syud Daoud took up fresh foot-marks of the hyena near the carcass of the donkey, and with the assistance of two or three other experienced men, tracked the animal a distance of four miles to some large ravines. Here they lost the foot-marks, the track being crossed by several others, and the ground being too hard to receive more than a faint impression; but after much searching, what with his clear sight, and his knowledge of the different dens in these ravines, Syud Daoud followed a track to a hole in the side of a bank, in which he decided that the animal, being gorged, had betaken itself to rest.

A semicircle was accordingly formed before the hole, two or three who had swords unsheathing them, and the boys standing fearlessly by them with stones and sticks, or holding back the yelling dogs. Syud Daoud ordered us to be as quiet as possible, in order that he might go into the den and tie the beast; but the hyena, alarmed at the barking of the dogs, came out upon us unexpectedly, throwing over a man who stood guard at the entrance with his sword. The boys, without the least appearance of fear, shouted and screamed, while they rained blows upon the brute's back with sticks and stones, the swordsmen every now and then making a cut at his hide, and they altogether so worried and confounded the animal, that after running up and down the rank without attempting to attack any body, he turned short and scrambled up the bank, rolled himself down on the other side, and set off at a long canter across a plain. It was some time before we could get our horses round, so that the hyena got a good start; he gave us a gallop of three miles, the greyhounds running alongside of the beast without being able to hold him, and he occasionally sidling his unwieldy body to the right or left to snap at them. At last the beast got into raviny ground, and we lost him; Syud Daoud said that he would not now stop till he reached a place some miles distant, so that we should not get him that day, and as his word was law on such matters, we returned home.

I mentioned that it was at first proposed to tie the hyena in his den. It appears a dangerous proceeding, but, according to the accounts of these people, it is not so for a man who has strength and coolness, for the hyena, though a savage beast, is easily frightened, and Syud Daoud was said to have tied three in the course of a day. However it is of course a very dangerous undertaking for one who cannot sustain great presence of mind, as they testified by mentioning the case of a man who a year or two before had died of a bite that he got in a clumsy attempt.

Syud Daoud himself described to me the mode of tying a hyena in his lair, as follows:—"When," said he, "you have tracked the beast to his den, you take a rope with two slip-knots upon it in your right hand, and with your left holding a felt cloak before you, you go boldly but quietly in. The animal does not know what is the nature of the danger, and therefore retires to the back of his den; but you may always tell where his head is, by the glare of his eyes. You keep moving on gradually towards him on your knees, and when you are within distance, throw the cloak over his head, close with him, and take care that he does not free himself; the beast is so frightened that he cowers back, and, though he may bite the felt, he cannot turn his neck round to hurt you, so you quietly feel for his two fore legs, slip the knots over them, and then with one strong pull draw them tight up to the back of his neck and tie them there. The beast is now your own, and you may do what you like with him. We generally take those which we catch home to the khail, and hunt them on the plain with bridles in their mouths, that our dogs may be taught not to fear the brutes when they meet them wild."

This Syud Daoud was a specimen of a character which I believe is not uncommon in Affghaunistaun: he cared for nothing but the pleasure of sporting, and from morning till night he would be out tracking wolves or hyenas, coursing, or hawking. He was the idol of the lads of the khail, who thought no honour equal to that of being allowed to accompany him on his excursions; but the elders, though they admired his daring, yet regretted that he was so engaged with field-sports, since he was of the best family, and ought to have been travelling about getting a good name to the khail, instead of wrestling for ever with wild beasts. Muheen Shah was quite pathetic in lamenting his disposition, which he said they had in vain attempted to amend: they had married him to the prettiest girl in the khail, in the hope of making him more domestic, but all for nothing, for he never cared for her, and would persist in being a regular junglee,—a wild man.

Syud Daoud was rather vexed that the hyena had escaped us this day, and for the two or three subsequent ones, he was out in the hope of finding and bringing the beast in. Some days after we had marched from Pisheen, a messenger overtook us at Quetta: he was charged with letters for different persons, and in one paper was written a message from Syud Daoud to me. "Tell the Sahib that I tied the hyena last Thursday, and that, Inshallah, we hunted and killed him at the khail. And tell the Sahib to send me some tea by the first opportunity."

CHAPTER VI.

Further residence at Pisheen—Affghaun superstitions—Alarm, and hasty preparations for continuing our journey.

PISHEEN being a centre to so much superstition, I hoped to obtain there a full account of the vulgar errors of the Affghauns; but while we were at our friend's house, the people were too busy to attend to me, and it was on different occasions during our journey that I noted the following superstitions, many of which are common to all Mohummudans, though their features may be altered in different places, to suit the character of a people, or the prejudice of a sect.

The Syuds of Pisheen, among their inherent supernatural powers, are believed to possess that of exorcising evil demons, Gins, Deeves, &c., in the various orders which have been assigned to them by the devices or the romance of man's imagination.

These beings are supposed to have propensities which induce them to mar the happiness of mortals, and therefore many of the ills and mischances of this life are attributed to their evil agency.

A Gin, as the name denotes, is a spirit, which enters into folks' bodies and possesses them. A person who has been thus taken, may be known by his foaming at the mouth, and losing the right use of himself; and as the gin usually takes hold of its victim's tongue, and uses it to utter foolish and blasphemous words, when a man speaks in such a manner, it is a great sign of his being possessed by a devil: but if there should be any doubt about a case, recourse is to be had to an exorcist, who looks into the patient's eyes, and if they are reddish, and like a cat's, it is certain that the spirit is there, for the gin substitutes its own eyes in the place of its victim's. Then the exorcist conjures the demon, and if it stubbornly retains its influence, he writes a charm upon a piece of paper which he burns under the patient's nose, and so causes the spirit to evaporate.

Sometimes the gin takes possession of the joints of a man, like the rheumatism; but in such case it is generally easy to expel him, by putting the afflicted person's fingers in the grasp of a strong man's hand, and pressing them. as in a vice, when the gin is heard crying out, and requesting that he may be allowed to depart: however, when the exorcist has a good hold, he is not a wise man if he frees the tormentor till he swears by Solomon's slipper not to come again.

It sometimes happens that the demon is not to be

so easily got rid of, and then the exorcist is obliged to light a fire, upon which he places a frying-pan with some clarified butter in it; when the oil is heated, the exorcist throws in a charm, by virtue of which the gin is made to feel the agonies of frying, and he is shortly heard exclaiming as before. Or he may be ejected by burning a charm under the possessed person's nose, as above described.

This is evidently a Jewish superstition; and either inherited by the Affghauns from (as it is supposed) their ancestors, the descendants of Israel, or borrowed, as so many of the Mohummudan traditions and superstitions are, from the Talmud. Josephus, in the Eighth Book of his "Jewish Antiquities," according to an edition of his works faithfully translated out of the Latin and French, by Thomas Lodge, Doctor in Physicke, A.D. 1632, in describing the character of Solomon, says, "Hee obtained also by inspiration the art of magicke for the profit and health of men, and the exorcising and casting out of deuils, for he deuised certaine incantations, whereby the diseased are cured, and left the methode of conjuration in writing, whereby the deuils are enchanted and expelled; so that never more they dare returne; and this kinde of healing to this day is very usual amongst those of our nation. For I saw a certaine popular and private man amongst the Hebrewes, in the presence of *Vespasian*, his sonnes, tribunes, and other souldiers, that cured divers that were possessed. And the manner of his cure was this:

he applied to the nose of the Demoniack a ring; under the seale whereof was a root of those things that Salomon had declared, which drew the deuil out of the nostrils of the sicke, as soone as he smelled the root: and as soone as the man was falne, he adjured him never more to returne, intermixing some mention of Salomon, and rehearsing those incantations that were invented by him."

The ability to exorcise malignant spirits, which the Pisheen Syuds are credited with on account of their supposed holy descent, is pretended to, more or less, by moollâs of all sects; for in Persia and Affghaunistaun, and I imagine in most other parts of the East, when a man is afflicted with any disease, or seized with a fit or sudden illness, which, from their slender knowledge of pathology, the doctors are unable to account for by natural causes, he is supposed to be labouring under demonomania, and treated accordingly. The moollâs themselves, being for the most part ignorant and superstitious, believe much that the common people do, and what they may doubt they assent to for their profit's sake, for they live in every way upon the ignorance of the vulgar.

Our excellent friend Moollâ Mohummud at Heraut, who certainly was as honest a man as could be met with in his class, would not allow me to express my doubts on such matters, and assured me that he himself had cured two or three persons in his lifetime. One case, he said, had occurred only the year before, at his own house in the city.

A man whom he had lately entertained as a servant, fell from the terrace of his house on which he had gone to sleep, and when he himself, being roused by the fall, went down into the court, he found the man writhing about in delirium, with eyes like coals. He at a glance saw how the case stood; therefore, calling two or three persons to raise the man and hold him, he proceeded to conjure the gin, and, after a hard battle of words, succeeded in expelling him, and restoring the man to his senses. I ventured to suggest that the man, being a stranger, might have risen in the night, and tumbled over; but the Aukhoondzâdeh scouted the insinuation. "*Een cheh gup ust?* What inconsiderate words are these?" said he. "The man was a man, and not a fool to take so little care of himself! What else but an evil spirit could have possessed him to tumble down several feet? Besides, did not I see the state of the man after he had fallen? No, no, friend of mine, hear reason!"

"If you doubt this, however," said Moollâ Mohummud, when he had recovered from the heat into which defence of his abilities had betrayed him,—"if you doubt this, how will you account for a circumstance which, in the knowledge of every one is of frequent occurrence? An unlettered fellow, who can just repeat '*Bismillah Irahmaun Iraheem*,' is suddenly seized with nobody knows what, and when a moollâ is brought to him, and begins to recite the Azîmut, he, that is not he, but the gin, speaking with his tongue, throws back a page for a verse, and proves himself the best read person of the two! How otherwise will you account for this, than by admitting that which is true; that which I tell you?"

"Then, I suppose," inquired I, "that if the patient be not cured, it is owing to the stupidity of the moollâ!"—"Undoubtedly; without doubt, to a certain extent; a man who has not studied, how can he fight a demon? but if one moollâ fails, a more learned one is sent for, and all measures are tried, for some gins are very potent. Once seven moollâs went to exorcise a gin who had taken possession of a man, but he was so *zubberdust* (powerful) that they could make nothing of him, and at last he got angry, and kicked the possessed person's foot with such force against the wall of the room they were sitting in, that it gave way, and the roof tumbled in and killed them. Nay, nay, Agha! you must not oppose your doubts to proven facts, *Een cheesha mushoor und*, these are things known to the world."

I remember being gravely told by a Persian at Meshed, that sometimes, when a gin lighted upon a person's head for the purpose of tormenting him, a clever moollâ would catch him by the following process: The moollâ takes with him an earthen pot, inside of which, when he has seated the person before him, he lights a lamp. He then proceeds to recite an Azimut, and, by a judicious application of texts, charms the gin from the patient's head into the pot, claps a cover on, and, hermetically sealing it with flour paste, sends it to some waste place; cautioning the bearer not to break the pot, lest the creature should not have been destroyed by the light, for gins are subject to death as well as mortal men.

A Deeve is vulgarly considered to differ from a gin in respect of his being of somewhat grosser fabric, but, strictly speaking, I believe they are creatures of the same class,—gin being the Arabic, and deeve the Persian word for them. A gin or a deeve can assume the form of any beast, bird, fish, or fly; he can take the semblance of a man or woman, of a cloud or a hill, in short, of any thing in nature, except that of a Nubbee,* or an Imaum.

There are good as well as bad spirits among the gins and deeves, and it is said that if one of them takes a fancy to a man, he will attend upon him as a sort of familiar, advise him, and help him to make a fortune. There is evidently a great deal of humanity about the creatures, for Mohummud ordered that the flesh nearest to bones of meat should not be eaten, but that it should be thrown out for the gins and deeves, whose perquisite it is; and it is a generally received notion, that they are so fond of sweets, that towards dusk they come into the bazaars of towns to buy them, so disguised that no one would know them unless he were a moollâ, and got an opportunity of narrowly looking into their eyes.

It is believed by all Mohummudans, that if a man will or can undergo the ordeal of the *chillah*, or forty

* Prophet.

days' trial, he may obtain power over all the genii. The trial is a very arduous one, for a man desirous of submitting himself to it must in the first place be a moollâ in the strict sense of the term, and he must moreover be a moral as well as a learned person. Then for the actual ordeal, he must sit for the space of forty days within a circle, and satisfy his appetite with a few grains of barley and a few drops of water daily. His occupation is to be the perusal of the Korân and select text-books, and he must be careful to perform every religious duty; for if he neglects the least one, or if he moves out of the circle, the genii have power to kill or madden him.

As he approaches the end of his probation, the gins and deeves exert themselves to the utmost to turn him from his purpose, coming round his circle in horrible shapes *à la* Freischütz, in order to frighten him; but if he keeps a good heart, and his presence of mind, their devices cannot hurt him, and on the fortieth day they disappear. Then the chief of the gins comes, in the guise of a venerable old man, perhaps, and with the insidiousness of a pleasing conversation endeavours to distract the probationer's attention from his books; or in the form of a beautiful woman tries to lure him into forgetfulness of a duty; but if he resists such temptations, and finishes his course, the head gin comes in his own appearance, and swears allegiance to him by the oath of Solomon's slipper, and then the genii, great and small, must attend at the call of the worthy moollâ to do his bidding, and he may send them all over the world,—to the peak of Demawand, or the pearl banks of the sea; into the heart of the earth, or to the fountain of Zuleimât at the north pole, to fetch him a goblet of the water of life.

Among the genii in whose existence the Affghauns believe, must not be forgotten the Peris; the best of whom are imagined to be beautiful creatures with forms like light, "who live in the air on odours," and are the friends and benefactors of mankind. They favour those to whom they attach themselves, by attending at the birth of their offspring; they sooth the children in their infancy, and attend on them in after-years as good geniuses, so that it is common for the Affghauns to say of a man who prospers in life, that he drank fairy's milk.

Like the beings of our fairy-land, the Peris are not above falling in love with mortals of earth. A woman of the Speen Tereen tribe, loved of a Peri, was taken away for five months to some fairy rath in Ginnistân, or elf-land, and, when restored, she was a "wise woman," and had the gift of discovering where stolen things were, so that people came from distances to consult her.

And I was told of a man then living, named Saudaud, with whom a Peri "*Murân Gool*" fell in love, and never left him till he married her. The youth had betrothed himself to a girl of his own tribe, and had prepared his camels to go and fetch his bride, when Murân Gool assembled a troop of Peris, threw over his gay kajavahs and broke them, and thus thwarted all his plans whenever he attempted to set out; so that Saudaud, who had turned a deaf ear to her entreaties for his love, was worried into a compromise, and agreed to marry both her and his betrothed. Murân Gool cunningly agreed to any terms which would put him in her power, and, when he had united himself to her, cast such a spell upon him, that he became blind to his mortal wife, and to all the other women of the world, having eyes only for herself, his enchantress.

It is supposed that our word fairy is derived from Peri, which, according to the construction of the Persian alphabet, may allowably be written Feri; there need scarcely be a doubt about it, for the beings whom either word describes are evidently the same:

> "They do wander every where,
> Swifter than the moon's sphere."

So that it would scarcely be an exertion for them to dance half round the beautiful parts of the earth in a night; and if the hills of Toba be truly such as they are described, without doubt Titania holds her revels there; and her pale orbs are to be seen on the emerald swards by the diamond-running streams.

The Affghauns have great faith in the malignancy of an "evil eye." I heard of a man so ill-favoured in this respect, that another person admiring a stone which lay on the ground, he did but look upon it, and it flew into a thousand pieces. This beats the gimlet eye! If a horse or other domestic animal chances to fall suddenly ill, an Affghaun says that an evil eye has stricken the beast, and one of these people would feel quite uneasy if a stranger looked long upon his horse or camel. They do not even consider that their own persons are exempt from the effects of a baneful look; and when a child, or, as it sometimes happens, a youthful person, begins to feel the influence of a disease which for a while had "slept in the blood," and to decline, they are apt to conceive such a one to be the victim of an evil eye.

The elements, of course, are taxed by the superstition of this country. It is a Mohummudan tradition, that when Cain murdered Abel, the elements were disturbed, and now, when a high wind blows for three days successively, Affghauns say it is a sign that murder has been committed. We witnessed an instance of their belief in this sign while we were at Pisheen, for it happening to blow very hard during three days of our stay, Syud Muheen Shah ventured to assert that "blood had been shed." It was a very warrantable guess in such disturbed times, and it so chanced that, before we left the place, intelligence was brought that some khan had been put to death by the Candahar Sirdars. Muheen Shah's expression was brought to mind, and he got credit for his second sight.

One of their fancies about the wind is quite an Irish one. They conceive that those little whirlwinds of dust and dried leaves, which spin about in autumn, are caused by a gin and his train, or by troops of the good people, taking the air, or travelling about on their own business; and they say that a moollâ, if he be sufficiently well read in Azimut, may make money by watching them; provided always that he be both poor and honest.

Holding in his hand a paper, on which is written an account of his good works, and a slight statement of his necessities, the moollâ goes to a plain where he is likely to meet with such whirlwinds, and standing patiently till one is passing him, throws his paper into it, and on the spot finds it transmuted into a heap of money. Should a man fail in such an attempt to enrich himself, he must not blame the good people, but return home, and study to acquire what is deficient in his learning or honesty.

Moreover, it is not to be doubted, that if a man who succeeded in making money of his charm, were to take a dried leaf from one of these fairy whirlwinds, and fasten it on the skin of his stomach, he might eat and drink without being surfeited, until it pleased him to to take it off again. What would not an English alderman give for the knowledge of such a secret?

The Affghauns share with other Mohummudans the superstition bequeathed to them by their prophet concerning the *Leilut-ool-kudr*, or the "night of power,"—the anniversary of the night on which the Korân is supposed to have been sent from High to the lowest heaven. In the Korân itself, this night is declared to be "better than a thousand months. Therein do the angels descend, and the spirit of Gabriel also, by the permission of their Lord, with His decrees concerning every matter. It is peace to the rising of the morn."

The *Leilut-ool-kudr* falls in the month of Ramazân, but the Mohummudan doctors differ in their opinions concerning its occurrence, some thinking that it falls either on the 15th, 16th, or 17th of the month, others being for the 21st, 22nd, and 23rd, and others again for the 27th, 28th, or 29th; but they are all agreed that in the month there is one night, and in that night one hour, in the which every prayer, every wish of the heart offered up, will find acceptance in heaven; so that even if a fakeer should petition to be made an emperor, his desire would be granted. Happy is one of the faithful esteemed whose fate it is to die on the blessed night.

It is not thought that the dead reappear to mortal beings, except in dreams; but the souls of the departed are believed to revisit their earthly homes, for love of those whom they left; at first often, but gradually making their visits more like angels',—"few and far between."

The Affghauns set great store upon dreams, especially those of reputed holy persons, such as the Syuds of Pisheen; for they conceive that the visions of such men are prompted by intelligence superior to that of mortals, and it is common for a man to ask a

Pisheen Syud to dream a dream for him. They imagine that the spirits of the departed appear to them in visions. Syud Muheen Shah, twice during the time that we were with him, pretended to have been visited by the shade of his elder brother, who enjoyed a saintly reputation while in the land of the living.

On neither occasion could I determine whether our friend was shamming, or whether he was suffering from a sort of nightmare, or waking dream, caused by his having brooded upon a superstitious belief of his brother's and his own supernatural endowments. The first time that he was seized in this manner was in the night; he awoke us as we were all sleeping near each other, by moaning and speaking thickly every now and then, heaving his breast in a manner that induced us to think that he was in a fit; but when one of our party would have shaken him, he was forbidden to do so by the Syud's people, who said that the Shah was *dreaming*, and was on no account to be disturbed. He appeared really unwell, and much depressed in spirits, for the next two days, which induced me to think that he had been worked upon by his imagination; but my friend Karaumut Ali insisted upon it that it was a scene which he got up periodically, for the purpose of keeping up his reputation.

Another custom which the Affghauns have in common with all followers of Islâm, is that of welcoming the new moon, when they offer a prayer to God to keep them from sin during the month of its continuance, and to dispose their hearts to his service. They pray God to preserve the moon from eclipse, and to cause its light to shine prosperously on themselves, their relations and friends, on the faithful, and on all just men in authority; after which they exchange good wishes—"May this month be a fortunate one to you," &c.

And I may mention another of their customs, which appears to have prevailed in all the East from time immemorial; though the Mohummudans, having adopted it, for the most part maintain that it was instituted by the founder of their sect, or by the Imaums who succeeded him. When a person is very ill, his friends release birds from their cages, as a propitiatory sacrifice to the mercy of God. Freedom from bondage, they say, is life; and they hope that as they release the bird's soul from the bitterness of its captivity, so the sick person's soul will be mercifully let free from the pains of its sickness.

To return to our journal.—We had been five days in Pisheen, when our host came with a face of much anxiety to say, that four of the Hâkims' men had arrived at the khail to demand us, insisting upon it that we were Jews, whom Muheen Shah had smuggled past the police-station, and desiring that he should accompany all our party to the presence of Abdoollah Khan. He and his friends, the Shah said, had protested that we were Indian pilgrims, who had remained but one day at the khail; therefore we must strike our tent, and go into his house, and on no account show ourselves outside his court, when Inshallah, and by virtue of his (eternal) *bukht*, he would arrange matters properly.

In the evening our friend came to say that all was going on well; that the men would remain that night to be his guests, and sleep in the mosque; that they did not suspect our presence, and that they had opened a negotiation about his not returning with them, the terms of which would be discussed at leisure, and, he had little doubt, be satisfactorily arranged.

In effect, he did induce the men to depart early on the morrow, by using an argument exactly suited to their understandings;—that it was better their bellies should be filled with a little, than their master's but indifferently satisfied with much; better they, their wives, families, and household stock, should gain the good wishes of a Peerkhaneh of Shâdeezye, by making a proper excuse for him, than that they should draw his ill-will upon themselves, by causing him to delay his departure, and suffer loss.

He swore, and I believe got a friend or two to back his oath, that we werel ndian Hadjees, who had gone on to Quetta; and assuring the myrmidons that they might tell their master he had also marched that way, since he certainly would do so on the morrow, he bribed, blessed, and dismissed them; esteeming a false oath in such a case no more perjury, than justifiable homicide murder. "Khoda Taullah," said he, "knows that I have never said a crooked word to take any man at disadvantage, but an oath to escape such an oppressor as Abdoollah Khan is *wajib* (incumbent)."

An apology for my friend's ethical imperfections must be borrowed from the one which he made for the men whom he had been obliged to bribe. The fault, he argued, lay less in the men than in their master: where governors were cruel oppressors, their servants would, of course, be rogues, and a man must do the best he could for himself when thrown into such society. Abdoollah Khan was a *man-eater*, who was not guided by a single just principle; who had no regard for Syuds whom kings thought it an honour to have seated by them; and who evidently being a person altogether without religion, deserved to be treated as a man worse than a kaufir.

I am beginning to fear that some uncharitable reader may be condemning us for having passively suffered ourselves to be benefited by such rogueries; but really, interference to prevent them would have been an act little short of "*felo de se.*" Now, having made an apology for myself and my fellow-traveller Karaumut Ali, I may continue that for Muheen Shah, whose private character, like that of any other great man in a peculiar situation, must not be judged by his public actions. The state of society in these countries is such, that however much virtue may be admired in the abstract, it is thought imprudent generally to practise it. A wise parent gives his son a sort of Janus education, telling him of a few virtues, but initiating him into the mysteries of every vice, in order that he may be a match for his demoralized neighbours; and thus nearly every person commences life prepared to be faithful to his friends, and an honest man or rogue to the world as may be.

For the Persian and the Lahoree I need not offer apology, since they assured me that none was necessary. To prove their words, they quoted a favourite Sheah text, that Huzrut Ibrahim forswore himself to Pharaoh; and when I remarked that he manifestly sinned in doing so, they replied, "Forbid that they should say a Nubbee was guilty of sin."

We felt much relieved when Abdoollah Khan's men had taken themselves away, for we could anticipate no favourable result from an interview with such a person. It would have been difficult to prevent his discovering me to be a European; and if he had done so, he in all probability would have taken me with him to Candahar, whither he had just been called by the rebel Sirdars, in order to lend his aid to their preparations to oppose Shah Kamraun. And had I assumed the character of an Armenian, I should have exposed myself to much ill-treatment, for Abdoollah Khan had the character of never allowing an unbeliever to pass until he had extorted all he could from him, and some of his modes of torture were described, which it was quite painful to think about. The mildest of his "tender mercies" were, we were told, putting stones under a man's armpits, and then pressing his arms to his sides, or laying a man on his back, and gradually placing weights upon his belly, until unendurable agony forced money or life out of him.

All infidels travelling through Affghaunistaun, would be glad to pay the poll-tax regulated according to the Shirra, if that were all; but, in the disturbed state of the country, every true believer demands it; and as the kaufir gets no receipt for his money, and his oath is of no value whatever, he must pay so long as he has money, and when it is all gone, accept the martyrdom of abuse and blows.

Jews make their way best, for they have some propensities in common with Mohummudans, while they affect poverty, and bear up against the injury which is their portion, better than any other people in the world. But a Hindoo whose fate brings him this way, travels at the risk of the worst treatment. As no disguise would serve him, he does not assume one, but pays the leader of a kafilah for his protection on the road, and endeavours either to make a circuit round police-stations, or to bribe the officers; but sometimes he is caught tripping, or he cannot bribe high enough, and then, if he is taken before a man dressed in a little brief authority, Abdoollah Khan for instance, but little mercy is shown him; for all his tribe are reputed to be moneyed men, and if torture should fail to wring a black coin from him, they would merely think that they had troubléd themselves to no purpose. What treatment could be too bad for such an usurious, and in every way abominable idolater?

Hitherto Syud Muheen Shah's protection had shielded us, but he honestly confessed that although his *bukht* had never failed to do great things for him, he could not answer for the conduct of a man who lived upon the bread of oppression, and who, since he did not fear God, could have but little regard for the holiest of men.

There are still parts of this country, the inhabitants of which retain their savage independence, but wherever the influence of any government extends, oppression is looked for as a matter of course, and a man in authority may, without much scandal, exercise it to a certain extent, by virtue of his office; it being an understood point between him and his subjects, that he is to extort, and they to withhold, as much as they mutually can by ordinary means; so that when a man is really notorious as an extortioner, he must needs be a monster of iniquity. Abdoollah Khan was in the enjoyment of, I should think, as bad a name as could well be given to a man; his countrymen said that he must have been suckled by a devil. The following anecdote, which is related of his former life, says much for the cruel cunning of his disposition, and shows also how easily an eastern despot can raise the wind.

When Mohummud Azeem Khan (brother to the

famed Affghaun Vuzeer Futteh Khan) was governor in Cashmere, Abdoollah Khan, who attended at his court, offered to give him eight thousand rupees for all the wind that blew over Cashmere. The governor, reasoning like Mertoun, that "since every thing in the universe is bought and sold, the wind should not be excepted if a purchaser can be found"—and partner, no doubt, in the villany that followed,—accepted the offer, and permitted Abdoollah Khan to issue a proclamation, warning all people that he had bought the wind of Cashmere, and threatening to punish any one who should winnow his grain, or in any other way use it without his permission. The order at first excited amusement, but when the governor, who had affected to think it a joke, said that he had been taken advantage of, but that he must be as good as his word, and allowed Abdoollah Khan severely to fine those who even presumed to fly a pigeon without purchasing his licence, the purport of the bargain was understood. The Cashmerians had been too long familiar with oppression not to know the only means of lightening its chains, and they subscribed a large sum of money to induce Abdoollah Khan to allow "the wind of heaven" to blow freely on them again, the governor promising that such another spell should not be put upon it.

The first thing that Muheen Shah did after the departure of the Hâkim's men was, to send advice to all horse-dealers in the valley that he was about to start immediately. Several merchants had assembled in order to travel under his protection, knowing that his influence as Peerkhaneh of Shâdeezye would greatly protect them, both on the road through their own disturbed country, and through Beloochistaun, and as they had for some days awaited his summons, they came at once to Shâdeezye, in order to make a fortunate start together.

The night before our departure, we went with Muheen Shah to dine with a Syud who was, in every sense of the word, the greatest man in the khail. He had a dozen children, and a great many sheep, and was so fat, that a Turkish lady might have envied him as he sat at the head of his hearth, a semicircle of fine sons standing respectfully about him, and seated by his side his pet child, a little rosy-faced boy, whose mother had thought to increase the effect of his large black eyes by streaking them with soormeh.

Our host's house was one of the best, its thick mud-walls being roofed over with large beams. We sat in a large mud-washed room, near the head of which was a hole containing a wood fire. The two eldest boys went round to pour water on our hands, and a stout negro lad and girl brought in two smoking bowls of fowl-soup and boiled rice. Such fare was not to be despised, and we fed, like Major Dalgetty in anticipation of several days indifferent living.

As all the company understood Persian, we conversed at our ease. They talked of the dangers of our road onward, especially of that which was to be dreaded in the close defile of Bolaun, in which the savage Cawkers had murdered hundreds of travellers; and they related anecdotes of the many different clans of this tribe, some of which were spoken of as wild but not bad people, while others were described as regular *Anthropophagi.*

I noted a story about one Hadjee Khan, a Cawker chief, who retiring from court to dwell among his tribe, took with him a small tent. This at first excited the wonder of the men of his clan, but when they saw what use was made of it, they were scandalized at such effeminacy and extravagance, and stealing the tent, cut it up for shirting.

Of some men of one of the more ferocious clans it was told, that they murdered a traveller for the sake of what they thought was a silver bowl, but finding it to be made of pewter, they imprecated a thousand curses upon the unfortunate man who had owned it, for giving them so much useless trouble.

After dinner the boys stood out, and danced the Attun for our amusement, the negroes standing together, with their thick lips apart, grinning their delight. We spent an hour more in pleasant conversation, and then retired to prepare for the morrow's journey.

CHAPTER VII.

March from Pisheen to Quetta, and halt there—Personal narrative—Blood—Feuds—Custom of Trysting.

Nov. 21.—About ten o'clock in the morning, the merchants being all ready to start, they assembled in front of the khail. The horses were led out by the families of those among the Syuds who owned them, gaily trapped with coloured beads and ribbons, and charms innumerable, to keep them from evil eye and all accident on the road, and ensure a speedy and good sale to "some Rajah, Inshallah!" in Hindoostân. The young women did not come near the men, but grouped at a little distance; while the elder dames took the privileges of their years, and came among their relatives, to reiterate charges about the sum that was to be got for a favourite horse, and the chintz or kimcob that was to be brought back with part of the money. It was a not-to-be-forgotten scene.

Two mounds of earth had been raised at a little

distance from each other, and on these stood two elders of the khail, each holding an end of a long scarf, in the centre of which was tied a Korân. Under this the horses were led off in succession, the friends of the owner of each animal ejaculating a "good luck" for him as it passed under the sacred volume; and when all this was over, the men embraced each other, or went into their harems for a last farewell. Our most particular friends among the boys, insisted upon stuffing our shulwars with raisins and little cakes fried in oil, assuring us that it was lucky to start on a journey with sweets in pocket.

Lastly, Syud Muheen Shah standing in the centre of the crowd, solemnly begged God's blessing on the journey, and a speedy and happy return to their homes, after which we mounted our horses and rode away. One or two old women followed to pour water after us, a custom similar to, and as efficacious as, that of throwing an old shoe, and relatives shouted their last words to each other as long as we were within hearing—"Adieu, my life! I have surrendered you into God's keeping!" "Inshallah! Inshallah! God preserve you from calamity, and give increase to your store, and grant that we may soon see your face where your back now is! Adieu! and may the great God preserve you!"

We marched between noon and sunset a distance of sixteen miles to Terkha Oba, a small kahreeze of bad water on the other side of the Ajrum hills. Our road was over a plain, which appeared barren to my eye, but on which, notwithstanding, many sheep were browsing. In the evening we were introduced to several of Syud Muheen's connexions, and to many other merchants, not Syuds, who nearly all volunteered intimacy with me, addressing me in broken Persian or Hindoostanee, and telling me that they were intimate friends of Elpistine Sahib,—and I had the misfortune of being the lion of the evening to those who had not seen a Frangee.

I now heard many wonderful stories related of Mr. Elphinstone and the English gentlemen who accompanied the British mission to Shah Shoojah;—how they shot birds on the wing, and understood the art of keemia,* and how they did and said various admirable things. One said that Mr. Elphinstone had a telescope, with which, by some magic contrivance, a man might see what was passing on the other side of a mountain. And a second declared that Mr. Elphinstone was a Soonnee, or at least that, in conversation with some khan who was quoted, he had said sufficient in praise of their sect to show that he inclined to it. They spoke of Mr. Elphinstone with the esteem, and I may say affection, with which all Affghauns use his name, protesting that he was a *Shé Ashrof*,—a real gentleman, and as full of understanding as generosity; though they confessed they

* Alchemy.

could not conceive why he had troubled himself so much about their hills and valleys, if he did not mean to come and take them.

I found that as far as professions went I might now count many friends; and if not very sincere ones, at least merry acquaintances for the time being. "You are for Bombay, of course," said one. "Inshallah! we will take you there safely, and then you shall sell all our horses to your friends. If you want a horse yourself, take that long-tailed gray, and pay me when you get to Bombay; or if you do not like mine, take Syud Azeez's colt with the thin tail, which you can cut off as your countrymen do;"—a sally which was received with shouts of laughter. "By your soul I am speaking the truth," added he, affecting to think that some doubted what he said; "by the life of your son! by the *char yar*,* I swear to you that some of the Inglis cut off their horses' tails as short as my thumb;"—and a second burst of merriment rewarded his wit.

Among Syud Muheen's relatives was a slight, resolute-looking young Syud, who prided himself upon being a perfect Sahib Shumseer, or master of the sword. He boasted that he could cut off a ram's head with a single blow, and hinted, moreover, that he could eat the best part of the animal afterwards; for in the east it is considered that a great hero must of necessity be a great eater. A *lion-eater* is a term

* "The Four Friends"—the title given by Soonnees to the first four Imaums.

for a distinguished man of war, signifying, doubtless, a man strong enough to kill a lion and eat him. The great hero Roostum devoured a wild ass to the very marrow; and to come down to warriors of later years, Nadir Shah, it is said, could eat a lamb stuffed with almonds. It is true that the Persian conqueror owed his death to the consequences of indigestion, but he was nevertheless a great hero, and had he been allowed to live on, would probably have added another bright page to the history of his wars.

The young Syud just mentioned, showing me his weapons one afternoon, vaunted that few men would like to cross swords with him, two having tried the experiment somewhat to their cost. This vain assertion was confirmed by others, who added, that the young man had so severely wounded his last antagonist, as nearly to entail a blood-feud upon himself, since had he killed his enemy, the nearest of kin would "never have left him." I at different times heard many anecdotes of Affghaun blood-feuds: some of the descriptions forcibly reminded me of the bitter enmities that we read of in the old stories of the Scottish highlanders. Few Affghauns but have a tale of this sort to relate, and the narrators always seemed to enjoy a fierce pleasure in detailing how such a one watched for and dissembled with his enemy, until he gained an opportunity of completing his vengeance.

Revenge for blood is, with an Affghaun, a duty which is rendered sacred by long custom, and sanctioned by his religion. If immediate opportunity of retaliation should not present itself, a man will dodge his foe for years, with the cruel purpose ever uppermost in his thoughts, using every cunning and treacherous artifice to entrap or lull him into confidence, and thinking it no shame to attack him in a defenceless state. The public leave men to settle their own quarrels, not interfering except, perhaps, in the case of a long-cherished feud between families which affects the interests of the community; and then they induce the man whose turn it is to retaliate, to accept the price of blood.

A friend told me that he was once in the bazaar of the city of Candahar in broad day, when a Ghilgie Affghaun, meeting a man with whom he had a blood-feud, suddenly drew his sword and killed him with a blow across the head, then escaping to the gate of the city, mounted his horse and fled; no relative was by, and strangers did not feel themselves called upon to stop the murderer. Another person told me that a nobleman with whom he was connected (one Arabkhan Allekkozye) having come to Candahar from his neighbouring village of Taubeen, had very nearly been murdered while in a public bath of the city; his servants and a barber having only just time to throw themselves between him and an enemy who had thought to take him unawares.

Moollâ Mohummud, our Heraut friend, told me the following story, the circumstances of which he said he could vouch for, as they occurred in a house which was close to one that he formerly lived in at Candahar, the females of which were intimate with his own. A Doorraunee of the neighbourhood of Candahar, had a blood-feud with a young man whom he had long vainly watched, in the hope of finding him off his guard. At last he heard that his enemy had sent sweetmeats to the house of a resident of Candahar, as a preliminary to espousing his daughter, upon which he left his village, and came privately into the city. The Affghauns, as before mentioned, have a custom called Naumzaud Bazee, (trysting)—the lover being secretly admitted to interviews with his mistress, which frequently last until a late hour in the night. The avenger watched in vain for an opportunity, till the very night before the wedding, when he gained access to a court adjoining that of the house in which the girl lived, and boring a hole through a wall, lay in wait there with his matchlock. In the evening the lover came as usual to tryst; he he had that day sent the customary present of the bridal dress and ornaments, but his betrothed "through modesty had declined examining them before all her female acquaintance," and when the young man asked if she approved of her trousseau, the mother explained this, and called her away to look at it then. This was late in the night; the moment she went out, the blood avenger took aim at his victim as he sat on a low couch, and in perhaps the happiest moment of his life, shot him dead.

22nd.—From Terkha Oba we marched twenty miles to the town of Quetta; the route taking us three miles across a narrow valley to a low range of hills running nearly parallel to Ajrum, called Musailaugh, two miles over and through them, and then fifteen miles across a plain to Quetta. Twelve miles on the road we crossed the Shâdeezye lora on its way from Ser-e-aub, and seven miles beyond, a smaller stream tributary to it. Five miles from Quetta, we passed through a village of forty houses, and in several directions we viewed small forts and artificial water-courses. We ended our march in the afternoon, and the horses being picketed on a plain spot near the town, the merchants went to pay their respects to the governor.

Quetta, the petty capital of the Belooche province of Shaul, is a town of four hundred small flat-roofed houses of one story each, surrounded by a thin mud wall, in which there are four gates. The residence, or as he himself was pleased to term it, the citadel, of the Hâkim who rules here on the part of the Khan of Kelaut-e-Nusseer, is built on a high mound inside, so that when his orders are shouted there, they may be heard all over the town. The residents are Affghauns, Belooches, and Hindoos. The latter, who may amount to a fourth of the population, are all engaged in trade, which is more considerable than a stranger would be apt to imagine from the appearance of the place.

Kafilahs to and from Hindoostan pass this way,

taking horses, dried fruits, and the few exports of Heraut and Candahar, such as assafœtida, saffron, &c,, and bringing back indigo, leather, English and Indian cloths and chintzes, spices, sugar, &c. The horses are nearly all marched down through Beloochistaun and Sinde to the sea-coast, where they are shipped for Bombay; and if they find speedy sale for their animals there, the merchants usually return home by the same route.

Quetta is also a rendezvous for merchants who, not liking to undertake long voyages, meet those who are on their return, and purchase a gross of goods which they retail among their own countrymen; while those who arrive from their journeys, are not sorry to take some days' rest here. On the whole, Quetta is a town of some importance, and were the country settled, and the roads from the different quarters opened to a regular trade, it could hardly fail to become a large place, seeing that the soil of the province is good, and water abundant in the hills which enclose it.

The town of Quetta, or as it is vulgarly called Quote, is situated at the head of a fine valley eight miles in breadth. Eight miles north-north-east of the town is the peak of Tukkatoo: it is in a high range of mountains, which, commencing abruptly six miles to the west of it, run easterly to the Indus. The Tukkatoo range is crossed by another very high one, called Umbàr, which comes up north by east, and which I conceive holds nearly the same course for many miles beyond. A branch comes to it from the Khojeh Amraun range, north-east in a bend across the valley, separating (as I understood) Pisheen from Burshore. Parallel to the Umbàr range, is one of equal altitude called Jingeer or Zunjeera, of which I shall make further mention presently. The climate of this place is said to be a fine one; during the nine days of our stay, the thermometer varied no more than half a point above or below temperate; we had a clear Italian sky and a cool wind in the day-time, while at night it was so cold that we were glad to sleep with our heads under our blankets.

We were detained nine days at Quetta. The merchants had duty to pay on their horses, and accounts to settle with debtors and creditors who met them here; all matters which required much discussion. At daybreak you might see the men rise one after the other from under the rugs they had covered themselves with, throw their indescribably dirty skin-cloaks over their dirty under garments, perform their ablutions, and say their prayers, and then get together in circles, and wrangle for two or three consecutive hours. It was amusing to observe a party thus engaged, for when the speakers became interested upon a subject, they declaimed in the most impassioned manner, giving effect to their words by vehement and in many instances very appropriate gestures.

I saw but few bonds given; the Hindoos, of course, did not fail to demand them, but in their dealings with each other, the Affghaun merchants did no more than strike hands in the presence of witnesses; a man buying a horse, or borrowing a sum in cash, and promising to pay so much at a given time, or on his return, whenever it might be; and I afterwards remarked, that few of those with whom we travelled took any account of the money they spent, further than that between such and such a place they had expended so many ducats.

These merchants can profit but little on the sale of such horses as they import into Hindoostân. Formerly they brought down valuable stallions bred from Toorkmun stock, but now they cannot obtain sufficiently high prices in India to make it worth their while to purchase many such, and those which they trade in are for the most part bred in their own khails. About six hundred tolerably good horses annually pass Quetta; a few of the best are purchased by the Hyderabad Ameers, and the rest are shipped for Bombay.

With every party of merchants there is one horse priced at a lac of rupees; declared to be the very brother of the famed steed which Tippoo Sahib purchased for that sum. Our lac-of-rupee horse was a tall roaring stallion, light brown, with white legs and forehead, and a back as long as an alligator's. He was dressed out with beads and amulets, and smarter body-cloths than the rest, and had the honour always to lead the march. The great merit of this animal lay in his paces, for he was perfectly trained to step and prance, and he ambled so fast, that a great man seated on him might glide along with ease and dignity, while his retinue, on their sorry steeds, kicked up the dust behind him at a canter. I afterwards heard that one of the Ameers bought the beast for three thousand rupees.

There were not fifty really good horses among the four hundred that we had with us, and considering the duties the merchants had to pay on the road, deaths, accidents, expense of shipping, and cost of long keeping, I question whether many were not losers on the whole. They said, indeed, they did not calculate their profit upon the sale of their horses, but upon the goods which they should bring back with them from India. They assured me, with a laugh at the expense of my countrymen, that at Bombay, the Bussorah merchants purchased some of their horses for four and five hundred rupees each, and sold them to the English gentlemen as Arabs for three times as much money.

Some of the horses were very rips, but their masters had a great idea of their value, and probably felt very much affronted when they were offered trifling prices for them in India. There was a man of our party who had three such animals; we parted from him at Shikarpore, and I saw him about fourteen months afterwards in Calcutta: he had marched down to the sea-coast, and taken ship for Bombay, whence he went to Mangalore, across the country to Bangalore, on to Madras, and thence along the sea-coast *viâ* Cuttak to Calcutta; as he said, here and there "selling a horse for nothing, that he might eat the proceeds." His third horse had died just after he reached Calcutta, and he brought me the tail as a present, begging me for old acquaintance sake to give him a trifle to help him home again. It was a case of *Nusseb kismut*, he said, and he might have better luck another time:—"Khire! Khoda kureem deh!" "All's for the best!"—"God is beneficent."

Jellâl Khan, the Hâkim, was a Belooche who had lately been a horse-dealer, and some of the merchants therefore expected to be indulgently taxed; but Muheen Shah shook his head at the idea, and seemed to think that the governor's being "Yorkshire too," was just the reason why they should not be able to talk him over. His opinion proved to be a just one, for after two or three days' hard discussion, the merchants found that their old pleas of hard times, &c., and their threats of not coming this road again, were wasted on a man who had been using them himself for several years, and they accordingly determined to pay the usual sum of half a ducat upon each horse, and to continue their journey.

But even this resolution did not suit the governor, for he had grain to sell, which they must needs buy as long as he could keep their horses there; so he devised excuses for deferring the settling time, and when pressed by the merchants to give them their *roksut* (congé), said that in truth he was unwilling to let them depart, because his information confirmed a report which had been some days in circulation, that one Poyindeh Khan, an ex-Hâkim of Pisheen, had put himself at the head of a banditti, composed of some desperadoes of the Cawker and other tribes, and had occupied the mountain-pass on the road to Dauder.

It was not doubted that there was some truth in the report, but as it was one which just served the interest of the governor, he apparently determined to make the most of it. In the evening it was rumoured that the Khan was "going out," and early the next morning he did indeed sally forth in his fighting apparel, at the head of some five-and-twenty Belooche matchlock and javelin men, when after capering about in front of our ground, with as much of the pride, pomp, and circumstance of glorious war as he could assume, he rode away for a spot about twenty miles distant, where some of the marauders were said to be. Late at night the governor returned without having seen any of the reported enemy; the rascals, as one of his suite said, having been too lucky to wait until the Khan got a blow at them.

The truth of that part of the report which related to the ex-Hâkim's league with the banditti having been ascertained, the merchants resolved to await the arrival of more of their fraternity, who were immediately expected; and a message was sent to an influential Cawker chief, to say that the merchants would give him money to escort them through the dangerous pass of Bolaun.

On the second morning after our arrival, I went with Syud Muheen Shah to visit the Hâkim. My friend said that as it was impossible the governor could remain in ignorance of my being there, he had thought it best to make a virtue of necessity, and be the first man to mention the circumstance; the Khan, he said, had received the intimation most graciously, and charged him to tell me, that he (the Khan) desired no greater pleasure than that of making the acquaintance of an individual of so esteemed a tribe as the Inglis Feringees.

Jellâl Khan received us on the terraced roof of his citadel, whence he could feast his eyes upon the best part of his domain. He was a tall and slight, hook-nosed, and vulgarly independent-looking man, who evidently did not want a good opinion of himself. After a few extravagant compliments had been exchanged, he waved his hand affectedly to direct my view upon the surrounding country, and asked me if I had ever seen such a place as Quetta. I answered, with truth, that I had not; and then he was pleased to assure me that I might bless the fortune which had brought me to his stronghold, since he was monarch of all he surveyed, and that if Abdoollah Khan, the Candahar Sirdars, or any body else, should send to demand me, he would spit upon the messengers, or, if I preferred it, blow them from the mouths of his cannon. (The Khan had one small gun which he kept in the court of his harem.) It had pleased him, he said, to travel much: he had seen and liked my countrymen, and had made himself acquainted with their customs; they were fine soldiers, and men of veracity, whom he approved of, and I might equally count upon his protection and friendship:— to all which I made a due proportion of bows and hyperbolical acknowledgments.—*L'amitiè d'un grand homme est un bienfait des Dieux!*

The governor gave the most sensible proof of his knowledge of English customs, by inviting me to cement our friendship by eating a meal together; and led the way down into a small mud-built apartment, the walls and roof of which were hung with matchlocks, swords, shields, and lances, and various trophies of the chase; one side containing a window looking upon the town, where the Khan was wont to sit to indulge his subjects with a view of his bust. Our repast consisted of fowl-soup, which was served in a large pewter bowl; we partook of the liquid portion by making temporary spoons of bits of bread as thin as pancakes, which were sent out to us hot and hot from "the within."

I have been particular in noticing occasions on which we got any thing very good to eat, because they were of sufficiently rare occurrence to make us consider them *dies festi.* Occasionally we got meat, but our usual fare was boiled rice or vetch, which we ate with cakes of heavy unleavened bread, and if we thought of breakfast for the morrow, we put a flap of the latter into our holsters or breeches-pocket. However we generally contrived to cook a kettleful of tea, which made amends for the badness of a dinner, and was most refreshing after a long march. We had fortunately provided a good supply at Meshed, for at Heraut neither tea nor coffee was to be purchased in the bazaar.

At Quetta I one morning remarked two evidences of our approach to Hindoostân. The first was seeing half a dozen thin Hindoos emptying pots of water on their bodies when it was hardly day, and the air so cold that others walked with their cloaks in their mouths; the second was seeing two idolatrous old women of the same caste walking round a tree, and pouring water on its roots, while they muttered charms or incantations.

On the sixth day of our stay, the expected horse-merchants arrived, and our party was made up to about two hundred and fifty men, who had charge of four hundred indifferent horses. As the greater number of the party had little to do, and they apprehended no danger, they dozed through the day, and kept us awake half the night with their songs and jokes.

From what I saw of the Affghauns, I should say that they are passionately fond of music; and there is this advantage attending their taste for it, that a little goes a great way with them. At Quetta there was one old musician, who played upon an Indian fiddle; he was so husky with a cold, that he could barely speak above his breath, yet he was made to play and sing every night. He would harp for more than an hour upon the same tune, varying the words of it for such as he could compose extempore, now and then warning the company, so as to allow them to bring in a chorus. Sometimes a loud laugh would interrupt the twang of the music for a minute or two, but it would be taken up again with the same melancholy, and had it not been played so often, pleasing air.

Rehmaun was an esteemed Affghaun poet, and his odes are often sung. At times the people of our party would sing the compositions of their village-poets; or, striking up a recitative tune, they would follow each other in extemporizing an irregular verse to a set chorus. One favourite and interminably monotonous chorus that used to keep sleep from us, I have reason to remember, ended with the long-drawn-out word *Shâdeezye;*—the meaning of the verses composed nightly to it would be something like what follows:—

Our home is now behind us,
We have quitted Shâdeezye!
Chorus.
We have quitted Shâdeezye.—(*bis*)

Where is a valley like it?
Where else is Shâdeezye?
Chorus.
Where else is Shâdeezye?

Long is the road before us;
Distant the land of Kaufirs we are going to;
Much trouble must we undergo in a land of strangers:
But we'll return to Shâdeezye!

Chorus.

But we'll return to Shâdeezye!

We'll return to Shâdeezye;
Our camels laden with silks and velvets,
With Kimcob, and spices, and choice things;
We'll return to Shâdeezye!

Chorus.

We'll return to Shâdeezye!—&c.

This is however but a cold outline of the style of such songs; for the performer endeavours to touch the feelings of his audience by introducing many little incidents associated with their recollections of home, often with success, as I could judge from the expression of their rough countenances, and their energetic demonstrations of applause.

At Quetta I first saw the Attun danced to perfection. It was bright moonlight, and while many of us lay upon a bank, thirty or forty men stood up in a circle to dance. They commenced by joining hands, and alternately advancing and retreating a step or two (as dancers do in the last figure of a quadrille), making each a deep and smothered sound from the chest, which I can compare to nothing but the groaning of a horse or other large animal. Gradually they increased the loudness of this, and stamped their feet in regular time, becoming more and more excited, and then with one accord they flung their hands loose, clapped their palms, and tossed their arms about, now making measured movements with their hands and feet, setting their teeth tight, frowning, rolling their eyes, and grunting, and then twirling their bodies round and round like drunken men, winding into each other's places, and shrieking and whooping as Scotchmen do in a reel; the spectators the while loudly applauding them with cries of "Barikallah! Barikallah! Shadbâsh!* Ai Shadbâsh!" "Well done!—well done! be happy! O be happy! Bravo Thamas Khan! well danced Thamas Khan! who said he was an old man? By Ullah he is the youngest man among ye! Shahbash Joomun! Barikallah Syud Azeez! excellent Thamas Khan!" and exciting themselves by the praises they lavished on the dancers, many threw off their cloaks and stepped into the ring. Thamas Khan, alluded to above, was a little old fellow with an immense white turban, upon whom every one thought himself privileged to cut a joke. His beard would have been also white had he not dyed it orange colour, but set him in an Attun ring, and he put the youngest to shame by the energy of his gestures and twirls. The dance lasted until the greater number of the performers were quite spent with the violence of their exertions, and lay down panting as they would after a hard run. The state of I may call it phrensy to which they excited themselves is

* Shadbâsh—be happy.

indescribable ;—if any thing could give an idea of the orgies of the Bacchanalia, it must be this dance.

I made several visits to the governor: he treated me with civility on all occasions, and was pleased to volunteer information regarding his province of Shaul, which he said extended from a spot called Kooshlauk, ten cross on the other side of the Tukkatoo mountains, to Ser-e-aub in the opposite direction,—was bounded on the west by the Ajrum range, and on the east separated by the Umbàr range from the country of the Cawkers. Further, the Khan said that he was lord of five thousand ryots of the Cassye tribe, who cultivated lands watered by fifty kahreezes, and who paid him annually 5000 cucha rupees, besides eight hundred khurwars of grain, and an equal measure of kau or chopped straw. The gross money revenue, including the sum levied by taxes upon the kafilahs which passed, averaged, the Khan said, the annual sum of 30,000 cucha rupees, or 1500 gold ducats.

A *budrukah*, or escort, of forty Cawker matchlockmen having arrived, and all duties having been paid, it was determined to prosecute our journey. The day before we marched, the governor invited me to breakfast with him, and Muheen Shah and I went together. Soon after breakfast, Jellâl Khan sent Muheen Shah into the town upon some business, and presently entered upon a secret and confidential discourse. He rejoiced, he said, that he had found an opportunity of speaking to me in private, because he wished to know whether I was satisfied with the treatment I had received at his hands, and whether there was any thing that he could do for me: he was not a wealthy man! but, please God, he descended from as good family as any of the chiefs who sat on the right hand of the Khan of Kelaut, and having met a man whose demeanour and conversation showed him to be of exalted rank, he was anxious to establish on lasting grounds, a friendship so auspiciously commenced.

This was the prelude. I answered it, of course, with suitable compliments of speech, and the governor proceeded to expatiate upon the natural fertility of his province, the revenue of which he doubted not might be trebled in good hands. He lamented that the Khan (of Kelaut) had so little art of making the most of his country, and wished that he possessed more of the understanding of my tribe, who undertook nothing without reflection and foresight; who by their wise conduct had won the esteem and confidence of all men; who did nothing uselessly, and who perseveringly went through with whatever they undertook;—as, for instance, I, who, having set out upon a journey through strange countries and unfriendly people, had persisted in making my way to Quetta, and doubtless, Inshallah, would shortly happily end my travel in my own country.

There was no mistaking the drift of the governor's discourse, but determining to let him come to the point himself, I replied that I thought he attributed too much sagacity to my countrymen, and overlooked a *shoke* (propensity) they had to wander all over the world to see people who had no great wish to see them, for the pleasure of novelty, or to indulge a disposition to study men and manners; but that though, as he had justly observed, a stranger was liable to suffer hardship and ill-treatment, still that he, on the other hand, might meet with persons whose justice, benevolence, and wisdom, were themes in every body's mouth: that I, for instance, had stored the recollection of many kindnesses received from different persons whom I had been so fortunate as to meet with, and that should I reach India, one of my particular pleasures would be to relate to my friends the lucky accident that had brought me to Quetta, and procured me the friendship of so accomplished a person as Jellâl Khan.

The governor could not look otherwise than flattered; he swore that every word I uttered more and more convinced him of my discretion and good breeding, but that, waving compliments, he would be glad if I would treat him with that ingenuous confidence that should subsist between friends, and tell him the precise object of my journey, in order that he might know in what manner best to serve me.

It cost me many protestations to convince the Khan (if indeed I did convince him) that I had not visited that part of the country with a view to some great political enterprise. He looked quite vexed while I was explaining to him the chance that had thrown me in the way of Syud Muheen Shah, and brought me that road, and coaxingly assured me that he knew the Feringees to be far too clever fellows to put themselves out of the way to no purpose. Had not we taken all Hindoostân, and was not Khorassaun a finer country, and was there not a tree near Candahar to which it had been prophesied that the Feringees should extend their dominion? God was with us, and it was decreed, and must certainly come to pass, as I knew, only I did not confide in him. I at last offered to take an oath that I did not believe my countrymen entertained the slightest idea of extending their frontier from rich plains into a barren country of mountains, as he must be convinced, if he used his excellent judgment; since, even admitting his erroneous supposition of their being "world-graspers," they did not want the sagacity of the wolf, who would not leave a sheep to dine upon a porcupine; and this so far satisfied him, that he did not press the matter further, but insisted upon my accepting of a small basket of preserved dates as a parting token of his friendship, and requested me to send him a fine telescope from India.

CHAPTER VIII.

Departure from Quetta, and march, through the defile of Bolaun, to the town of Baugh, in the plain of Kutch—Halt at Baugh.

On the morning of the 2nd December, we took leave of Quetta, and marched down the valley formed by the Umbàr and Zunjeera mountains, eleven miles a point west of south, to Ser-e-aub. The soil of the valley was good, and, on the right, under the Zunjeera hills, were several little hamlets. At Ser-e-aub we encamped near the source of the Shâdeezye lora, which rises from several springs in a bed which you may jump across, but which soon widens and deepens.

There was a sensible difference between the climate of Quetta and this spot. It was so cold at night, that every one's care seemed to be how much clothing he could heap upon himself. At evening, our now large party looked very picturesque, lying round their clear burning fires, between the pickets of their horses; the wild-looking Cawker guards having post apart, a little distance from either end of our bivouac. And later, when the moon was up, the scene was only varied to appear more beautiful. The men, wrapped in their rugs and blanket-cloaks, lay in all directions among packages, saddles, and various weapons, stretched in the deepest repose; and the stillness of the sharp night-air was only interrupted by the sound of camels chewing the cud, or the occasional thick breathing of a dreaming horse. Here and there—

> ——— "a man
> Clad in a flowing garb did watch the while,
> While many of his tribe slumber'd around:
> And they were canopied by the blue sky
> So cloudless, clear, and purely beautiful!"

The next day we marched eighteen miles to the Kurklekkee hills, which may be described as the first of a close and high series that cover the country as far as the plain of Dauder, and which have a general inclination up to the Tukkatoo chain. After riding six miles, we passed round the end of the Umbàr range. The Jinjeer line has a longer course: below Ser-e-aub it takes the name of Speersoond, with which it runs down about twenty miles, when it is crossed by another high but (I imagine) short range. It is difficult to ascertain the courses of these mountains, for some of them rise at once to their greatest altitude, and, perhaps, after a few miles end abruptly.

They are all high, and their general direction is north and south; but others come across these, cutting out valleys from ten to fifteen miles in length, and seven or eight miles in breadth. Three miles and a half before we reached the Kurklekkee hills, we passed through a break in a parallel line, called Dewângee; the plain between it and the continuation of the Jinjeer hills is called Dusht-e-Coochooti. On different parts of it were small mud towers, built by the husbandmen as places to flee to in case of their being attacked by marauding Cawkers from the adjoining mountains. After a march of eighteen miles, we reached the foot of the Kurklekkee hills, and crossing a narrow ridge, found ourselves in a stony slip of a valley, at the head of which we halted for the night.

This march we brought skins of water with us. Hard by there was said to be a small natural reservoir on a rock, but we did not visit it. Great vigilance was observed throughout the night; a strong guard was posted at the narrow entrance into the valley, and the merchants and their grooms relieved each other on watch from time to time, as they had received some confirmation of the report which had alarmed them at Quetta.

Before it was light next morning the whole camp was astir, and when all were ready, the order of march was arranged; the riders who had fire-arms forming an advance and rear guard, while the grooms, leading the horses and camels, walked together in a body on foot. From the valley in which we had slept, we at once entered the close defile of Bolaun. At first there was but breadth for a dozen horsemen between the rocks, which rose like walls on either side to a great height. Afterwards the road lay broadly between the mountains, occasionally opening out. It was like the beach of a sea, formed of loose pebbly stones and sand, and it ran in sharp angles from one hundred and fifty to two hundred yards in length. This was the style of the pass for ten miles to Ser-e-khujoor. The minutest description could hardly convey a just idea of its strength; it is a defile which a regiment of brave men could defend against an army.

At Ser-e-khujoor, a full and rapid stream gushed out from the foot of the rock. It ran a short distance, and then lost itself in the ground, appearing again two miles lower down, near a single date-tree, called Khujoor-e-pauin. At Ser-e-khujoor the hills broke off from the road, but they still commanded it for nineteen more miles, and the same beach-like road lay between steep banks, as if it were the bed of a deep but dried river.

Sixteen miles on the road was Khaukee Deho, and thirteen miles further on Beebeenaunee, both places where there was abundance of good water, used as halting-points by camel caravans. Many graves were here and there pointed out as those of murdered travellers, and I afterwards learned that beyond Khaukee Deho we passed a burying-ground named Kutlgau, or the place of slaughter, from the circumstance of a large party of travellers having been murdered there.

At Ser-e-khujoor we had halted a minute or two to water the horses, and then continued our march in the same order as before, with the exception that, where the nature of the ground admitted it, we had skirmishers thrown out on either flank on the bank above us. Muheen Shah rode at the head of the party, from time to time giving such advice and orders as he deemed expedient. He looked anxious, but said that he had seen a dream in the night, and that it was *khire,** *Inshallah.* At Beebeenaunee the mountains parted off to the right and left, and here ended the dreaded defile of Bolaun. Many keen eyes had been all the way directed to the tops of the hills, from whence we expected to see enemies overlooking us, but not the shadow of a foe appeared, and we returned thanks to Providence with minds much relieved, though still highly excited: when we were safely at the end of the dreaded pass, Muheen Shah called a halt, and recited a short prayer, which was answered by two shouts that made the hills ring again.

At Beebecnaunee we parted company from the Cawker guard, and, continuing our march more leisurely, rode on till an hour after sunset, when we halted for the night at Keerta or Gurm-aub, a soft

* Propitious.

sandy spot near a moderately high range of hills, running up north-north-west to Tukkattoo, named Gurm-aub from the circumstance of there being a thermal spring close by.

We marched from Kurklekkee at break of day, but the road at first wound so frequently, and the mountains were so high, that I could not exactly ascertain our course. At Keerta I compared notes with my companion Karaumut Ali, and we agreed that we had not marched less than forty miles. Judging from the recollection of our indirect route, and from the bearing which I the next morning took of a small peak, said to be just above the little stony valley in which we had slept, I laid down Keerta, in a direct line, twenty-eight miles south-east by south of Kurklekkee.

From Ser-e-khujoor to Beebeenaunee our pace was so quick a walk, that the camels were almost pushed into a trot. This was partly owing to every body's anxiety to get forward, but chiefly on account of the great descent of the road. I should have mentioned that the rise of the country from Quetta to Kurklekkee is very apparent. The Kurklekkee hills, thus standing upon the highest ground, have been fixed upon by the natives as the natural boundary between Khorassaun and Hindoostân.

There is another pass which joins that of Bolaun at Beebeenaunee, but it is said to be a more difficult one:—"You travel six miles south from Ser-e-aub, and then the road turns off to the right, to a spring at the foot of the mountains, which is the first halt. The second march occupies camels ten hours; the road is over steep hills, and only camels half laden can take it. You halt at a spring called Nagahoo. The next march is to Koogelee, whence you go *viâ* Beebeenaunee to Keerta: the road is on a great descent. At Koogelee there are khails of Belooches and Muhrries; there is abundance of water, and much good rice is cultivated. The road all the way from the first spring is so difficult, that it is only taken when danger is apprehended in the defile of the other one. Horses all lose their shoes whenever they come this way."

From Keerta we rode south through a deep and narrow valley. The bed, as before, was like a beach, and on it lay many ponds of clear water, which we were continually crossing. After ten miles, the road between the high rocks was blocked up by a lake too deep to be ridden through. We made a circuit of three miles, by a craggy path up and down rocks, and got into the valley again where, widening out, it allowed the water to spread into a shallower pond, which we forded where the water reached to our saddle-girths. Some babool trees, named in Pushtoo *Cundye*, gave name to this spot; but they had been swept away two years before by a torrent, which caused the lake to form in the area that its violence had deepened. To judge from the traces of the ravages, a great flood of water must have rushed through the valley; for in parts it had furrowed up the large stones of the bed, and thrown them up like a wall to the height of several feet. In answer to my inquiries where this water came from, I was told that it was rain-water, and it struck me as probable that the periodical rains which come up from the Indian Ocean, are stayed by and gathered in these mountains. They deluge the plain of Dauder, but are hardly felt at Quetta. The rocks are high and barren. In summer the sun acting upon these pent-up waters, causes a pestilent air, and the road between Quetta and Dauder is shut.* Native cossids are, indeed, to be found whose poverty will tempt them to carry letters, but they often remain on the road as food for hyenas. We saw many foot-marks of these animals, fit inhabitants of a region so desolate, that had they not the power of going far for their food, they must eat each other.

From Cundye a road goes direct to the town of Baugh. When we had crossed the broad lake, we followed a turn of the valley for four miles, then the mountains breaking, we left them, and, following a small but rapid brook, rode across a bare plain, seven miles to Gooroo, a village distant three miles from the town of Dauder.

Dauder is a town of the same size as Quetta; likewise governed under the authority of the khan of

* When this road is shut, travellers go from Quetta *viâ* Moostung and Kelaut-e Nusseer to Gundawa. The latter road is taken by caravans of laden camels, and it is not described as a difficult one.

Kelaut-e-Nusseer. The Hâkim was a man who had been brought up as a slave in the house of the Khan. Two-thirds of the inhabitants are Juts,* and Belooches, and the rest Hindoos. Viewed from hence, the mountains which we had left presented the appearance of one very high range, coming up north from the sea, and crossing the Tukkatoo chain at a right angle, so as distinctly to separate the mountainous from the plain country. We now felt that we had quitted Khorassaun :—climate, soil, and produce, and the dark, oily, naked people, all forcibly told of Hindoostân.

Dauder is situated in the arid white plain of Kutch, the crusted surface of which is cracked like the dried bed of a marsh. Even the natives feel the heat of this plain in summer as dreadful, and it would scarcely be habitable were it not watered by the stream which we brought with us from the hills, and by a river called Nâree, which, coming from the Tukkatoo, or, as they are here called, the Lâree mountains, runs south to forty-two miles beyond Baugh, and then goes off to the right towards what I may term the great Sinde and Kutch chain.

During the periodical rains this bed is filled: the cultivators build strong earthen dams across it, and so retain the water for a second crop. Scarcely any wheat or barley is now grown: the staple food of the

* The aborigines, long ago converted from the Hindoo, to the Soonnee Mohummudan, religion.

people is jawarree, which is cultivated to a great extent round Dauder. Bajra and cotton are also cultivated. We halted one day at Gooroo, and the Hâkim's men levied a tax of half a ducat upon each horse.

Dec. 7th. — Thirty-six miles to Baugh. After riding eleven miles, we saw at the distance of five miles on our left, the village of Heeree, which is used by camel caravans as a stage between Baugh and Dauder. The country was quite bare till we were within eight miles of Baugh, when it was flooded by water from the dams of the Nâree, and cultivated all the way with jawarree and bajra. From the approach, the town looked well, adorned, as it appeared, by fine trees, and several little temples, and built upon a rising ground, above the oasis which had been formed around it; but when we approached, the illusion vanished, and we found a dirty town of low mud houses, built partly within, and partly without, a crumbling mud wall, the many gaps in which had been stopped by furze bushes. In the trees, however, we were not so much disappointed, and we picketed our horses in a large grove.

Baugh is a town of two thousand houses, and three hundred shops. A third of the inhabitants are Hindoos, and they seemed to enjoy a brisk trade, chiefly in the common sorts of grain. The Affghauns take many camel-loads of jawarree hence to their own country, both using it to make bread for themselves, and giving it to their horses. The Hindoos also profit by the sale of gunpowder, much of which is manufactured here, and exported to Affghaunistaun and to Sinde.

We halted seven days at Baugh, in order that the horses might recruit upon the nourishing stalks of the jawarree plant. When we arrived, the Hâkim, who had also been a slave in the family of the Khan of Kelaut, was away, fighting some of his rebellious subjects, but he returned on the third day, at the head of a faithful body of his men at arms, looking as victorious as possible, preceded by a state elephant, and by a brace of musicians, who made a dreadful noise with Indian trumpets. The horse-dealers were lavish of their adulations: "The Khan was come from beating his enemies! Inshallah! was it not always thus that his fortunate foot returned to his abode of wealth and delight!"—The Khan condescended to be as gracious as a proper sense of dignity would allow him, and subsequently evinced his satisfaction by accepting something less than the regular duty of half a ducat upon each horse.

Great was the astonishment of some Affghauns who had not before seen an elephant. They stared at the animal open-mouthed, sighed, and shook their heads, and seemed with difficulty to persuade themselves that it was a natural creature.

On the road from Pisheen I had been astonished at the physical powers of the Affghaun grooms: many of them had the difficult task of leading two strong horses during a march that occupied the day, and at night they relieved each other on guard, their food consisting only of half-baked cakes of unleavened bread. Here many seemed inclined to bring up the balance of their fatigue hours, reposing day and night among the bundles of jawarree stalks that had been piled up for the horses, while a few would amuse themselves by bathing in the deep lakes which had been formed in the river's bed, or by prowling round the banks to get a shot at wild fowl. I saw a young man of the party shoot two ducks with ball: at the end of his matchlock was a long fork on a pivot, which he used as a rest, and he invariably fired with great precision.

At sunrise every morning Hindoos would visit us with pots full of curds, portions of which they ladled out to a pea's weight, insisting upon money first, and taking special care that their vessels were not touched. The last caution was thought a great presumption by some of the rough mountaineers, who had been accustomed to think very contemptuously of a Hindoo, and they became quite indignant when the idolaters presumed to elevate their voices, and bandy angry expressions with them. "Oh! that I had you up in my own place!" was nearly the malediction of one of Muheen Shah's men, when called off from a Hindoo radish-merchant whom he had been bullying: "Oh! that I had you up in my own place!" By Aboo Bukr, I would flay you, and then flog you to death with your own black hide, vile dog of jehannum!"

Not having had the good fortune to visit Wales, I cannot tell how far I am justified in the following comparison, but judging from written descriptions of the people of our sister country, I am inclined to think that, as the Persians have been named the Frenchmen, so the Affghauns might be termed the Welshmen of the East. In their love for cheese, though they have not yet learned to toast it, the Affghauns are very little behind the Welsh; they are brave, ridiculously proud, and as hasty as tinder to catch fire; and, like the Welsh, they have a peculiar way of altering the letters of words, so as to make them sound short.

Furrah (the ancient Purra) they call Purrah; and the famed Vuzeer Futteh Khan, whom they so loved, and whom they still so often talk about, is commonly called Putteh Kan. The Persian alphabet, which they use (having no written character of their own), admits of several substitutions of one letter for another; but the Affghauns are frequently not guided by rule, and as they generally speak in a nasal tone, and mispronounce the words of any other language but their own, a good story is easily made out of their expressions. The following anecdote, ill as my translation of it may read, is an inimitable one as told by a Persian who has lived among Affghauns.

When Ahmud Shah founded the Doorraunee monarchy, he modelled his court upon the Persian style, and several gentlemen of the latter country came to obtain service under his Majesty. The greatest of these was an old kuzzilbash nobleman, named Ali Merdaun Khan, who having signified his desire to the proper authorities, had a day appointed for audience of the Affghaun monarch. The Doorraunee ceremony of presentation at court is a very strange one, borrowed, apparently, from the Chinese Tartars,—the person upon whom the honour is to be conferred, being placed between two officers of the court, who run him up at a trot to within a certain distance of the king, shout out his name, and then, twisting him round, hurry him back again at the pace he came: at least this is the Persian account of the ceremony. Ali Merdaun Khan's dignity was considerably shaken by this (to him) unusual mode of proceeding, and he lost all control over his temper when he was announced as Ali Pertan Kan, from Ispilan. Indignantly shaking off his conductors, the old noble exclaimed, with more warmth than decorum, "*Not* Ali Pertan Kan, from Ispilan! but A-li Mer-daun Khaun, from Is-pha-haun,"—laying a dignified stress upon every syllable of his full-sounding name and birthplace, and then, with a reverential bow to the king, awaiting his dismissal, and gravely retiring as he would have done from the presence of the Shahan Shah. Ahmud Shah, it is said, was much amused at the Khan's bearing, and wished to retain him near his person, but the old gentleman's pride was hurt, and he refused to stay among a people too barbarous to pronounce his name properly.

Besides curd-sellers, we were daily visited by

venders of fried peas, and of immense radishes and turnips, which the Affghauns devoured raw in great quantities; and morning and evening we were waited on by all the indigent of the place, among whom were several uncombed and debauched-looking fakeers, who used to prowl about until they caught a party about to eat, when with the exclamation of *Yah Huk!* they would coolly thrust their gourds forward, and wait until something was put into them. One red-eyed old beggar of the crew was even less ceremonious, for one evening, when a party near us had prepared for themselves, as a treat, a mess of bread sopped in mutton broth, he waited till they gathered round it, then stepping up to where they were seated, dropped on his heels, and with a devout "Bismillah Irrahmaun Irraheem!" threw up his sleeve, and dipped his fingers into the dish. The party were disposed to be angry, but seeing that they drew back, their self-invited guest with the most imperturbable assurance pressed them to eat;—"Bismillah! Bismillah! fall to! pray, fall to!! what Ullah has provided let no man be unthankful for!" and, whether moved by the piety of his speech, or by hunger, one of the hosts repeated Bismillah! and they were presently all eating together with as much concord as diligence.

Apropos of turnips above alluded to,—I at this place heard a curious anecdote related by a Ghilgie, who accounted for the defeat of his tribe, when on the last occasion they rose under Abdooraheem Khan, the lineal descendant of their ancient kings, and endeavoured to overthrow the Doorraunee monarchy; for the interesting account of which, see Elphinstone's Caubul.—"You'll be late, and will lose your bargain if you remain there higgling for turnips," said a Syud to a Ghilgie Affghaun whom he wanted to accompany him to the town. "And if I am," retorted the man, "I cannot lose more than I have done by turnips." The laugh that the answer excited, induced me to ask the meaning of it, and the Ghilgie himself gave it to me in the evening. He commenced by describing how his clans were induced to get together, what Khans were among them, and where they met and fought the Doorraunees, &c.; but the part immediately relating to his answer was this: "We had the best of it, and got near Caubul, and after fighting and beating the Doorraunees till the heat of the last day, we went into a turnip-field to refresh ourselves: news came that the Doorraunees had rallied and were upon us; we did not believe it, but stayed to eat our turnips, and I was among the few lucky ones who can tell the tale."

Some ill-natured person of our company told the Hâkim that Muheen Shah had a Feringee with him. Fortunately the worthy governor was a *Moreed** of our patron's, and he took no further advantage of the communication than to exact the promise of some particular blessings for his son. He

* Disciple.

even sent two horsemen to see us safely out of his country,* only requesting that Syud Muheen would pass his son under his leg: this the Shah told me he did three times, and, Inshallah! no sword would cut, no bullet shoot the lad, and he would become a distinguished man if it was his *nusseeb kismut*.† And thus we happily bade adieu to Baugh.

* I have since learned with regret, that this kind deputy was put to death by his chief, for sending a complimentary present to the unlucky ex-monarch, Shah Shoojah, on his last fruitless attempt to recover the Affghaun monarchy.

† Fate and fortune.

CHAPTER IX.

March from Baugh to the town of Shikarpore—Remarks on the political and social condition of Beloochistaun.

Dec. 14.—We rode from Baugh, sixteen miles, to the village of Muchee. On the road we passed the villages of Kâzee-ke-wustee, and Gilpore, at each of which there was an unbricked well. We nearly followed the course of the Nâree river: in parts the water had been kept, from others it had been drawn off. The natives here and there dig wells in parts of the bed which have been lately drained: the water thus obtained is not good, but it is better than could be got by digging elsewhere. There was much cultivation of jawarree and cotton on the way.

15th.—Twenty-six miles, *vid* Hâjee-ke-Sheher, Ghurree, and Meerpore, to Cunda. The three first places were well-sized villages, and at the last were two mud towns of the same name. This march also we had with the Nâree, the bed of which was dry for about two-thirds of the distance. The Nâree river now goes off to the right, nearer to the mountains, and, some said, reaches the sea.

At Cunda there was an old large, and a small new

town, both surrounded with mud walls. We could not buy any milk here, and the inhabitants said that they were all in a state of beggary; a tribe of marauding Belooches having driven away seven hundred head of cattle a few months before, and the jawarree crop having been blighted.

Here a demand was made by two different parties for duty upon our horses. The Syuds agreed to pay the chief of the strongest set, on condition that he kept off the other, which he consented to do; but when he had persuaded his rivals to withdraw, he insisted upon receiving half the sum that they had demanded besides his own, threatening to bring them back if his demand was not complied with. The Syuds were now obliged to assume their bullying tone: they declared that they would fight both parties rather than be robbed, hinting that common weapons would avail little against theirs; and, getting together, they took counsel about formally cursing the exactor Nawaub Juwanee, as the chief was named.

This got wind, as it was intended it should, and not long after came a messenger from the Nawaub's mother, to offer a trifling present to the head Syuds, deprecating their curse, and promising to use all her influence over her son, to bring him to reason. This she apparently did, for in the evening the Nawaub sent to say that if the Syuds would pay him his due, and a trifle more, he would escort them with twenty horsemen to the end of the next stage, and this was agreed to.

16th.—Twenty-one miles to Saatee. For the first nine miles we rode through a fine tamarisk and thorn wood; the country onward was bare. Saatee is a moderate-sized village. Here a party came to demand duty: Nawaub Juwanee took three ducats to dismiss them, and when he had with much difficulty succeeded in doing so, he sent to request that some *chirs** might be given him. The Syuds were shocked at its being supposed possible that they could have any thing so unlawful in their possession, but they sent him another ducat in lieu, fearing altogether to cast his highness off. The title to which this debauched extortioner answered was, *Ghurreeb Nawâz*,—"Cherisher of the Poor."

17th.—Twenty-nine miles to Poonoo. After riding ten miles, we came to a jungle of low trees, which, running east and west, marks the boundary between Beloochistaun and Sinde, and which southward extends to the river Indus, whose banks it fringes. We had stolen away from Saatee a little before the moon rose, and reached the wood about sunrise; hardly had we entered it, when we heard two or three shots fired behind us, and the cry ran that our rear was attacked: the fighting men hastened back to the post of danger, priming their pieces as they went, while the others pressed on as fast as the narrow path would admit, camels and horses crowding upon each other; but after a few

* An intoxicating drug.

minutes of suspense, we learned that the alarm had been needlessly given by two or three stragglers, who had been stripped of their clothes by robbers. We continued our march without further disturbance, and when we had ended it, the merchants congratulated each other upon being out of Beloochistaun.

Poonoo is a large Hindoo village, surrounded by a few acres of land cleared from the jungle, inhabited by people who had the air of a society of Quakers, compared with those whom we had been accustomed to look upon. Here was much to assure us that we were really in India: we encamped in a fine grove of neem and mango trees, near a very large brick well, to and from which the women passed at evening, gracefully carrying jars upon their heads, and sometimes singing as they went in groups; many gray squirrels were chasing each other round the trunks of the large trees, the foliage of which was filled by doves, minas, and little green paroquets; the sun, the heat of which, even at this season, we felt unpleasant when long exposed to it, went down like a ball of fire, tinging the sky one beautiful deep orange colour; and at night the ground we slept upon was wet with a heavy dew.

The next morning we parted company from the greater number of the horse-dealers, Syud Muheen Shah resolving to accompany me to the north-west frontier of British India. A few of the merchants came with us to Shikarpore on business, while the rest went on to the town of Larkhana, where they proposed to make a halt of ten days or a fortnight, before proceeding *viâ* the capital of Sinde to the sea-coast. Muheen Shah selected half-a-dozen of his best horses to take with him, and sent the rest on to Bombay, under charge of his brother.

From Poonoo we rode about five-and-twenty miles to the town of Ghurree. Our path lay through a thick jungle, the soil of which was very fine. Tracks crossed each other in all directions, and we frequently lost our way until we obtained a guide; once we were obliged to make a circuit to avoid a marsh or lake, which had been formed, we were told, by the inundation of the Indus. We thought it must be rain-water, but were assured that, above Shikarpore, the right bank of the river was low, and that there much water was let in upon the country.

There were many wretched hamlets on and near the road, occupying small spots cleared from the jungle. At each there was a shallow unbricked well, and round about most of them small patches cultivated with the commonest grain. A few buffaloes, goats, and fowls, seemed to constitute the wealth of each village.

Ghurree is a moderate-sized, thriving town. We saw there much good sugar-cane, and noticed twenty common Indian mills at work, expressing oil from sesamun seed. Here we first saw a wheeled carriage. A hundred Affghaun families are settled at Ghurree; their chief, Jooma Khan Baurickzye, was residing in a neat little fort near the town, affecting submission to the authority of the Ameers of Hyderabad.

From Ghurree we rode eight miles north to Shikarpore: half way was the fortified village of Kerne. In approaching Shikarpore, we rode for some distance through open groves of tall palm-trees, and the appearance of the town was imposing, as we occasionally got glimpses of its high houses rising above each other among fine trees. Two miles from the city we were met by a party of the governor's confidential people, who were going off express to Poonoo, on the report that a large company of horse-merchants had halted there. The chief of the party, who was a consequential and fat little Belooche, deemed our coming reason sufficient for his returning; therefore inquiring where the horse-merchants would be met with, he sent his men after them, and himself took charge of us, riding round us as we proceeded, to judge if any of our steeds were worthy the Ameer's notice; for these princes are very arbitrary in their orders about the horses which come down from the north countries, allowing none to be taken out of their dominions until they have seen them. I happened to be riding the best of Muheen Shah's horses, and the man singled me out:—"Ho! you sir! what is your fortunate name?"—"Meerza Sâdik," muttered I, taken rather by surprise.—"Then Meerza Sâdik, just walk your horse out, hold up his head, and put him to his amble:—higher,

higher, man! phoo! are you a horse-dealer; or do you not want to show his paces? I believe that is it, for you Puthans are deceitful fellows." Here it was explained who Syud Muheen Shah was, and the Belooche sobered his tone, declared that he had a great esteem for holy men, and that we were welcome to Shikarpore. On reaching the city, our bustling conductor left us, to announce our arrival, and we put up in a small grove just outside the wall.

Shikarpore is a very large town, surrounded by a thick, but much broken mud wall, in which there are eight gates. Much of the interior is waste ground, and part is occupied by large trees. Almost every house has a shop attached to it, and through the centre of the city runs each way a low bazaar, covered in with rafters and palm leaves. The shops seemed to be well filled with the necessaries of life, and various merchandise, and the people had that busy air which characterizes men engaged in active trade.

Around the city are fine gardens, and groves of luxuriant Indian trees, which make the environs very beautiful; but the heat of the climate during the greater part of the year is such as would kill any body but a Hindoo. So great is the heat, that every inhabitant who can afford the expense, builds upon his house a very high story, on the roof of which he sleeps without clothes. "In summer," said an Affghaun resident, "the sun will roast an egg, and turn a white man black;" about the *ne plus ultra* of solar heat.

Shikarpore is chiefly inhabited by Hindoo bankers and merchants, who have commercial connexions all over the east. They are sleek, smooth-shaven, and what an American would term prosperous-looking men, and if report does not very much belie them, they are an immensely rich body. Like the blood-sucking Sircars of Bengal, they are said to attach themselves to the fortunes of others, and to grow fat, in proportion as their patrons grow poor:—*au reste*, they are civil, good people, and very clever at languages, there being but few among them who do not understand Persian, Beloochee, Pushtoo, Hindoostânee, and the dialects of Sinde. Several corruptions of the Sinde language are in use, the most common one of which is called Shikarporee. We heard it spoken at Dauder, and after we had crossed the Indus, as far easterly as Buhawulpore; it is a sharp, quickly-spoken dialect, differing from Hindoostânee about as much as Bengalee does.

More than a fourth of the inhabitants of the city are Mohummudans, and among these are from five to six hundred Affghaun families. In the province, we were told, are settled as many as four thousand families: great jealousy exists between them and their late tributaries the Sindees, but they can do nothing but grumble, and pray that the Doorraunee King may have his own again. When the relatives of the Affghaun vuzeer dethroned Shah Mahmood, Shikarpore fell to the share of the Candahar brothers; but the Hyderabad Ameers, who had only been obedient to the Affghaun monarchs occasionally and upon compulsion, declared themselves entirely independent after the revolution, and ejecting the Affghaun governor from Shikarpore, placed a servant of their own in his stead, not fearing the rebel claimants, who, they judged, would have enough to do to take care of themselves in their distant province of Candahar. The Hâkim who now rules at Shikarpore on the part of the Ameers, collects from the town and province three lacs of rupees yearly. The further sum of 50,000 rupees accrues annually to the Ameers from the customs of the city. When the Affghauns had the rule, double the latter sum was collected.

The soil of the province is very fertile, and it may in most places be irrigated by means of wells; water lying sufficiently near the surface to be raised by the Persian wheel. Sugar, cotton, indigo, tobacco, and opium, are cultivated, as also wheat, barley, and peas, a little rice, and much jawarree and bajra. However the finest land of the province is waste: the rich banks of the Indus, which are alluvial for some miles' breadth on either side, and which might be cultivated to great purpose, are allowed to remain covered with jungle, that game may be preserved for the sport of the Ameers.

I would now take a slight review of the country

between Candahar and Shikarpore, premising that as Mr. Pottinger wrote a full description of Beloochistaun, I confine myself to the detail of such parts as came immediately under our observation.

Our calculations make the distance from Candahar to Shikarpore (bends in the road, &c. included) about three hundred and ninety miles. It has been shown that the rule of the Candahar rebel Sirdars does not extend to Quetta; and that although the authority of the Khan of Kelaut-e-Nusseer commences at the latter place, the road from it to the capital of the next of his petty states is commanded by wild Affghaun and Belooche tribes, who occupy the hills on the left and right of the formidable pass of Bolaun. Hâkims rule at Dauder and Baugh in the name of the Khan of Kelaut, but they have each enough to do to sustain their limited authority, and the more southern and western parts of Beloochistaun are in a very disturbed state. Belooche tribes war upon each other, or plunder the Juts, and many who can find means to pay a few retainers, set themselves up as chiefs, and call a small circle of country their own.

The good order of Beloochistaun, I mean of that part of it which may be considered as belonging to the government of the Khan of Kelaut-e-Nusseer, and which I will call Beloochistaun proper,* would

* Say Kutch, on the east of the great (Sinde and Kutch) chain; and west of this, to the longitudinal line of 64°, the country between Kelaut and the sea: for the western Belooches are, and, I imagine, ever have been, as independent as Bedouins.

appear to depend upon that of Affghaunistaun. When, on the death of Nadir Shah, Ahmud Khan Suddozye founded the Doorraunee monarchy, Beloochistaun, under Nusseer Khan, became virtually subject to the reigning power in Affghaunistaun;—an agreement being made by which the Khan of Kelaut engaged to furnish a large quota of troops to the King of Candahar's army, whenever it should be employed in foreign war. Ahmud Shah made the Belooches sensible of their inferiority to the Affghauns, and while he reigned, his authority was generally respected. So long also as Nusseer Khan lived, Beloochistaun was well governed, but during the last twelve years of this chief's rule, another king sat on the Affghaun throne—Timour Shah, who by his irresolute conduct gave encouragement to turbulently-disposed chiefs to throw off their allegiance, and the Belooches, long accustomed to consider that alone to be power which was sustained at the sword's point, began to think lightly of the protecting government, and many of them to set at nought their liege-lord the Khan of Kelaut.

Mahmoud Khan was a mere boy when he succeeded his father Nusseer Khan, and consequently he was not able effectually to check the revolt of his chiefs. The sons of Timour Shah Doorraunee occupied themselves in civil war, and when the last of them was driven from the throne by rebels, Affghaunistaun was divided into several states, which were not separately strong enough to enforce obedience from the Belooches.

However, Mehraub Khan, the present Khan of Kelaut, not being cordially supported by his chieftains, finds it expedient to be friends with the Candahar Sirdars; as well to prevent their spoiling his country, as to have in them an ally against the Ameers of Sinde, who have shown a wish to encroach upon his territory. Mehraub Khan has also found it necessary to conciliate Runjeet Sing, and, all things considered, it seemed to be thought that he wished for the restoration of the Suddozye dynasty in Affghaunistaun.

The bulk of the inhabitants of Kutch are Juts,—the aborigines. It is not exactly known at what period these people were converted from the Hindoo to the Mohummudan religion; at present they are divided into many tribes, and profess themselves Soonnees. They live in villages, and are the agriculturists of the country.

The Belooches bear but a very small proportion to those whom they conquered, and, with the exception of a few who reside in the small forts which are scattered over the country, they live in khails, and rove to pasture their oxen and sheep.

The condition of either people seems far from a prosperous one. They are just able to feed and clothe themselves, and that but indifferently. The Belooches live under felt tents. The habitations of the villages are mere sheds, generally built of sticks and grass, and the inhabitants can change their situation almost as easily as if they lived in tents.

The terms on which the land is tilled are these: Persons wishing to cultivate land near a stream, (the Naree, for instance,) throw a dam across the bed, and run up a few houses near the spot. The produce of the land upon which water is turned, is divided into three shares:—the first one the cultivator halves with the Hâkim, or with the proprietor of the soil, to indemnify himself for the expense of constructing the embankment; and of the two remaining shares, the Hâkim, or proprietor, takes nearly seven eighths. A traveller might note the sites of villages which, perhaps, would not be found twelve months afterwards; for in case of oppression by the lord of the soil, or of accident, such as the breaking away of a dam, &c., the ryots are likely to remove and establish themselves elsewhere.

The country to the right of our road, near the mountains, is I imagine not ill-cultivated, for we learned that from the base of the mountains, all the way from Dauder to the sea, run many little rivulets, the waters of which are dammed, and kept for agricultural purposes. I mentioned that we brought a stream with us from the mountains, which went off towards them again after having watered the land about Dauder. I believe that this is joined by another stream, which comes out of the hills by a pass called Moollâ, and that it then runs parallel with, and at no great distance from the mountains, half way to the sea.

The river Nâree comes south from the high mountains of Tukkatoo, or Lâree, past Sewee, a proverbially hot place, where much rice is cultivated. Eastward of the Nâree we heard of two moderately-sized streams (which I imagine must run to the Indus), and many small rivulets are said to irrigate the lands at the foot of the mountains. The general course of all the water in this plain is south.

The staple food of the people of Kutch is jawarree or bajra bread. The first grain is much cultivated, and sold very cheap. Wheat and barley are little, if at all, grown. We could only obtain wheaten flour at the towns, and then not much; even barley meal, which is far cheaper, was not to be had ready ground in any quantity.

At the towns of Dauder and Baugh, a little mutton or goat's flesh was exposed for sale in the bazaar. The people of Kutch possess many cattle, but owing to their poverty, and perhaps to the heat of the climate, they do not eat much flesh. Some of the horse-merchants of our party brought with them pieces of dry salted meat, to which they occasionally treated themselves.

One day we had the luck to taste fresh mutton, such as it was. A stout Caubul ram, which was being led to India for sale, warranted to break the head of any male of his species he might butt against, happened to receive a severe kick from a camel, and as he looked very likely to die, it was determined to kill and eat him. Muheen Shah was called upon to officiate. Standing in the midst of a crowd, the gasping ram lying at his feet, he bared his arm, and flourished his knife, with the dignity of an ancient priest of Jupiter, then uttering a loud "Bismillah Ullah Ho Acber!" he stooped and turned the victim's head towards the *kebla*, while he dexterously drew the sharp blade across the throat, so as not quite to divide the thorax, and then declared the flesh to be lawful meat.

CHAPTER X.

Halt at Shikarpore—March to the river Indus, and on to the towns of Khirepore and Rohree—Fortress of Bukkar—Ameers of Sinde—State of the people—Rohree well situated for commercial purposes—Remarks on British and Russian trade with central Asia.

We halted three days at Shikarpore. Our friend had business to transact, and the Hâkim made some difficulty about allowing him to take his horses across the Indus, until he promised to go *viâ* Khirepore, in order that the Meers of that place might see the animals.

We had ample leisure to survey the town and its environs. I do not believe there is any thing very curious to be seen at Shikarpore, unless it be the library of one Meah Hadjee Fakeer Oollah, who boasted that he possessed seven hundred volumes, six hundred and ninety-nine of which were upon theology, and one upon history.

On the 20th of December we rode from Shikarpore to the river Indus. The distance was about fifteen miles, and our road lay through a jungle, which in many places was inclosed and planted with sugar-cane, to preserve wild hogs for the sport of the Ameers. Just as the sun was setting, we found ourselves at the end of the wood, and upon the high bank of the Indus, which was flowing past us in one calm broad stream. The spot where we stood commanded a view of two other broad reaches, and the scene altogether was one that for quiet grandeur and beauty could hardly be surpassed.

We slept upon the bank, and the next morning were ferried over in boats which held two camels and three horses. We were towed up the bank for some distance, and then loosing, went across diagonally with the help of the stream. We were rowed by a large pair of oars, assisted by a long rudder which the helmsman used as a paddle, and we were exactly eight minutes from bank to bank.

The water appeared to run at the rate of two miles and a half per hour, and the breadth of it was half a mile. The boatmen said that the water was then at its lowest, and that it would not rise till the mountain snows melted in the spring. We had not the means of ascertaining its actual depth, but we found no bottom near the centre of the stream with a pole twelve feet long, and were told that we were not near it. Though the right bank was high, the left was here scarcely defined; the bed was of earthy sand, and the water in appearance like that of the Ganges.

We rode on nine miles beyond the river, through

a low open wood not far from the bank, and crossed a dry bed which we saw again at Khirepore: water is dammed up in it for cultivation, as in the Kutch water-courses. Seven miles on the road was a large village named Hohrara or Oleera; we halted at the village of Dublee, where we spent the night unpleasantly enough in a drizzling rain. Muheen Shah tried an address to the skies, but they would not pity us, and we had nothing for it but to get well under our blankets.

22nd.—Eight miles by a winding road through jungle to Khirepore, a very large open town built among trees,—the seat of the descendants of the late esteemed Sinde chief Ameer Sohraub.

At his death Meer Sohraub bequeathed his country to his eldest son Meer Roostum, and all his collected wealth to his second son Meer Morâd; decreeing however from the revenues of the eldest, provision for forty other descendants. The two brothers at first quarrelled, but when we were at Khirepore they were living in the same house, though on very dubious terms. A wall divided their several ranges of apartments, and the entrances were kept by a body of either chief's retainers; indeed we were told that Meer Morâd dreaded to go out hunting without his brother, lest the latter should take the opportunity to seize his treasure.

Yet we heard from several persons an anecdote of Meer Morâd, which, were it not for the indubitable fact that it is not in the nature of Asiatics to confide in each other, would induce a doubt whether a man who had acted so generously, could harbour such degrading suspicions against a brother who could not wrong him if he acknowledged the weakest dictates of honour or gratitude, as the following story may show.

Meer Roostum received no money with the territory that his father bequeathed to him, and when he quarrelled with his brother, he found himself so ill able to pay the fighting men whom he had entertained, that he applied to a neighbouring chief for a loan to enable him to carry on the war. Meer Morâd, hearing of this, sent to request that he would not lower his dignity by taking money from a stranger, for he would lend him whatever sum he required, whether they were to continue enemies, or to become friends;—and this it was, according to the story, that led the way to a reconciliation.

We arrived at Khirepore early in the day: scarcely were our horses tied up, when we heard loud shouts and the barking of many dogs, and presently came a party of troopers to say that the Meers were going out hunting, and had ordered our horses to accompany them, that they might see their mettle. Remonstrance was useless, so the horses being saddled, were ridden off, and put through their paces till evening.

Muheen Shah was very indignant, and the next day took an early opportunity of applying for permission to continue his journey. When he went, he was offered five hundred rupees for his best horse, and excusing himself from selling any, on the plea that they had been bought on commission for some Rajah in British India, he was ordered to pay a very heavy duty upon each animal. He complied, and was told that he should receive a pass, but as he was about to leave the palace, he was taken by a party of Meer Morâd's men, who demanded duty on account of *their* master, and the consequence of his refusal was, that in spite of his *bukht*, he was put in a guard-house, and kept there all night.

We did not at the time learn more than that our friend had been imprisoned, and therefore suffered much uneasy conjecture as to the cause. The Affghaun grooms were very dejected, and evidently attributed their master's ill-treatment to his connexion with me.—We were all sitting round a fire late in evening, " chewing the bitter cud of unpleasant reflections," and listening to a serenade of jackals, when a stout Affghaun stranger walked up and gave us a Salaam Alekoom! One of our party looking up, with an exclamation of surprise recognised the man, who when he had exchanged a few questions in Pushtoo, sat down among us, and unrolling a cloth from his waist, produced a packet of English letters addressed to me. For a moment or two I could scarcely think myself awake, so great was the surprise; but breaking the seals, I recognised the signatures of friends whom I had left at Tabreez, and was presently able to appreciate their kind efforts in my service.

The letters contained bills on Heraut for the money we had required, and our friend Moollâ Mohumud had sent them after us to Pisheen, whence again they had been forwarded by the Syuds.—Karaumut Ali also got remembrances from his friends, and for a while poor Muheen Shah and our sorrow on his account were forgotten; but the happiness that I experienced in receiving these letters, was dashed with regret that I could not but feel on learning from them the death of the British Envoy, Sir John Macdonald, to whom I had been indebted for many kindnesses.

The next morning Muheen Shah thought it better to pay for his release, and thus obtaining it, he lost no time in getting the promised passport from Meer Roostum. The Shah looked very pale and unhappy when he returned to us, and refused all offers of refreshment, vowing that bread should not pass his lips until he was away from such a place. We accordingly made ready to start, and engaging the services of a guide who said he knew all the roads between that and Buhawulpore, we set out for Rohree.

The distance from Khirepore to Rohree is about sixteen miles. We rode for ten miles through a country which had been partially cleared for cultivation, and then entered a grove of gigantic palm-trees, on either side of which were large walled gardens of many fruits, and occasionally a few houses. We rode for six miles through this beautiful grove, and got out of it upon a broad area of loose sand shelving gently down to the Indus. To the right of this, built upon a flint rock, was the old town of Rohree,—a ruined collection of tall, desolate-looking houses, with broken latticed windows, and wooden balconies,—and on the left stood a thick clump of trees, partly shutting out from view the massy fortress of Bukkar, which, strongly built of brick and stone, rises from an island in the centre of the river. Our horses clambered up the rocky path into a narrow street, which was crossed by a long bazaar, lowly roofed over with rafters and palm-leaves: not being able to ride under this, we found our way through the town by narrow lanes, and halted on the other side of it, near the bank of the river.

25th December.—We spent Christmas-day at Rohree, for Muheen Shah going early to present our pass to the governor of the fortress, was told that it was informal, and that we could not proceed; upon which our friend saddled a running camel, and trotted back to Khirepore again, leaving us to survey the wonders of this extraordinary place.

Rohree, the ancient capital of the Sogdi, if not the town which, according to Arrian, Alexander the Great built when he rested hereabouts on his way to the ocean, has fallen into decay, and does not contain more than six or seven thousand inhabitants, four-fifths of whom are Hindoos. The flint rock upon which it is built, is washed by the river, and it runs curiously back to some miles' distance, having somewhat the appearance of an old line of bastioned fortification. The flint of which this and the other rocks are composed is of so good a quality, that travellers on the river commonly take away a quantity in their boats.

We did not visit the ancient town of Bukkar, but we viewed its extensive ruins at some distance from the opposite bank.

The island fortress of Bukkar is built upon an oval flint rock three quarters of a mile in circumference, which divides a stream eight hundred yards in width. The fort itself is strongly built, but it is overlooked by the bank upon which stands the town of Rohree. It commands the river, and all boats that pass up and down pay a toll. The water covers part of the rock at one end, and forms a little islet, on which is a Mohummudan temple embowered in trees: this is the resting-place of so great a saint, that the very fishes come up from the sea to swim a *Ziarut* round it, and to mark their respect for the shrine, they never once turn tail on the journey up.

Near the bank, a little below the fort, is another rock, which becomes an islet at the swell of the river. This hill has long been used as a Mohummudan burial-ground, and is covered with old tombs. You ascend to its summit by seventy steps: a little way up dwells a hermit, who makes visiters take their shoes off, and accepts their charity, bidding them pray for the souls of the departed.

The natives of Rohree are an amphibious race of

beings who spend their days upon the river catching fish, which they salt and preserve. The mode in which these fishers exercise their art is very curious: they lay their stomachs upon large empty jars, and holding a line or net in hand, they use their feet as paddles, and float about with their faces close to the water. We wondered at the ease with which they seemed to control the force of the stream. Sometimes a man would lie still upon the water, as if he was tight anchored to the bottom, and then, abandoning himself to the current, he would drop down as far as it suited him, when he would land, walk up the bank with his jar, and launch himself afresh.

From its situation, Rohree should be a healthier place than Khirepore; the chiefs however prefer residing at the latter place, and not only is the town of Rohree neglected, but on the bank of the river beyond it, jungle keeps waste rich land which might be very profitably cultivated, as well with articles for export, as with the better sorts of grain. The Ameers of Sinde appear to live only for themselves, and to be as blind to the capabilities of their country, as they are regardless of the welfare of its inhabitants: to indulge their passion for sporting, they suffer much of their richest land to be covered with jungle, and the revenue thus sacrificed is made up, as far as is possible, by heavy drains upon the profits of such lands as are left to the peasantry. The people feel the check of this ignorantly oppressive system, yet attempt not to better their condition, and in that happy spirit of filial piety for which Indians are distinguished, resign themselves to the life that their fathers endured.

The staple food of the people of Sinde is bread made of jawarree or bajra. Buffaloes being very cheap in this country, the poorest people have them, and some possess a few goats and fowls. Their dwellings are of the meanest order: the neatest are those of the people who reside upon lands which are liable to be flooded;—little thatched sheds raised upon bamboo frames some five or six feet above the ground, into which the occupants ascend by small ladders.

From what we observed, and were able to learn of Sinde and its people generally, I cannot help thinking that the amount of the Ameers' income has been exaggerated; though there need be little doubt that it would more than equal the reputed sum, if these princes could fully understand their interests. It is lamentable that provinces which, from their situation and natural fertility, ought to be filled with rich and happy people, should be subject to the misrule of a few ignorant despots: but the Indus must be shortly thrown open to our trade, and then will be levelled that unsocial barrier within which the jealous chieftains of Sinde have so long fenced themselves; we shall enlighten them with notions of just policy, and thus raise the condition of their people. Hitherto the Indus has been suffered to flow from its source to the Indian ocean, contributing little to the wealth or civilization of the countries which lie upon its banks; the short-sighted chiefs of the Indian states which it bounds, have been distrustful of each other, and mutually jealous of the power which has resources and enterprise sufficient to embrace the whole of the river in one grand commercial scheme; but happily their distrust is giving way before the tried good faith of the British Government, and we may hope that many years will not elapse before all parties are zealously engaged in an extended trade, which will bind their interests closely together, and be the means of introducing commerce and civilization into a new world.

Rohree is a city which appears in every way designed to become a place of wealth and importance, surrounded as it is by a fertile country, standing on a noble river which is navigable from the ocean to Attock, and situated at mean distance from many places of political and commercial importance. On the verge of the natural frontier of Hindoostân, and commanding the great Candahar road, it is well situated on what would be adopted as a line of defence against foreign invasion; and conveniently placed with regard to some of the principal cities of India, it offers an admirable position for an emporium which would make our manufactures accessible to the countries which stretch far to the north and west.

The natives of Affghaunistaun chiefly trade with southern India, taking the roads through Beloochistaun and Sinde, to the ports of Kurâchee and Mundavie, where they embark for Bombay. The Hyderabad Ameers endeavour to keep the trade in these roads, and the Ameers of Khirepore, by injudiciously exacting large and irregular duties, have discouraged the merchants from opening a new one through their territory to the northern provinces of British India, &c., and thus Shikarpore flourishes; but Rohree is in every respect better situated for commerce than Shikarpore, and were it once established as a mart, would scarcely fail to attract the wealth of the former place, and to become one of the largest commercial towns in India.

If the Affghaun merchants could obtain at Rohree the European and Indian goods they traffic in, many of them certainly would repair thither in preference to following the tedious and expensive route to the sea-coast. Those who brought things which they could not sell or exchange at Rohree, would travel up to Buhawulpore, and thence by the newly opened road across the Indian desert to the provinces of Upper India; and probably they would return to the frontier mart to purchase an investment for their own country. Thus a grand trade road would be established *viâ* Quetta to Candahar, and the latter city would become an *entrepôt,* whence our commodities would be dispersed to other quarters.

I will here venture a few opinions upon the distinct question of our trade in the countries beyond the Indus, for having viewed it in connexion with the other advantages which should be consequent upon the opening of the river, my preceding words may have made me seem too sanguine about it.

Our trade beyond the Indus must depend first—upon the state of the Affghaun country; for until that is in some degree restored to order, traffic cannot be greatly extended in or beyond it. Not only do merchants risk open and violent robbery, which they must pay to guard themselves against, but they are exposed to the arbitrary exactions of so many persons in authority, that it is only in consequence of their obtaining large prices for the small quantity of goods exported, that they are enabled to make profit.

The extension of the trade must be gradual; for as yet the pastoral tribes of Affghaunistaun are not rich enough to purchase a very great quantity of our manufactures, much as they covet them; nor does their country afford many things that we could to any extent receive in barter from them.

If encouraged, the Affghaun merchants could import into India any required number of really good horses, at a fair price, but the demand for these must necessarily be limited, since the Indian cavalry cannot be dependent upon a foreign country for their supply of horses, and the Government studs breed nearly as many as are required for the public service.

The whole of Hindoostân is now supplied with dried and preserved fruits from Caubul, by the following roads, *viâ* the Punjaub to Loodeeana; *viâ*

Damaun, Mooltân, Buhawulpore, and Hissar, to Dehlee; *viâ* Quetta, Dauder, Baugh, and Larkhana,* to Sinde, and on by the usual road to Bombay and Madras. Apples, quinces, and grapes are packed in cotton, and as they are easily damaged, the profit on them is uncertain; but pomegranates, pistachio-nuts, almonds, dried apricots, figs, raisins, &c., are brought without loss: the demand for them is certain, and the profit good.

Assafœtida and saffron are the chief exports from

* I may here insert a memorandum of the duties levied on the road we took from Quetta to Shikarpore, which was by mistake omitted in the first edition.

At Quetta 9½ *cucha* rupees, named huft senna (18 of which go to a Bajoklee or gold ducat), are levied for the Kelaut chief, on every horse, or laden camel, going to Hindoostân. Ditto on laden camels coming from Hindoostân; except when they are charged with indigo,—the duty on a camel-load of which is 13½ rupees; or with cloths or leather,—the duty on which is 9 rupees per load. Unladen camels pass duty free.

At Dauder (formerly levied by the Affghauns, and sent to Candahar, now sent to Kelaut), 4 rupees are demanded for every horse, or laden camel. During the Doorraunee monarchy, *pucka* rupees were current in this province, and then the same number of those were taken.

At Baugh 3, at Cunda 2, rupees per horse or laden camel for the Kelaut chief.

At Shikarpore (which clears Larkhaneh), for the Hyderabad Ameers, are levied in rupees of which 5 go to a ducat (about the same as siccas),

	Reals.
Per horse	9½
Per camel laden with either raw or wrought silk . .	17
Do. with assafœtida, fruit, Ilwerd, crimson dye-wood, &c.	9

Uncut Turquoise stones, Khak e Ferooza, imported into Hindoostân upon camels in large quantities, pay duty at the general rate of 7 or 8 annas a seer, according to the guessed value, for it is a speculation how the rough stones will cut up.—Note to Second Edition.

Heraut: the quality of the carpets made there is very fine, but I am not sufficiently well informed about our trade in this article, to know whether it would suit us to revive the manufacture at Heraut, so as to obtain carpets thence by land-carriage, and ship them at the mouth of the Indus for Europe.

At Candahar is grown tobacco, which is esteemed to be little inferior to that of Shirauz. Very good opium is cultivated at Candahar, and the mountains in the north-eastern part of Affghaunistaun contain inexhaustible mines of the purest rock-salt. I am not qualified to judge to what extent it would serve the purposes of the Honourable Company's Government to receive the last two articles, but I presume that every encouragement would be given to people willing to relieve us of our manufactures, and perhaps some sacrifice submitted to in one branch of trade, for the establishment of another.

It is difficult to judge what wealth there may be in Affghaunistaun and the countries beyond, because the state of society there is such, that men will bury their money rather than be thought to possess much; and having little security for their neighbours' honesty, they are careful how they lend what they are afraid openly to speculate with themselves: but money there doubtless is in those countries,* and were security established, it would quickly find its way into circulation. Affghaunistaun is a coun-

* I asked an Affghaun merchant whether there was still wealth in this country. "Is there any doubt about it?" was his answer: "if there were not, what would so many Hindoos do there? Flies do not swarm about an empty honey-pot."

try which, were it settled, and freely open to those which surround it, would soon attract trade and wealth. The climate of the countries beyond the Indus is such, that our woollen and cotton cloths, &c., will always be in request there, and gradually, as the condition of the people betters, will markets open for our exports.*

Of late years the Russians have been sedulously endeavouring to extend the sale of their manufactures in Toorkestaun, Persia, and Affghaunistaun, and they have now four channels for their trade.

1. *Viâ* Orenburg to Bokhara, whence their commodities are taken to Meshed and Heraut, to Caubul, and even to Cashgar.

2. From Astrakhan *viâ* Mangishlak, on the east coast of the Caspian, to Khiva.

3. By the port of Reshdt, on the south coast of the Caspian, to Tehraun and Isphahaun, &c., and to Meshed, &c.

4. By the land-route from Tiflis, *viâ* Tabreez to Tehraun, &c.

The articles that they export are mentioned in my account of the trade of Meshed, and according to the statement of Baron Meyendorff, the commerce between Bokhara and Russia employs three thousand camels.

According to the same authority, the value of merchandise imported by the Bokharians into Russia, upon about three thousand camels, may amount in a

* See Appendix A.

good year to near eight millions of paper roubles, or 333,333*l.* As the goods which the Bokharians import into Russia, are more valuable and less bulky than those which they export thence, it may be conjectured that they receive in barter as great a quantity of Russian commodities as will load their camels, and that they are paid the balance in gold. Gold ducats coined in Russia, are, I know, brought from Orenburg: this coin passes current all over the East, and it is generally sold at a good premium, on account of the purity of its metal.

Baron Meyendorff says that the Bokharian merchants realize a clear profit of thirty per cent. upon their trade with Russia, "Généralement," he observes, "ils gagnent moins sur la vente des marchandises Russes en Boukharie, que sur celle de leurs en Russie; *ce qui doit faire conclure que l'importation de celles de Russie en Boukharie a presque atteint son maximum.*"

This may be owing, first, to the greater facility which has of late years been given to the other channels of Russian trade eastward, and secondly, to the circumstance of English chintzes and other cloths having found their way in greater quantities to Bokhara. The Russian manufactures have as yet little to recommend them but their cheapness, and ours are every where bought in preference, notwithstanding the great difference of the prices.

According to the best of my information, the least profit the Affghaun merchants gain upon the sale of our goods at Candahar and Caubul, is one hundred per cent. upon prime cost. Owing to the irregularity of the trade, our commodities are sometimes cheaper at Caubul than at Candahar.

My friend Muheen Shah, in the year 1828, at Bombay, invested a capital of seven thousand rupees, chiefly in English piece-goods, which he took by sea to the port of Soomeeanee in Beloochistaun, and thence on camels *viâ* Bayla, Kelaut, Pisheen, Candahar, and Ghuzni, to Caubul. Here, according to a list of prices shown me, he disposed of part of his investment at the rate of one hundred and ten per cent. profit upon prime cost, and the rest, consisting chiefly of English chintzes, he sent on *viâ* Bulkh to Bokhara. His goods reached the latter city about the time that the Russian caravan arrived there from Orenburg, but they sold immediately at a profit of from one hundred and fifty to two hundred per cent. upon prime cost, and comparatively with Russian manufactures of the same kind, at the rate of a fifth higher price.

Muheen Shah, it is to be observed, made profit upon goods which had come to market by a month's sea voyage, and a land route of from thirteen to fourteen hundred miles, notwithstanding many arbitrary exactions that he was subject to on the way, and the expense of four months' detention at one place, on account of the disturbed state of the country. From him and other merchants I learned, that English goods generally sell at Bokhara, at the rate of one hundred and fifty per cent. profit upon prime cost at Bombay, and at the rate of a fifth higher price than Russian manufactures of the same kind. They told me also that, two years ago, some Russian chintzes brought to Caubul could not even be sold for the *Bokhara* price, because there was much English chintz in the market. I offer their statements to show the different degree of estimation in which English and Russian manufactures are held in these countries, and to show that, if we had the navigation of the Indus, we could afford to lower the prices considerably: we should thus throw our manufactures among a fresh class of persons, and if we could further reduce our prices to the level of the Russian rates, we should in a great measure turn our rivals out of the market.

I have taken Bokhara as an extreme point: of course, if we can gain any advantage over the Russians in our trade there, it must be increased to us the nearer we come to the Indus. The trade is now confined to men who undertake distant and irregular speculations upon petty capitals, which they have first to realize by selling the things which they export from their own country; but were the commerce extended, moneyed merchants would engage in it, regular investments would be imported and stored, and the present traders would for the most part become carriers from one entrepôt to another.

In a previous chapter, I quoted a passage from

Baron Meyendorff, where he says that the trade of Russia with Bokhara would require fresh impulses, if the communication between the two countries were made safe by the subjection of Khiva to the Czar. If the Russians do by any means succeed in establishing their authority at Khiva, they will assuredly navigate the Oxus;* and here we must keep in sight a point of great importance, upon which Baron Meyendorff speaks positively; *viz.*, that there is no water communication between Bokhara and the Oxus;—the river which flows past the city of Bokhara, expending itself in the lake of Kara Koul. This gives Khiva such an advantage as a place of trade, that it would in all probability attract the commerce of Bokhara, and, becoming stocked by Armenians, Jews, and other commercial people, would rise into a place of considerable importance.

The Oxus would easily lead the Russians to Bulkh, which, there is licence to suppose, would become a large town, corresponding to Khiva, and a mart at

* According to the accounts that we received of the Oxus, it is navigable during eight months of the year. From above Bulkh to past Khiva, the river has an average breadth of half a mile. [One informant, who stated this, said that he first crossed the river above Bulkh, and again on his way from Bokhara, at Charjoob.] When the snows melt on the mountains from which the Oxus flows, it runs in a broad and very rapid stream, which it would be dangerous to come down, and very difficult to ascend: this excess of water runs off in two months and a half or so, and then the river runs broadly and moderately, having depth sufficient to float boats of large burden. There are boats at the ferries that take across twelve camels.—The general account said, that there were no fords, but that travellers often crossed on inflated skins. In winter the Oxus is frozen.

which much Indian produce would be exchanged for Russian exports. This would cause a great revolution in the trade of Central Asia, and give the Russians advantages, the effects of which would be best counteracted by those which we should produce by throwing open the Indus.

Our trade in the countries beyond the Indus, I have observed, must be gradually extended; but we should at once nearly double it by establishing an emporium on the bank of the river, since we should enable the Affghauns to make two voyages where they now make one. But it is not in these countries only that we shall extend the sale of our exports by opening the Indus to our trade:—goods brought by ship from Bombay, or from England direct, to the mouth of the Indus, could be taken up the river, and landed at Rohree so cheaply, that we should lower the prices in Sinde and Rajpootana, in the Central and Upper Provinces of British India, and in the Punjaub; so that it may be reasonably concluded, that the gross demand for our manufactures would be very much increased.

CHAPTER XI.

March on *viâ* Buhawalpore, across the Indian desert, to the British frontier—Conclusion of journey.

December 26th.—From Rohree we made a march of about forty miles to a very large village named Cawnpore. We passed eight small villages on the way: the road lay through jungle, which was suffered to keep waste a fine soil.

27th.—Forty miles to Raatee. Syud Muheen Shah fancied that the Ameers would somehow or other hear of my being with his party, and send men to bring us back; he therefore desired the guide to avoid the main road, and we went from hamlet to hamlet to ask our way. The soil of the country we rode through was fine, but, excepting where cleared for a little cultivation of cotton or jawarree, it was overrun with jungle. About sunset, as we were making the best of our way up a long open glade, one of our running camels slipped upon the turf, and snapped its leg in two, so that we were obliged to unload the poor animal, and give it to some villagers.

Raatee was a large village, where we got food for ourselves and horses at a Hindoo shop.

28th.—Twenty-eight miles to the village of Zorekote. Fifteen miles on the road was the village of Zeera-ka-kote, which marks the frontier between the territories of the Khirepore Ameers and Buhawul Khan. There were numerous hamlets on the road, and the jungle was greatly cleared for cultivation. At Zorekote we met a party of Affghauns, who had come from Caubul *viâ* Damaun, and were going to Hyderabad with hawks and a *kaufir** slave-girl for sale.

29th.—Twenty-five miles to Sultanpore. Three miles before the latter place was the small walled town of Nohshehera, where, halting to rest a little under the shade of a tree, we fell into conversation with a Persian stranger, who, according to what we could discover of his condition, was a gentleman of the Zand family, travelling *pour se distraire.* In two minutes Keraumut Ali and the stranger became as old friends, cracking their jokes, and complimenting each other on their wit: a little persuasion induced the traveller to turn his pony's head, and go back with us one stage, and I do not remember many pleasanter evenings than this which we passed in his society.

Khoosroo, as the stranger styled himself, was a

* From *Kaufiristaun*, or Infidel land; a part of the Hindoo Koosh mountains, inhabited by a race of idolaters, supposed to be descended from a colony of Grecians. Vide Elphinstone's Caubul.

tall, very handsome, and goodhumoured-looking man, with a beard worthy of one who claimed descent from a late royal family. He had travelled through Toorkestaun, part of Affghaunistaun, and the Punjaub, and was full of very entertaining anecdote relating to his travels. From the little he had seen of English society at the outpost of Loodeeana, he undertook to describe the ways and means of the Feringees who ruled over India, and if his remarks were severe, they were very amusingly made.

"The Feringees," he commenced, "are, I beg leave to represent, by no means a pleasant people to be among; for they have nothing to say for themselves, and, considering that they are unbelievers, have more *damaugh** than enough. One of their sirdars, learning that I was a great traveller, sent to invite me to visit him: so I went, and saw a great little man, who was very civil, but as *khooshk*† as a stick: he seated me on a chair near him, and gave me tea, which, I beg leave to state, they make deliciously: he then asked me whether I had not visited this and that place, and when I answered *bulli*‡, he rejoined, "Ha!" We sat thus for some time; first came in one captân, and then another captân; they looked at me and at each other, and every now and then delivered themselves of a syllable or two; while one man was pacing up and down the room as if he was possessed. At last some of them

* Pride, or self-sufficiency. † Dry, stiff. ‡ Yes.

gave their hand to the master of the house, and went away; so I thought I might as well take leave also.

"I have learned that formerly these men were a small tribe of merchants, servants to the kings of this country, but now, maledictions on their fathers! they have it all their own way. The secret of their rule is this: They have information of every thing that passes every where, and they make the most of the news. If two men quarrel about a country, they step in to adjust the dispute, and turn both out. It is a pity we had not the land! Ullah! how rich some of those fat Lahore idolaters are!

"Soldiers, I request permission to observe, the Inglis are not; though no doubt they are great merchants, and shrewd people. For a long time they paid us some crores a year, to keep the Oroos off them; but old *Suleiman** there has enough to do to keep them off himself, and the Feringees, having been acute enough to see this, no longer waste their money. They say that Abbas Mirza has married the Imperatoor's† daughter! Is it true? These are wonderful times! we were kings the other day, and now I am—let me remember—ay, Khoosroo Shah, sometimes compelled to hide my religion, and beg civility from a set of dogs like—what is the happy name of your friend the peer

* A term of derision for Futteh Ali Shah, in allusion to the number of his women.

† The Emperor of Russia.

there asleep? Muheen Shah; Moobarik bâsh, Muheen Shah, (aside,) if you hear me, and a curse be upon you if you are asleep!"

We parted the next morning. Keraumut Ali was as sorrowful as if he was about to separate from a brother, for it was long since his heart had been gladdened with so much khoosh-sobut,* and when we had marched on some distance, he broke a long silence by exclaiming, "Hei Irân! Irân! your people may be rogues and liars; but I swear you are such pleasant companions, that one would live among you on any terms!"

30th.—Twenty-six miles to Cawnpore, which is a small town with a good bazaar. For the last two marches, the soil had gradually become lighter and more sandy, and the villages now were generally built upon sand-hills, which warned us of the vicinity of the desert. Even in this country the Syuds of Pisheen are much esteemed: many of the Mohummudan people would come to be patted on the head and blessed by our leader, and sometimes a man would stand in the road while our line passed, asking a blessing at every stirrup.

31.—Twenty-seven miles to Chowderee, where were a few huts, near a bungalow erected for the occasional use of Buhawul Khan on his sporting excursions. For the last thirteen miles, our road

* Pleasant converse.

lay on the edge of the desert: close on our left was the good soil, cultivated as far as the eye reached, and separated from the desert as if by a line.

January 1st, 1831.—Twenty-eight miles to the city of Ahmudpore. Five miles to a village on the edge of a desert, as many east into it, and then twelve miles N.E. to a village named Cohee, where we got upon the good soil again.

Ahmudpore is a very large open town, in the environs of which are many fine trees, and a park containing a handsome white stuccoed building, the palace of Buhawul Khan. The Khan generally resides here, consequently the town is in a flourishing condition: it appeared to be filled with inhabitants, and the neighbouring lands were most industriously cultivated. We halted here three days to rest our cattle, and knowing Buhawul Khan's respect for the English, I declared myself a British officer, from Persia overland, travelling through his country to our frontier. The Khan was away at Derawul, a fortress in the desert, which is esteemed strong on account of its situation, and where the Khan is said to keep his treasure. A messenger who was despatched on a running camel to report my arrival, was sent back with a message expressive of the Khan's hearty welcome, and regret that he had been led so far into the desert in pursuit of game that he could not return soon. He sent his minister orders to supply all my wants, and furnish me with a free pass through his dominions, and during the time of our stay here, his people loaded us with civility, sending me presents of sheep, rice, and sweetmeats, insomuch that, as my companion observed, "the Affghauns began to think that they had arrived at the confines of Paradise!"

5th.—Thirty miles to the city of Buhawulpore, through an open country of mixed good land and sandy soil, which was greatly cultivated. One day's halt. We accounted the distance from Roree to the city of Buhawulpore to be about two hundred and forty miles. We came by a road to the right of the great one: the latter is flooded in the rains so as to be impassable, and the one that we took must be very bad at that season. This is a country to puzzle those who lecture upon the ill effects of malaria: a vast quantity must be engendered in the jungle which extends from the road to the banks of the river, yet in this wood are concealed innumerable little hamlets, the inhabitants of which seem to care as little about damp as their buffaloes do. For the first ninety miles, to the boundary of the Khirepore Ameers' territory, we continually came upon a herd of these hideous animals, lying in a stagnant pool, with their satanic-looking heads just above the water, tended by a creature nearly as black and untamed as themselves, and it was cheering to get out of so waste a country. As soon as we had crossed the frontier into Buhawul Khan's territory, we were struck with the improved appearance of the land: the ground was cleared, and cultivated with the better sorts of grain; the people also seemed more orderly and respectable, and they all spoke of the Khan in terms of regard.

Buhawulpore is not now the city that Mr. Elphinstone described it to be: the walls have fallen, and there is a general appearance of decay in the town, in spite of its manufactures, and the trade which passes through it. This is owing to the Khan's preferring to reside at Ahmudpore, where he is further from his hated neighbours the Sikhs, and nearer to his fancied stronghold in the desert. The river Hyphasis has hardly proved a barrier to the encroachments of Runjeet Sing, and it is said that the dismemberment of the Punjaub has been the Khan's prayer for many years.

The day that we halted here I rode to see the river Hyphasis. There was not much in the appearance of this classic stream to reward a ride over a very deep sand; but fortunately it was a Hindoo festival, and the banks of the river were lined with many groups of the townspeople in their gaily-coloured, fluttering dresses, which made the scene very picturesque.

On this occasion I was told of a Hindoo superstition, than which, I should imagine, there are few more extraordinary in any of the creeds of this world; *viz.*, that it is a highly meritorious charity to feast a

Brahmin until he dies of a surfeit! I doubted the statement of the first person who described a feast of this sort, but the statements of others confirmed his, and I wrote down the ensuing fable, which accounts for the custom, from the translation of a learned Brahmin, who read it from the Bhagwut.

In the era of Krishna, the eighth Avatar of Vishnu the preserver, there was a Rajah named Kurrun, who daily gave away a mun and ten seers* of gold in charity, before he broke his fast. By the decree of Providence, he was killed in fight with a Rajah of the Chettree caste, and went to Paradise, where he saw hundreds of mountains of gold. The Pluto† of this Elysium said to him, "These are all for thee! the million-fold multiplication of the gold which thou gavest away in charity upon earth!"

Presently Rajah Kurrun felt very hungry and thirsty, and asked for food; to which request the guardian of Paradise answered,—"When thou wert in the world, didst thou ever for charity's sake give away *meat and drink*, that *its* increase should be laid up for thee here? Reflect! Do you ever remember giving food away in charity?" After much

* About 100 lbs. avoirdupois.

† Yumu, the Indian Pluto, is a dark-green man, clothed in red, with inflamed eyes; he sits upon a buffalo, has a crown on his head, and holds in his right hand a club, with which he drives out the soul from the body, and punishes the wicked. This is his form of terror, as king of the souls of the dead; but he is also worshipped in a form less terrific, which he is said to assume when he passes a sentence of happiness on the meritorious. Vide "Ward's View of the Hindoos."

consideration, Rajah Kurrun said, "This much I remember, that one day when a person in my neighbourhood was entertaining Brahmins, a very hungry man came to me and asked, 'Is it in thy house that Brahmins are this day entertained?" I replied, no! but with my little finger I pointed to the house in which the feast was being held." The Pluto of Paradise on hearing these words, said, "For this, much reward has been reaped for thee: put thy little finger into thy mouth and suck it!" Rajah Kurrun did so, and instantly the painful feelings of hunger and thirst left him.

Rajah Kurrun then thought to himself, if I, by the trifling act of pointing with my little finger to the house of entertainment, have gathered such reward, how great will be the portion of him who gave the feast! Upon this reflection, he requested fifteen days' leave of absence from Paradise, and returning to earth, spent the whole time in feeding Brahmins. The anniversary of this period is held sacred by Hindoos, and it is chiefly on these days that persons who are anxious to go to such a real Hindoo Paradise as Rajah Kurrun's, spend their money in giving feasts to Brahmins. A man invites a party of these holy men to dine with him, by requesting them to come and sit in the light of his eyes, and put the soles of their feet upon the crown of his head; when they are arrived, and seated on the ground, with leaves of the palm-tree before them as plates, he serves them with rich dishes, and uses his utmost endeavours to make them eat to repletion.

The more the Brahmins partake of his charity, the greater the host considers his reward will be; and as he cannot do more than kill his friends with kindness, he does his best to persuade them to so happy a death. When the guests protest that they have eaten their fill, the host beseeches them to bring blessings on him by eating a little more; from entreaties he proceeds to offers of reward, and actually bids his guests sums of money to eat further portions, increasing his offers according to his disposition and means, sometimes to very large sums, for if he fails to kill his Brahmin guests with his meat, he still looks for the virtual increase of what they eat, and of the money with which he bribes them; and "men,"—to borrow an expression from my best informant, "after spending the greatest part of their lives in an economy which scarcely allowed them to keep flesh upon their bones, have been known to dissipate at a sitting, the gatherings of many years of their usurious existences."

It may occasionally happen that the greediness of a novice induces him to kill himself by eating overmuch; but the old Brahmins must be too discreet to sacrifice themselves for the benefit even of the most generous entertainer; and doubtless, on a good occasion, they "all keep a corner" to make money by.

Syud Muheen Shah, not having calculated upon

the exactions of the Khirepore Ameers, had not borrowed sufficient money from his agent at Shikarpore, and we were only just able to pay our expenses to Buhawulpore. This gave me an opportunity of judging how well our patron's name was known to his own countrymen, for an Affghaun of the Bukhteeauree tribe, who was here on his return from Dehlee, hearing that Syud Muheen Shah had arrived, came and advanced him a loan of two hundred rupees, though he had never seen him before. Muheen Shah hinted that the man might expect a great increase of his camels and sheep, and such other things as he considered among the blessings of this life; and he allowed him to kiss the hair of some deceased saint's beard, which he carried with him rolled up in about a dozen handkerchiefs.

Learning that the road eastward through the desert might now be safely taken, we determined to end our travel by journeying across it to the British frontier, and on the 7th of January rode from Buhawulpore, thirteen miles, to Parwallah, a village of one hundred huts in the desert, where there were four deep wells of good water. Two miles from Buhawulpore we got off the good soil, and then our road lay through low heaps of loose sand, which had formed upon a hard subsoil. At Parwallah the water of the wells was poured into clay cisterns, and large droves of camels and oxen, which had been driven in from the grassy jungle of the desert, were being watered at these.

8th.—Taking water and grain with us, we marched twenty miles into the desert, and halted where there was much coarse dry grass, with which we fed our horses. At midnight we loaded our camels, and marched on fifteen miles to Maroot, a small town with a bastioned wall, where we got the commonest necessaries of food for ourselves and horses.

Between Parwallah and Maroot there was more hard soil than loose sand, but what there was of the latter was heavy. This is esteemed the only difficult march on the road. At Maroot duty was demanded upon our cattle, but on showing the Khan's letter, we were allowed to pass free. There were several wells of good water here; we paid a trifle for watering our horses, and marched on eleven and a half miles to Meerghur. Six miles on the road was the little square brick fort of Jamghur, within which were a few houses, and near to which we observed a small wood of babool trees. At Meerghur there was a strong little brick fort: within it were a few shops, and outside, many dwelling-houses. Here we saw large droves of cattle, which had been driven in to water. The road between Maroot and Meerghur lay for the most part over firm earth: occasionally it was crossed by a broad layer of heavy sand, but this bore no proportion to the good soil. Many tracks crossed the road, leading to wells dug in different parts of the desert for the use of cattle.

10th.—Twelve miles to Phoolera, a small town with a fort; and twelve miles beyond it to Sirdar Kote. There was very little loose sand this stage; the road lay for the most part over hard earth, which sounded under our horses' feet, and for the last twelve miles of the way there was much good dry grass, of which we cut a supply for our horses. Sirdar Kote is Buhawul Khan's frontier town: formerly the place was named Walour. Outside a fort are many mud houses and several wells, but the water is bad. Here we escaped another duty by showing the Khan's pass.

11th.—Eleven and a half miles to Anopghur, the largest town on the road. Here also there is a brick fort. We watered our horses at one of several wells, and then continued our march: when we had got about two miles from the town, we saw that we were pursued by three ragged spearmen, mounted on lean ponies, who riding up to us with very fierce gestures, would have taken us all prisoners, for attempting to defraud their master, the Bikaneer Rajah, of his rightful dues. Muheen Shah and I rode back under their escort, and were taken before the chief of the place, whom we found seated on a low terrace, just above the street, from which we addressed him. There was a shout of derision from some eight or ten persons who composed his court, when I declared myself to be an English officer, and we were told that we deserved to have our ears and noses cut off, for pretending that we were going to remain, and then stealing away to evade payment of the regular duties; a crime which had not, I believe, entered into any body's thoughts. When the governor had done speaking, we appeased his indignation with soft words, persuading him, by means of Buhawul Khan's passport, that I was an English gentleman and not a merchant; then being released, with many apologies for the mistake, we galloped after our own party, and rode on with them ten miles to Rehrer, or Kummaul Ser, a small Mohummudan village, where we halted for the night.

The water at this place was very bad; and there was only one shop, kept by a little famished-looking old Hindoo, who would not sell us any bajra for our horses, because he could not give change for a rupee. This "atomy of a man" sat on guard before half a dozen earthen pots that contained his stores, callous alike to the civil and blustering words of the Affghauns who in turn assailed him, and he only came to terms when they agreed to spend the whole rupee in his shop.

This last day's march there was much good dry grass on the sides of the road: the soil was for the most part hard, thinly dotted here and there with little hillocks of shifting sand which the wind had blown up.

12th.—Twenty-two miles to Hulwana, where we found a mud fort, many houses, and some wells of excellent water. Three miles and a half on the road was Beloocha, and twelve miles beyond, Boogea; both villages where the water was bad. Throughout the whole of this day's march the soil was sandy: eight miles distant, on the right of our road, was a strongly-marked line of high sand-hills.

13th.—Eight miles to Soorutghur, a town with a small brick fort. We rode beyond this thirteen miles to the village of Gooree Bunga, where we got provisions from a Hindoo shop. The water here was good. This day we got near the sand-hills on our right, and, in chase of a fox, rode into them. They appeared too firm to be moved by the summer tuffâns,* and perhaps prevent much sand from being drifted from the southward.

14th.—Ten miles to the town of Futtehghur, *viâ* the villages of Kallee Bunga ke Sheher, Beloor na ghoor, and Sujjee Poona. At Futtehghur the road branched: one route went up to Bhutneere, and the other, which we followed, led more directly to Tibbee. We passed within three miles and a half of the large fortress of Bhutneere, and crossed the British frontier at Tibbee, where we found a rasallah of Colonel Skinner's irregular horse. Among the men of this troop, I found two or three with whom I had been

* Strong winds.

acquainted in camp some years before, so that I presently felt quite at home. They insisted upon giving us a zeafut,* and making much of us, and getting together round a good fire, we spent a very sociable evening together.

At the calculation of two miles and a half per hour for camel's pace, we made the distance from Buhawulpore to the British frontier one hundred and seventy-six miles. The first eighty-three belong to Buhawul Khan, and the rest to the Bikaneer Rajah.

The preceding route shows that this is not, as has been thought, altogether a desert of deep sand. What loose sand there is lies upon a hard subsoil, and it bears no proportion to the good land.

The country is greatly covered with low jungle of weedy bushes and grass, in which many thousand camels and oxen are pastured. The best of this grass is like good hay, and a coarser sort, which produces a small bur, is a favourite food of oxen. Wells are dug in many parts of the desert, to which the cattle are driven to water every second or even third day, according to the season of the year. Water lies at a great depth below the surface, from one hundred and fifty to two hundred and fifty feet, and we were told that further south it was only found at a depth of three hundred feet. But for this circumstance, much of the soil might be cultivated; as it is,

* Entertainment.

crops of bajra, and môt,* are raised by the periodical rains.

The preceding route also shows that there are several towns upon the road. Some of these have been much enlarged of late years, and if only the commonest necessaries are procurable at them, it is because there is yet no demand for others. The staple food of the people is bajra, and upon this, or upon jawarree, we were obliged to feed our horses, for these animals being seldom brought this road, no provision has been made for them.

So long as the Bhuttees were in force, it was dangerous to travel this road, but since the British Government put these marauders down, it has been quite safe, and it may now be travelled by a single man. One of the first signs of our approach to a civilized country, was similar to that which has been recorded by a former traveller. The bones of three Bhuttee murderers were hanging in chains on the side of the road, and we learned that such an unheard-of punishment had a wonderful effect upon the people of this wild tribe.

From Tibbee we marched to Raneah, formerly the seat of the Bhuttee Nawaub, whose revenue was chiefly derived from his regular share in whatever his subjects stole. The Bhuttees are a very dark and savage-looking race, who profess the Mohummudan religion. We were told that they are very strict in their religious exercises, one of their prayers being a

* A small pea.

petition that the British power may be destroyed in Hindoostân, and the good old times revived again.

We continued our march through this country, and on the evening of the second day reached the station of Hissar, where in the hospitable mansion of Captain Parsons, Superintendent of the Government Stud, I had once more the satisfaction of hearing my own language spoken.

Hence I marched on through British India to Cawnpore on the Ganges, where taking leave of Syud Muheen Shah, I embarked for Calcutta. Near Dehlee I had an opportunity of introducing both my native friends to the Governor General, Lord William Bentinck, from whom they received marked honour and great kindness.

The reader will have formed some idea of the care, and of the difficulty, with which Syud Muheen Shah conveyed us from Heraut to Dehlee, but I could not in words express the kindness and delicacy of this man's conduct towards us during the whole of the journey. Wherever he met friends, they laboured to convince him that I was an impostor, and he was exposed to extreme vexation and danger on my account; yet he never relaxed in his endeavours to promote my safety and comfort, he paid all our expenses, and avoided alluding to my debt to him. I have to express my gratitude to many English gentlemen in different parts of India, who have made a point of showing attention to this friend, and I am happy in the assurance that he is in every way satisfied with the result of his generous conduct to a stranger in distress.

Syud Keraumut Ali, my tutor and steadfast friend, some months after our arrival at Calcutta, went in a political capacity to Caubul, returning from whence he settled in the distinguished office of Mootawullee, or administrator, to a large Mohummudan endowment at Hoogly, which I trust he will happily enjoy to the end of a good old age.

AFFGHAUN HISTORY.

AFFGHAUN HISTORY.

THOSE whom the following sketch will interest, will have read Elphinstone's History of the Affghauns. We in vain sought for information that would throw a light upon the origin of this people: the Tuarikh-e-Khan jehan Khan, a Persian work to which we were referred, is so full of fable and improbable circumstances, and so inaccurate with regard to early dates and genealogies, that little reliance is to be placed on it; and as it apparently is the book from which Mr. Elphinstone extracted his notices of the supposed descent of the Affghauns, I cannot do better than refer my readers to that gentleman's work. We made careful inquiry about the modern history of this nation: the accounts which I obtained from the best-informed men we knew, tallied so nearly with those given by Mr. Elphinstone, that I trust I may be excused for borrowing from that author's narrative, such details as will give a connexion to my continuation of it.

The last of the Sôfis resigned his crown to Mahmood Ghilgie, at Isphahaun, A. D. 1722. Five years after, Nadir Shah rose to free Persia, and not only drove the Affghauns thence, but, after some hard fighting, defeated them in their own country. The Affghauns were then known as two great rival tribes, the Ghilgies and the Abdaullees. In 1737, Zulfacar and Ahmud Khans, brothers, of the Suddozye (the chief) tribe of the Abdaullees, entered Nadir Shah's service, and followed him in his wars, with a large body of their clan. Zulfacar Khan was subsequently appointed Hâkim at Heraut, and fell in a battle with the Ghilgies: Ahmud Khan's conspicuous gallantry endeared him to Nadir Shah, and he remained in high rank and favour with that monarch until he was murdered in his camp at Couchan (June, 1747). Ahmud Khan then withdrew from the Persian army, followed by the Affghauns at that time serving in it, and hastening to Candahar, as head of the Suddozyes, took upon himself the exercise of chief authority there. The sum of thirty lacs of rupees (according to Khojeh Abdul Kurreem, from the revenue of Peshower Caubul and Sinde) arriving at Candahar at the time for Nadir Shah, Ahmud Khan took possession of it: this enabled him to equip a body of attached troops, composed of the veterans who had fought under him for Nadir Shah, and before that year was ended, he caused himself to be crowned King of the Affghauns at Candahar, assuming the title of Dooree

Dooraun (the pearl of the age) and changing the name of the Abdaullees to Doorraunee.

Ahmud Shah reigned twenty-six years, and during the whole of that period scarcely knew rest; marching continually east and west, to subdue foreign enemies, and to subject domestic ones: twice he marched conqueror into Dehlee, and four other times to different points in India. In the west, he carried his arms as far as Neshapoor and Astrabad. In his fiftieth year, his constitution sank under constant fatigue of mind and body, and in June 1773, he left the great monarchy which he had founded to his eldest son Timour.

Timour Shah had neither the enterprise nor the mental vigour of his father, and was content to reign in indolent magnificence for more than twenty years, during which time he laid the germ of "a decay that has advanced with rapid strides under the reigns of his successors."—Timour begot many children, who fought for the inheritance. Those whom this history concerns were—Hummayoon, the eldest, by one wife; Shah Zemaun, and Shah Shoojau, by another; Shah Mahmood, and Prince Ferooz Oodeen, by a third.

Timour Shah died at Caubul, May 1793. The succession not having been fixed, Shah Zemaun proclaimed himself King at that city, and, through the influence of Poynder Khan (breveted Serafrauz Khan), Chief of the powerful tribe of Baurickzye, secured the support of the other lords there. His first act was to send his Vuzeer, Wuffadar Khan Suddozye, with an army, to take Candahar. Hummayoon had there proclaimed himself King, but being ill-supported, he was beaten by Zemaun's troops: he fled from Candahar, and lived a precarious life for a year, when he was seized and blinded, and his name does not again occur in this history.

At Heraut, Mahmood was Hâkim; but as he acknowledged Zemaun's authority, he was allowed to retain his government. Prince Ferooz Oodeen was with him; shortly after, on some disagreement, the latter went to Mecca, and on his return lived in Irân. From that time he is generally spoken of as Hadjee Ferooz.

Shah Zemaun was popular, and might have retained his kingdom had he set about organizing it; but he left that care to a man every way unworthy the office of Vuzeer, and gave himself up to a project of invading India. So often as he advanced east, he was recalled by danger in the west, and he dallied with it till he lost his crown.

Mahmood, who in acknowledging him King had only made a virtue of necessity, rebelled as soon as he could muster a force. He made three attempts for the throne, in 1794, 97, and 99, but was unsuccessful in each, and finally took refuge at the Court of Irân. In 1800, he accompanied Futteh Ali Shah, on his second expedition into Khorassan. His hopes had revived, for the Persian monarch promised him assistance, and great discontent prevailed against Zemaun Shah, in consequence of his severity to six conspirators, all men of rank, and headed by the same Serafrauz Khan who had been instrumental in securing him the crown. Their intention was to murder the Vuzeer, and to depose the King in favour of Shoojah. Zemaun upheld his minister, and put them all to death; a vengeance as fatal in its effects as severe: not only did it lose him the crown, but to it may be traced all the misery which has since afflicted Affghaunistaun through Futteh Khan.

Futteh Ali Shah's promises came to naught, and Mahmood, left helpless, retired to Tubbus, with his eldest son Prince Kamraun, and a few stanch followers; but he shortly received an invitation from Futteh Khan Baurickzye, who offered to assist him against Shah Zemaun, with all his tribe.

Futteh Khan succeeded to the chieftainship of the Baurickzyes, when his father was executed by Zemaun Shah: in assisting Mahmood, he saw a prospect of gratifying both his revenge and his ambition, and setting out from Tubbus with his royal confederate, after they had solemnly sworn on the Korân to stand by each other, he marched with him through Seestaun to the Helmund. At Girishk the influence of Futteh Khan showed itself; Baurickzyes, Ishaukzyes, and Alizyes, flocked to Mahmood's standard, and possessed of sufficient force, the rebels advanced and invested Candahar: after forty days, Futteh Khan obtained entrance into the city at night, by stratagem; the royal governor fled hastily away, and the place was theirs without bloodshed.

Zemaun Shah was near the Indus, preparing to invade Hindoostân, and it was not till he heard of the fall of Candahar, that he was roused to a sense of his own danger. Leaving his brother Shoojah at Peshower, in charge of the most valuable crown property, he hastened to Caubul; but, even had the Doorraunee lords been willing to overlook his recent severity, it would have been impossible for a man so detested as his Vuzeer to have met the danger properly. His fears were shared by the King, and they showed them by attempting to treat with the rebels. Popular opinion was turned against the Shah, and when at length he marched on Candahar with thirty thousand men, the effects of his conduct were shown in the desertion of many to the usurper. When the Royal vanguard neared Futteh Khan's army, it went over to a man.

On the news reaching head-quarters, the conscience-stricken Vuzeer gave up all for lost, and imparting his alarm to the King, they fled back to Caubul. Meeting there but little sympathy, they continued their flight to the Shainwarree country: the attendance of so odious a person as the Vuzeer was in itself sufficient to prevent many nobles from sharing the fortune of their master; they nearly all went over to the usurper, and the dethroned King, strange to say in an Affghaun country, was given up by the man whose hospitality he had sought. He was blinded and confined at Caubul, and Futteh Khan took the life of the ex-Vuzeer in atonement for his father's blood.

Shahzadeh Kyser, a son of Zemaun Shah's, was ruler at Heraut. His minister now intrigued with Hadjee Ferooz, and that prince coming to Heraut, was confirmed by Mahmood in the government of the province. Kandahar was given to Kamraun, Mahmood's eldest son.

The new King gave himself up to indolence and enjoyment. Akrum Khan Alizye, a lord who had shared his worst fortunes, and Futteh Khan, were at the head of Affairs, but these ministers soon quarrelled, their rival parties weakened the state, and the people, who in a change of government had hoped for relief, found themselves at the mercy of an undisciplined soldiery, whose excesses Futteh Khan* winked at, that he might attach them more particularly to himself.

Such a reign could not last. Futteh Khan upheld it by military force for more than two years, during which time he defeated three endeavours of the Prince Shoojau to overthrow it, and two insurrections of the Ghilgies, who vainly hoped through the dissensions of the Doorraunees to restore

* Futteh Khan was a profligate and ambitious man, of desperate valour, and unbounded liberality. His character was so correctly drawn by Mr. Elphinstone, that it may be traced in his every action since the period at which that gentleman wrote.

their* dynasty. At last Akram Khan died, and Futteh Khan being away with the army settling the provinces, Moukhtar Oudoulah, (son of Shah Wullee Khan)† who considered Futteh Khan as a usurper of his hereditary right as Vuzeer, set on foot an insurrection, in which he was assisted by the Meer Waez, a saint of reputed strict manners, and of great influence over the people.

The population of Caubul is greatly of the Sheah persuasion, and as Mahmood's body-guard was chiefly composed of Persians, he gave favour to their sect. Offended at this, the Meer Waez zealously concerted with the Mookhtar Oudoulah, and inflaming the Soonnee population of the neighbourhood, raised a religious tumult in which Mahmood was deposed: the Mookhtar Oudoulah brought Prince Shoojah to Caubul, and on reaching the city, he was conducted in triumph to the palace as king.‡ Shoojah imprisoned Mahmood, but spared his sight; a rare act of clemency, and one which he unfortunately had afterwards cause to regret: he immediately restored his brother Zemaun to liberty, and his only act of rigour, if such it may be called, was to punish the man who had basely given up Shah Zemaun.

Futteh Khan went to Kamraun at Candahar; but as they could not make head there, the Prince

* Vide Elphinstone.

† The office of Grand Vuzeer was originally made hereditary in the family of Shah Wullee Khan, of the Baumizye tribe; but first Zemaun, next Mahmood, departed from this rule.

‡ Vide Elphinstone.

repaired to Furrah, and the ex-Vuzeer offered his services to the new King. They were not accepted, and he retired to his castle at Girishk. Shahzadeh Kyser was made ruler at Candahar, and Hadjee Ferooz was allowed to retain the government of Heraut.

Mookhtar Oudoulah was appointed prime minister, and the commencement of Shoojah's reign was promising; but he made an enemy of his Vuzeer, by wishing to act independently of him, and there were not wanting persons to increase their jealousy. Gaining the crown after so many years of adversity, Shoojah found himself surrounded by men to whom he was under obligations, but who were too many for his resources; those for whom he could not provide, intrigued to weaken the existing ministry, in the hope of bringing themselves in, and thus Shoojah, with the best desires, felt himself unable to restore the tone of a government which his predecessor had so much weakened.

Futteh Khan, whose life was intrigue, set on foot many rebellions, and, in the summer of 1805, aided Kamraun to eject Prince Kyser from Candahar. Shoojah marched in person against the rebels, who were assisted from Heraut with six thousand men, under Mullick Cossim (Hadjee Ferooz's son); but these latter being recalled by a threatened invasion of the Persians, the intriguers found themselves without an army; Kamraun fled to Furrah, Futteh Khan again tendered his services to Shoojah, and the latter, hoping to make a friend of so dangerous an enemy, accepted them.

During Mahmood's unsettled reign, the Persians had taken Meshed, and established there a governor of Persian Khorassaun, and they showed that their further encroachments would depend upon the Affghauns' means of resisting them. They now threatened Heraut under Mohammed Khan Cujjer, Naib of Khorassaun.

Hadjee Ferooz, necessitated to be warlike, exerted himself with much policy to meet the danger. He declared it a war of faith, and called upon Sooffee Islâm,* a famous saint of the neighbourhood, to use his interest with the followers of the blessed Imaums. Most of the townspeople were Sheahs, and could but wish well to the Persians; but among the Soonnees, Moollâs exchanged their books for

* Sooffee Islâm was of Oosbeg origin, and formerly famous as a freebooter. Renouncing this character, he took that of a Derveish, and assuming the name of Sooffee Islâm, settled in Bokhara, where, as his doctrines were of the easiest, he soon attracted many disciples. Shah Moraud Beg of Bokhara, who was more ambitious of fame as a saint than as a king, condescended, it is said, to strike the innovator upon the mouth with his shoe, and publicly to abuse him for his morals: certain it is that he expelled him the city, and the Sooffee retired to Koorook, a province of Heraut, where he rose to great esteem with all ranks. The Soonnees vied with each other in sending him presents of grain, sheep, &c., and as he gave freely of what cost him nothing, he got a character of great charity. He was so free from the common prejudices of religion, that he married eighteen wives, daughters of his devoted admirers. He is described as a small man, pale, with a little beard on the chin. Being lame, he rode in a palkee; great the honour of those who carried him. Some time before his death he shed a tooth, which was buried with honour in his garden: a tomb raised over it commemorates the fame of so great a saint.

swords, and those of the country round flocked to the Sooffee's standard. In all were collected eleven thousand men (Affghauns and Eimauks); but only two thousand were soldiers, and with these Hadjee Ferooz marched to encounter the Cujjers, who were superior both in numbers and discipline. A battle was fought beyond Shikkeewân: the Soonnees, who were excited to the highest pitch of fanaticism, charged furiously upon the Sheahs, but fighting with more zeal than tact, they were divided and sadly cut up. Sooffee Islâm fell a martyr, and his body was ignominiously burnt hy the victorious Persians, who now advanced and threatened the city of Heraut. The Doorraunees rallied to defend it, but Hadjee Ferooz, rendered cautious by his defeat, paid fifty thousand rupees to be quit of the invaders.

Shoojah had at this time too much to occupy him at Caubul to think of resenting the foreign affront:—jealousies had increased in his councils, and an attempt (favoured it was said by his Vuzeer) was made to raise one of the confined princes to the throne. This, though it failed, had serious consequences; for in the confusion caused by it, Mahmood escaped from prison, and fled to his son Kamraun at Furrah.

In the beginning of 1808, Shah Shoojah went to Sinde, but allowed the Ameers to withhold much of their tribute due, upon pretence of bad seasons. Futteh Khan, who accompanied him, irritated at his thus yielding, or more probably seeing a chance of his former power in the restoration of Mahmood, took an early opportunity of quitting the army with three thousand men, and marched to join Mahmood.

The Mookhtar Oudoulah had remained at Caubul, but perceiving that his influence with Shah Shoojah had greatly decreased, he resolved to place a more compliant master on the throne, and accordingly intrigued with Prince Kyser.

Intelligence reached the Shah that the Mookhtar Oudoulah had proclaimed Kyser King at Caubul, and they that had taken Peshower: Shoojah marched directly to the latter place, defeated the rebels, and entered Peshower in triumph, with the Vuzeer's head borne behind him on a spear. Next Shoojah marched an army against Mahmood, who, joined by Futteh Khan, had again taken Candahar: he defeated the rebels, and retook the city, and then returned to Peshower, 10th January, 1809, shortly after which period the Honourable Mr. Elphinstone arrived at his Court, on a mission from the British Government.

The object of this embassy was to secure the friendship of the Affghaun monarch, so as to prevent the intrigues of the French, who threatened to carry the war into Asia, and a very excellent understanding was established between the Doorraunee Court and the British mission, during the stay of the latter at Peshower: unfortunately, however, the good footing which Mr. Elphinstone had gained, was lost to us in consequence of an immediately succeeding revolution which dethroned Shah Shoojah: our negotiations in Persia at this time prevailing over those of the French, the event was not of immediate consequence to us, but it is to be regretted that any thing should have occurred to break off a friendship so happily commenced, and that the subsequent state of this interesting country has been such as to preclude us from entertaining any definite relations with its rulers.

For the office of Vuzeer, Shoojah now selected Akram Khan Baumizye, a man of courageous, but arrogant, and close disposition: as a check upon him, he gave his confidence to several Persian lords who were at his court, and he was considered firmly established on the throne; but he had been rendered too confident by his late successes, for he sent Akram Khan, with his army, to reduce the rebellious province of Cashmere, which was held by Atta Mohummud Khan, son to the late Vuzeer Mookhtarlung, and Futteh Khan, who was never disheartened, got together more troops, and again advancing, retook Candahar for Mahmood.

This news reached Shoojah at Peshower. While he comforted himself with the hope that Akram Khan would return and defeat the rebels in the west, came news of the entire discomfiture of his army in Cashmere. This was closely followed by news that the rebels were advancing upon Caubul. Shoojah, unprovided with money, and without zealous ministers, was surprised; but he equipped as effective an army as the haste would admit of, and resolved to try a battle at Peshower, where he hoped that those to whom he had shown so much kindness would rally round him. In case of a reverse, his harem was sent towards Ràwil Pindee, and Zemaun Shah accompanied it.

Shah Mahmood entered Caubul on the 17th of April, 1809, with an army of between five and six thousand horse. One of his first acts was to seize and put to death Meer Allum Khan, an influential Noorzye chief; a very impolitic deed, and one which gave great offence, as it was felt to have been instigated by the private animosity of Futteh Khan. It caused a blood-feud between the Noorzyes and the Baurickzyes, and many of the latter tribe expressed strong disapprobation at the conduct of their chief, for hitherto no Doorraunee had been molested on account of the part that he had taken in civil war. Shoojah marched from Peshower on the 15th of June: on the 29th of the same month, Futteh Khan met his troops on their march, in the hills halfway between Caubul and Peshower, and attacking them briskly before they could form, put them to confusion: Akram Khan was killed, fighting bravely in a vain attempt to restore the day, and Shoojah seeing all lost, fled over the mountains south of the Khyber pass to Hessauruk. He staid at the latter place a few days, and was joined by some of his adherents, when finding that Mahmood remained at Caubul, he returned to Peshower. As he had some reason to impute his defeat to treachery, Shoojah was inclined rather to retire into Hindoostân than to trust his countrymen in another struggle for the throne, but the earnest persuasions of those who remained faithful to him, induced him to try his fortune once more, so quitting Peshower with a small party, he took the direct road to Candahar.

The reason why Mahmood did not follow up his victory was, that he feared to venture from Caubul: much disaffection existed among his Sirdars, in consequence of the execution of Meer Allum Khan Noorzye, and the tribe of the murdered chief, burning for revenge, had gathered under Abdoollah Khan, his father, and threatened an insurrection. There were indeed grounds for alarm, for as soon as the insurgents had made head, they were joined by Yehyah Khan Baumizye (brother to the late Vuzeer Akram Khan), Sauloo Khan Ishaukzye, and other Doorraunee lords of note, and feeling themselves strong, they advanced upon Candahar. Prince Aiyoob,* who had been left in charge there, marched out with a small force to oppose the rebels, but seeing their superior strength, or perhaps hoping to gain their favour for himself, he joined them, and they amicably accompanied him on his return to the capital.

A few days after this event, arrived Shah Shoojah. Misfortune seemed to follow the steps of this

* A son of Timour Shah's, half brother to Mahmood.

monarch, for on the tenth evening of his march from Peshower, when he and his followers had retired to rest, one Noor Mohummud Khan Doorraunee, who had a blood-feud with his Nussuckchee Bâshee, came upon that nobleman by stealth, and murdered him while he slept; depriving the king at once of a faithful friend and an influential partisan. However Shoojah continued his march to Candahar, and when his approach was announced to the insurgent chiefs, they went out a great distance to meet him, and escorted him with all honour to the city. Prince Aiyoob, who at first distrusted him, being reassured by many kind promises, embraced the good cause, and it still looked well, for many of the provinces yet held out for Shoojah: the Norzyes, who were bound to his side by the strong desire of avenging their chief's death, mustered in considerable force, and the lords who took part with him subscribed so liberally, that he shortly saw himself at the head of a well equipped army: he had the advantage of position, being at Candahar, in the centre of the Doorraunees, and his character stood in every way higher than did that of his enemy, who, in addition to his late cruelty, had been rendering himself odious by heavy exactions upon the people of Caubul. Mahmood's only strength lay in the genius of Futteh Khan, but here again the fortune of that extraordinary man predominated. The armies were drawn up for battle, when Sauloo Khan Ishaukzye (probably by concert) went over to Mahmood's side, a treachery so unlooked for, that it caused much confusion among Shoojah's troops, and Futteh Khan seizing the moment to charge, bore down impetuously upon them at the head of his whole force, and put them to the rout. The unfortunate Shoojah, again forced to fly, took the road south to the Indus, and, crossing the river at Bukkar, proceeded to rejoin his family at Rawil Pindee.

Shortly after his arrival at this town, (February 2nd, 1810,) Shoojah had an interview with the Sikh monarch Runjeet Sing, who received him with many professions of esteem, and kept him a guest in his camp for ten days. On returning to his family, Shoojah found messengers from Atta Mohummud Khan, the rebel governor of Cashmere, who had sent him both money and troops, desiring him to try his fortune again. The Shah accordingly set out, and, fording the Indus on the 20th of March, eight miles above Attock, he marched to Peshower, and took undisputed possession of that city; Mohummud Azim Khan Baurickzye, Mahmood's governor, evacuating the place on his approach.

Shoojah kept Peshower till the month of September in that year, when Mohummud Azeem Khan, coming from Caubul with a strong force, drove him beyond the Indus again. He made a third attempt in the month of December 1811, but suffered a defeat at Akora, and was at last fain to rejoin his family at Rawil Pindee. In the spring of the year, he was invited to Cashmere by Atta Mohummud Khan, and as that chief had given him many proofs of devotion, Shoojah did not hesitate to go; but when he reached the valley, the treacherous governor seized and confined him; for no apparent cause, except perhaps that he bore in mind the tragical, but merited, death of his father the Mookhtar-lung.

When the news of this fresh misfortune reached the royal family at Rawil Pindee, they began to fear lest some violence should be offered to them, and remembering the attentions which Runjeet Sing had bestowed upon Shoojah, they determined to seek refuge at the Sikh court; accordingly, in the month of September 1812, they retired to Lahore, where Runjeet received them kindly.

Mahmood was now King again at Caubul, but (to judge by his conduct) had not learned to profit by his reverses; Kamraun assumed the government at Candahar; Hadjee Feerooz was still allowed to keep Heraut; and Futteh Khan was grand Vuzeer. This chief had regained entire sway over Mahmood, and took the surest way of strengthening his own power, by placing his near relations over the provinces of the kingdom.

As soon as Mahmood was relieved from fear of Shoojah, he felt it necessary to direct his attention to his country east of the Indus; for Atta Mohummud Khan was still iu open rebellion in Cashmere, and Runjeet Sing, perceiving the disunion of the Affghauns, had commenced his long meditated encroachments upon the Doorraunee provinces in the

Punjaub. Many skirmishes took place between the Affghauns and the Sikhs, but in the end of the year 1812, Futteh Khan made a truce with the Maharajah, and engaged to give him nine lacs of rupees, if he would assist in expelling the rebel governor from Cashmere. Runjeet Sing agreed to the proposal, and intrusting his dewân, Mokum Chund, with the command of ten thousand men selected for this enterprise, returned to his capital.

The allied forces commenced operations against the rebels in Cashmere, and the first month of the new year saw them in possession of the valley. Atta Mohummud Khan fled when the last passes had been forced, carrying off his treasure by the direct road through the mountains to Peshower. When Futteh Khan and Runjeet Sing's dewân arrived at the capital of Cashmere, they learned that the unfortunate Shah Shoojah was imprisoned in a neighbouring fort. Futteh Khan released the monarch, and it appears made some overtures to him, but Shoojah had been taught to distrust this chief's professions, and longing to be with his family, determined to accompany Runjeet's dewân on his return to Lahore.

When Atta Mohummud Khan was forced to fly from Cashmere, his brother Jandaud Khan held the fort of Attock; now, instigated by motives of revenge and avarice, he offered to give up this important post to Runjeet Sing, on condition of receiving a rich jahgeer in the Punjaub. The Maharajah too well knew the value of this fortress to hesitate about securing it; he made great promises to Jandaud Khan, and immediately sent a strong force to garrison the place. When Futteh Khan was informed of this arrangement, he refused to pay the stipulated sum for the assistance of the Sikh troops, declaring the spirit of the treaty violated; then leaving his brother Mohummud Azeem Khan with the troops, in charge of Cashmere, he posted to Caubul, and returned with another army to retake Attock; so war was declared again between the two nations.

Runjeet was prompt to defend his newly-acquired position, and sent his best troops, under dewân Mokum Chund, to encounter the Affghauns: a desperate battle was fought between the two armies, and victory was at first doubtful, but all the gallantry of the Affghauns did not avail them against the discipline of the Sikhs, and being completely routed after an obstinate resistance, they fled leaving one thousand of their best men upon the field. Futteh Khan, rendered careful by this defeat, collected a large force at Peshower, in order to support his countrymen in the Punjaub, or in Cashmere, and to take advantage of any opportunity that might present itself of recovering the fort of Attock, or of annoying his enemy.

This victory was a great triumph to Runjeet, and the pride of Futteh Khan seems to have been broken as well as mortified, if we may believe him to have dictated the following cool proposal, which was shortly after sent secretly in a letter, as from Shah Mahmood, to the British Government:

> "Since we worship the same God, it is our duty jointly to extirpate the infidels who are so many thorns in the garden of the Punjaub. As soon as the flame of war shall have been kindled, and troops under Vuzeer Futteh Khan put in motion towards that quarter, God willing, we shall soon put the idolaters to confusion, and then we will divide the Punjaub between us."

The Vuzeer, however, kindled a flame to little purpose against the thorns of the Punjaub, and his attention was shortly called to the aggressions of foreign enemies in another quarter.

During the late events, Hussan Ali Meerza had succeeded to the government of Persian Khorassaun: in the beginning of 1818, this Cujjer prince wrote to Hadjee Ferooz, desiring that the titles of his father, the Shah of Persia, should be stamped upon money coined at Heraut; that his name should be read in the Khotbeh,* and that tribute should be given him: further, it was desired that Ferooz, in ratification of these hard terms, should give his daughter to Hussan Ali Meerza's son.

Ferooz answered evasively, and sent a young son (Mullick Hossein) to Caubul, requesting assistance against the Persians. Futteh Khan being sent for from Peshower, proposed to march fifteen thousand men to Heraut; Mahmood assented, but in recollection of some very unworthy treatment that he

* A public oration regularly delivered in the mosques, in which the reigning king is prayed for.

had received at his brother's hands after his escape from Caubul, desired the Vuzeer, if opportunity served, to seize and confine Hadjee Ferooz, then to fight or make terms with the Cujjers as seemed most expedient.

Futteh Khan accordingly marched with Mullick Hossein, to whom he paid assiduous attention, putting in practice all his artifice to impose upon the young embassador. He threw out hints that, slighted by Mahmood, he longed for an opportunity of transferring his allegiance to Ferooz: Mullick Hossein eagerly caught at this idea, and to confirm him in it, Futteh Khan, instead of halting at Candahar, sent his troops forward eight miles from the city, where joining them after a hasty audience of Kamraun, he gave out that the Shahzadeh wished to seize him.

Kamraun was much troubled at this report, for he had become very jealous of the Vuzeer, and conceived that this was a plan to embroil him with the king his father: he in open durbar disclaimed all idea of injuring Futteh Khan, and sent Mohummud Hossein Khan (a Persian noble, his servant, and a friend of the Vuzeer's) to beg him to dismiss such an idea from his mind, and to name the author of the slander.

Futteh Khan had made a long march, and the envoy reaching his camp about sunset, found him seated before his tent, in company with his brothers Dost Mohummud, Sheerdil, and Poordil Khans, and others. Before he could deliver a word of his message, Futteh Khan assailed him with reproaches, for having forgotten old friendship, and made party with the prince against him; "but," said the Vuzeer loudly, "If such is to be my reward for long and tried service to Shah Mahmood, I renounce it; —there are others who will prize it more." He would not hear the envoy, but made a point of his remaining his guest for the night; some hours after, he made his tent private, and sent for his old friend whom he received with the greatest cordiality, and jeered for his want of discernment, "This firman," said he, "sends me to seize the Hadjee; it was necessary to blind so wary a person, so do you return to Kamraun, and tell him that I am his servant."

Futteh Khan was more than ever attentive to Mullick Hossein, persuading him that he would beat the Persians, and then march back with Ferooz to depose Mahmood: the young prince was completely blinded, and thus they reached Heraut. News of the rupture with Kamraun had preceded them, producing the effect that Futteh Khan wished; Mullick Hossein was earnest in persuading his father how entirely the Vuzeer was devoted to his service, and the suspicions of even so cautious a person were laid asleep.

The camp was formed two miles from the city, and profusion reigned in it; the townsmen were feasted there, and they in turn invited the soldiers to the city. This unreserved intercourse lasted for ten days, the engrossing subject with all being the expected conflict with the Persians. At the end of this time, Futteh Khan contrived to seduce the khans most in Ferooz's interests to the camp, for a council of war. He arranged that many of his men should be in town, and proceeding with his brother Dost Mohummud, and a large retinue, to pay his respects to Hadjee Ferooz, he seized that prince suddenly at audience,* and made himself master of the citadel, before those who were in camp suspected his design.

Futteh Khan next brought his men close under the walls of the town, and, having imprisoned Ferooz and his family, he sent for the Persian envoy, whom he thus addressed:—"Money is coined in *Mahmood's* name, *his* name is read in the Khotbeh, and to *him only* is tribute given;—I, his servant, acknowledge no other authority; if your master wishes to dispute it,—Bismillah! In God's name!"

Mahmood was very indignant when he heard that his instructions had been exceeded to an extent that cast dishonour upon himself; more so when, as his portion of the spoil, he received only a few horses; but Futteh Khan felt himself beyond the king's indignation, and with what fell to his† share of

* Feeroz, alarmed at the number of the Vuzeer's attendants, attempted to retire by a private passage to his inner apartments; but he was pursued by Dost Mohummud Khan, and a large party, into the actual harem, there seized, and plundered of his valuables to the very ornaments upon the women: Dost Mohummud Khan himself, it is said, insulted Ferooz's daughter-in-law, by attempting to cut a bunch of pearls from off part of her dress.

† Dost Mohummud Khan, rather than account with his brother for the share that he had secured, fled with it by a direct road to Peshower.

Ferooz's money, doubled his force, and marched out to Ghoorian to meet the Persians.

Hussan Ali Meerza marched from Meshed on receiving Futteh Khan's answer, with a mixed force amounting to fourteen thousand men. He had four thousand of the Shah's regular footmen (Semnaunees and Damghaunees)* under Sirdar Zulfacar Khan, and the rest of his army consisted of cavalry. There were three hundred Koords under Hussan Khan Chinnaraunee (a reputed hero, with a double-headed spear), some Arabs of a tribe seated near Berjend, and horsemen from the neighbourhoods of Neshapoor, Subzawar, Meshed, and Toorshish. He was accompanied by Meerza Abdul Wahab, Moatimudood-Dowlah,† who had been sent by the Shah to put Khorassaun in order, but who brought only his talent and sanctity to the field.

Hussan Ali Meerza, who perhaps had judged too hastily of the Affghaun character from Hadjee Ferooz's former conceding behaviour, sent an envoy to Futteh Khan, urging him to avoid bloodshed by agreeing to the required terms; but the Vuzeer sent back the envoy with his former answer, and talked of following in the steps of Mahmood Ghilgie: he had increased his army to thirty thousand men, and it would be difficult to say what were the projects of so ambitious a man, with such an army at command.

* Provinces of repute for furnishing good soldiers.

† Confidential state minister.

The rival forces mutually advancing, came in sight of each other at Kahreeze, about "chaust" (breakfast) time on the 25th of May, 1818, and by noon the Carools* were engaged in a sham fight,—"careering their horses, firing their matchlocks, shaking their lances, and shouting, to show their manhood." The Affghaun force the while was breaking into line opposite to the one which Hussan Ali Meerza had formed. A Cahreeze of water, which gives name to the place, ran through the field; both parties performed the ablutions prescribed for the dead, in case they should fall in battle, and exchanged their usual clothes for fighting apparel. Hussan Ali Meerza doffed his prince's suit for the dress of a common trooper, but Futteh Khan, "Sirdar-e-Sirdaraun" (chief of chiefs), dressed all in black, and mounted on a famed charger, "was proud to make his tall figure conspicuous in front of the centre of his line."

The Persians had eight light guns, and two hundred camel-swivels. The Affghauns had but four guns, and one hundred swivels, but they were better mounted, and in numbers far superior to their enemy: the artillery of each line was in front of its centre, but Hussan Ali Meerza, of his excess of cannon, planted two guns on either wing.

Booneeard Beg Hazaureh, with three thousand of his tribe, had come near the field of action, probably

* Vanguards.

to dispose of his services. The Prince royal sent and desired him to side with neither party,—to plunder the conquered and welcome. So he kept aloof with his men, waiting like vultures to fall upon the vanquished.

An envoy came from Futteh Khan, to propose, as an adjustment, the cession of Ghourian. Hussan Ali Meerza was disposed to agree, and so were his sirdars, with the exception of Zulfacar Khan, an old nobleman whose desperate valour had gained him the reputation of a madman: however, the Moatimudood-Dowlah was called upon to *istakhaur*, or cast the event; he did so, and it came up, "That it was good to cede Ghourian." Next Futteh Khan sent to desire that the Persian force should fall back: again the Moatimudood-Dowlah istakhaured, and pronounced, "That it was good to fall back;" but Zulfacar Khan became like a madman at the idea of such an act, and would not hear of it. "To retire," he said, "would be to acknowledge themselves inferior; which, please God, the 'Shahan Shah's' troops never were, when opposed to the scum of the earth; then, in the fulness of his heart, he damned the Affghauns for Soonnees and infidels, swearing that he would burn their fathers, and dishonour their houses; and he ordered the gunners to show the envoy how warm a reception his countrymen might expect." Three or four guns were rapidly let off, and the envoy coupling this display with the old Khan's hostile speech, thought it safest to put spurs to his horse and ride back to his party; the bravado fire was returned from the Affghaun side, and the battle began.

A general discharge of artillery was kept up for some time, without doing much execution on either side; there was a little distant skirmishing, and then more than half the Affghauns, headed by the Vuzeer's brothers, Sheerdil, Cohundil, and Poordil Khans, and by the old Sirdar Yar Mohummud Khan Allekkozye, put their horses to the gallop, and loosening rein as they got to full speed, they placed their left arms across their foreheads, and, flourishing their swords and shouting, charged furiously upon the Persian line. Their greatest numbers were directed against the left wing, where Zulfacar Khan was with his infantry. "They knew that there was but one *man* in the line, and their object was to break it where he was."

Muddud Khan Saugzye (Doorraunee) had a few years before come to Meshed, and was in the Persian ranks against his countrymen. When Zulfacar Khan cursed the Soonnees so warmly, his heart turned; he was the first to fly, and his desertion, with the impetuous charge of the Affghauns, struck a panic into Hussan Ali Meerza's army, which rapidly spread through his mixed ranks, and, one after another, the two centre and the right divisions broke and fled. The camel-swivels were carried off, but the great guns were deserted; Hussan Ali Meerza made some attempts to stop his men, which greatly endangered his own life; it was gallantly saved by the hero of the two-headed spear, whose horse he mounted after his own had been wounded, and he escaped from the field with a small party about him.

Zulfacar Khan had firmly stood the charge of the Affghauns, and, returning a steady fire of musketry, had sent them back in confusion upon their own line, when he secured his guns. About this time Futteh Khan was struck in the mouth by a spent ball, which caused him to fall upon his horse's neck; those about him supposing him killed, and seeing their countrymen return in disorder from the charge, lost heart and fled, and though Futteh Khan regained his seat, and waved his sword to his troops, he failed in rallying them; he saw victory snatched from his grasp by an event as singular as unlooked for, and had no alternative but to lay the accident on his "fate," and take the road to Heraut after his men.*

Hussan Ali Meerza succeeded in rallying part of his troops about three miles from the scene of action, and shortly learned that the Affghauns had fled; upon which he returned to his faithful Sirdar, who kept the field, and arriving there when it was well night, fired off his remaining powder to victory.

Some of the earliest fugitives reached Meshed in

* Booneeard Beg plundered both armies in their retreat. In Futteh Khan's tent he got part of Hadjee Ferooz's wealth, which had been brought to the field, and on the Persian side he captured the Moatimud-ood-Dowlah, who was afterwards restored. The Persians, who must have their joke, declare that Meerza Abdul Wahab *istakhaured* which road to take, and chose the wrong one.

an incredibly short space of time, and sang "tout-est-galore." The Vuzeer was for flight, and great consternation prevailed, but Meerza Hidayut Oollah, the high priest, reminding the inhabitants that no person of any sect called Mohummudan had ever dared to commit the impiety of firing at the sacred walls of Meshed, proposed to remain defended within them till help should arrive from the Shah; at any rate to await certain intelligence. It was not till the prince returned, that this victory was believed; then Meshed was illuminated for joy, and all sorts of congratulation and feasting went on. A large picture, which still hangs in the citadel, was painted to commemorate the event, and Hussan Ali Meerza got the title of "Sword of the Throne."

Futteh Khan, finding that the Persians did not pursue, lit up Heraut for his share of the victory; not long after it, came Kamraun from Candahar, sent by his father, lest Futteh Khan, having ejected Hadjee Ferooz, should keep Heraut on his own account. The prince put up in a summer palace in the Baugh-e-Shah,* refusing to enter the town; probably because the citadel was in the hands of the Vuzeer's nephew, Ameen-ool-Moolk. Futteh Khan, who went daily (as was his duty) to salaam, was repeatedly asked for a share of Hadjee Ferooz's property, but he first answered evasively, and at last directly, that what his sword had earned he would

* "The king's garden,"—situated a mile from the city.

keep. He was frequently warned by his friends, that the dishonour he had put upon the royal family in violating Hadjee Ferooz's harem, rankled in the hearts of Mahmood and Kamraun, and he was requested to appease the latter with part of the spoil; but his scornful answer was—"I twice placed Mahmood upon the throne, and his kingdom is now in the hands of my kinsmen; who is Kamraun, therefore, that in a dream he should think of injuring me?"—Kamraun wrote to his father that Futteh Khan was in reality king, and proposed putting him away. Mahmood left all to his discretion, and the prince consulted rather his revenge. Shortly after, Futteh Khan, coming as usual to morning salaam, found the prince with those lords most in his interests; among them Atta Mohummud Khan Noorzye, who had the blood-feud of Meer Allum Khan to avenge. The cruel scene which then took place, had evidently been planned: the conversation was led to the subject of the late battle with the Persians, and one of the Khans took occasion to throw out a taunting allusion to the Vuzeer's flight; this was followed up by a sarcasm from another of the party, and when Futteh Khan turned fiercely upon them, the prince took their part, assailing him with violent reproaches for having brought lasting disgrace upon the Affghaun name, by flying before an infidel army not half so numerous as his own. Fired at this, Futteh Khan replied with indignation, that as no man could control the decrees of Providence, so he could not be held answerable for them, and he added proudly, that with regard to the imputations cast upon his courage, Shahzadeh Kamraun could hardly need to be reminded of what the sword of Futteh Khan had done both for and against him.* Nothing more was needed to complete the prince's rage; he rose up in his anger, and gave the word to his ready attendants, who immediately seized the Vuzeer, and on the spot blinded him: Atta Mohummud Khan, on a sign from the prince, thrusting the point of a dagger into his enemy's eyes. Futteh Khan was then put upon a horse, and sent to confinement in the citadel. Mohummud Hossein Khan, a Persian nobleman (the same who had followed him with a message when he marched from Candahar), was appointed to command there, and Poordil Khan, with his nephew Ameen-ool-Moolk, were seized and added to his charge.† When the news

* Alluding to occasions during the civil war, on which he had worsted the prince. Vide Elphinstone.

† I relate the following anecdote in the words of the man who gave it to me; he had served Mohummud Hossein Khan, the father of our host, at Heraut:—"When Futteh Khan was brought to the citadel, and put under charge of my master Mohummud Hossein Khan, I was appointed peishkhidmut to him, and I was with him till he was taken away. A few days after I had first waited on him, a party came to the apartment. One said, 'Salaam Alikoom Vuzeer.' 'Alikoom Salaam!' answered Futteh Khan, 'who are you?' 'I am Cossim Khan.' 'What Cossim Khan?' 'A man of the Vakeel's:—Shahzadeh Kamraun sends to say, that for what is past he is sorry;—he hears that your eyes pain you much, and deprive you of sleep, because there still remains part of the flesh, and he begs you will let me remove it, that you may be put at ease.'—(It was rumoured that Atta Mohummud Khan had not entirely destroyed the sight with his dagger.) Futteh

reached camp, it broke into small parties and dispersed. Sheerdil and Cohundil Khans effected their flight to Girishk.

Five months after, Kamraun returned to Candahar, taking with him his unfortunate victim in a litter, the brother and the nephew of the Vuzeer, and also Hadjee Ferooz. The latter was released on his arrival at Candahar, probably because he was not worth keeping, and he retired to Meshed. The other captives were tortured for money: Futteh Khan's mother offered a lac of rupees for her sons alive, but Futteh Khan sent to desire her not to give any thing, as both money and life would be taken, and as in his then lamentable state he set little store upon existence.

The immediate consequence of Kamraun's cruelty was that all Futteh Khan's brother's rebelled, and

Khan did not at first reply, then he answered bitterly, and in a changed voice, 'The prince takes too much thought on my account, does he wish to put salt upon a wound? My eyes can be no worse, but now, they are well as they are.' Seeing that the imposition would not pass, they did not dissemble further, but threw him down, and drew his eyes out of their sockets. Futteh Khan did not even groan, though he evidently suffered great torture. '*If ever there was a man in this world, that was he!*' I was left alone with him: the whole of that night he walked up and down the apartment, wringing his hands, and asking what crime he had committed to be thus tortured. At whiles he would imprecate curses upon the authors of his calamity, then pray that he might die. Towards morning he was exhausted, and slept many hours: he was afterwards calm, but very melancholy; very regular in his prayers. He seemed most to feel the falling off of severa friends, who were afraid to have communication with him, and he often said that Mahmood would lose Khorassaun by his precipitate cruelty."

Mahmood soon found himself but nominally king. He was pressed to return to Caubul, but he put off his march thither till the cold weather rendered it impracticable. Dost Mohummud Khan, imboldened by the inaction of the royalists, and joined by two other brothers, raised a party and threatened Caubul, and then only Shahzadeh Jehanguire (Kamraun's son) was sent with a small force to relieve Prince Sooltaun Mohummud Khan,* who had been left there in command. The prince reached Caubul, but the cold was so great that some of his party died on the road.

With Jehanguire was sent Atta Mohummud Khan Baumizye to direct him in his government. To this man the rebel brothers wrote that revenge was their sole object, and that if he would send away Jehanguire, they would consider him in the right of an elder brother, take the city for him, and then turn their strength upon Candahar.

Atta Mohummud Khan allowed himself to be seduced by their fair words, and made party with them. His defection disheartened the royalists in the town, and it was easily taken: Jehanguire retired to the Baullah Hissar,† but the rebels vigorously besieging him there, blew up a bastion, when the prince, mounting his horse, put himself at the head of a few devoted followers, and gallantly cutting his way through the rebels when it was dusk, escaped at the city-

* Descended from Timour's son Aiyoob.

† Citadel.

gate, leaving Dost Mohummud Khan and his brothers masters of Caubul.

They had now to dispose of Atta Mohummud Khan, who was not less occupied in projecting means to get rid of them. They were however beforehand with him, and failing in an attempt to blow him up at a feast, seized him there and blinded him.* Dost Mohummud Khan then doubting how far he, not being of the Suddozye tribe, should at first be recognised as ruler at Caubul, ostensibly appointed Sooltaun Mohummud Khan governor, but kept the real authority in his own hands.

In the spring Mahmood, convinced of the necessity, marched his troops to the vicinity of Caubul. He was accompanied by his son Kamraun, and Futteh Khan was taken with them in a litter. Gool Mohummud Khan, Populzye, was left Naib at Candahar.—As soon as the royalists had marched from Candahar, the Girishk brothers got together two or three thousand men, and put themselves between the city and the army; they then sent to the Naib, de-

* There were two brothers; one in the service of Atta Mohummud Khan, and the other a servant to Dost Mohummud Khan. Atta Mohummud Khan, having accepted the rebel brothers' invitation to a feast, had seated himself and his party on powder enough to blow them through the roof. The man in Dost Mohummud Khan's service seeing his own brother of the party, called him out, and told him that the host's leaving the room on an excuse, was only awaited as a signal to fire the train. The second brother, having eaten his master's salt, returned instantly to save him, and told him of the plot. The rebels, finding that their treacherous intentions were suspected, thought it as well to throw off the mask; so laying hands on their guest before he could make his escape, they on the spot deprived him of sight.

siring him to surrender the capital. Gool Mohummud Khan, with the tact of a real diplomatist, agreed to give the city to them in case Mahmood should be defeated, and satisfied with this promise, they withdrew to await the event.

Dost Mohummud Khan could oppose but three thousand men to Mahmood's large army, but he knew how Futteh Khan had been loved by the King's troops, and calculating upon much defection from them, he resolved to abide a battle. The armies were separated by a line of hills, and for ten days thus remained, messages passing to and fro, but all attempts at reconciliation proving vain. At the end of the time spent so foolishly, a noble named Shahpussund Khan told Mahmood that many of his Sirdars were disaffected, and he mentioned Atta Oollah Khan Alizye (a Sirdar of influence), as among the number. The next day, Dilowar Khan Shahghaussee went over with fifty horsemen, and Mahmood, with his characteristic want of energy, instead of sifting the matter, gave up all for lost. After evening prayers, he assembled his Sirdars to council in open plain, and Futteh Khan was placed in the midst: Mahmood addressing him, said, that he was weary of seeing the blood of his people shed; that what had passed could only be regretted, but that if the Vuzeer would bring his brothers to their allegiance, they should be continued in their respective governments, and higher honours than ever be heaped upon himself. "You offer what is gone from you," replied Futteh Khan, "and what has a blind man to do with power? Before you deprived Futteh Khan of sight, you should have secured the authority in the hands of his kindred. Do you act as you deem best to quell the storm you have raised; I wash my hands of all consequences, and will abide my fate." —Mahmood, enraged at his obstinacy, then completed his vengeance, by ordering "the man who was his friend to step out and strike the first blow;" twenty swords were drawn, for many that stood there had life-reckonings with Futteh Khan, and he was literally cut to pieces.

Though he should have been re-assured by the part his Sirdars had taken in the murder, which put a feud between themselves and the rebel family, Mahmood could not shake off his disquiet at Shahpussund Khan's intelligence; perhaps remorse at his cruel return to one who had twice gained him a throne, added to his natural timorousness, made him distrustful of those about him, and fearful of the dreadful reckoning which the rebels would exact should he be betrayed into their hands. On the second night after the tragedy, he and his son Kamraun, escorted only by a small party of their most trusty retainers, fled by the direct road through the Sheah Hazareh country to Heraut. Their departure was so little suspected, that it was midnight before the news spread in the camp, which was then suddenly broken up: some few went over to the rebels, but the greater number followed Mahmood to Heraut. With them came Atta Oollah Khan Alizye, and then the King, convinced how hastily he had acted, was with difficulty dissuaded from putting Shahpussund Khan to death. This nobleman is described as an intriguer gifted with so rare a speech, that he could talk any body into his projects. He well knew how to play upon the weak intellect of his master, and, little doubt is entertained, purposely deceived him in this instance; but his plans evidently failed, nor is it, I believe, generally known what they were.

Dost Mohummud Khan and his brothers were glad to return to Caubul, so unexpectedly ceded to them; and Gool Mohummud Khan, faithful to his promise, gave up Candahar to the Girishk brothers.

Mohummud Azeem Khan, full brother to Futteh Khan, and next in age of the family, had marched from Cashmere with a strong force when he heard of Kamraun's cruelty, leaving Jubbar Khan (a half brother), governor in "the valley;" but, before his arrival at Caubul, he heard that Dost Mohummud Khan had taken the city. Mohummud Azeem Khan then wrote to his brother, warning him that Aiyoob's* son would league with his fellow Suddozyes, and counselled that he should be put to death to revenge Futteh Khan's blood: this Dost Mohummud Khan's regard for his good name forbade his doing, but he feigned to fly from his elder brother, and allowed him to take possession of Caubul.

* Sooltaun Mohummud.

Mohummud Azeem Khan upon this took thought how to rid himself of Sooltaun Mohummud Khan, and at the same time save his own reputation. He found an instrument in another of the Suddozye princes, who was induced by the prospect of succession, artfully held out to him, to murder his brother. Next the intriguer, with the same temptation, instigated an uncle to assassinate his fratricide nephew, and lastly, sending a person to assure the old man in confidence that Azeem Khan was only looking about for another Suddozye to murder him, he frightened him from the city, and it remained his own.

Dost Mohummud Khan now returned from Ghuzni; he was nominally governor of the latter place, but he lived with his brother, to whom, in consideration of his seniority, he ceded the exercise of chief authority at Caubul. Sheerdil, Poordil, and Raheemdil Khans established themselves as joint rulers at Candahar, and other brothers of the family were appointed to the governments of Peshower and Jallallabad.

Thus was overthrown the Doorraunee monarchy. —The ex-king and his son had, by their cruel and dastardly conduct, forfeited claim to the sympathy of the people, who also, in the continual struggles and changes which had taken place among the royal family since the death of Shah Timour, had lost much of their respect for the sovereign tribe; and the rebel Sirdars, by appropriating the revenues to the maintenance of select troops, were able to retain the governments which they had usurped.

Shah Shoojah, to whom some now looked, was in Hindoostân: he was, indeed, induced to venture back to his country in the winter of 1818, but his endeavours to reinstate himself were as unsuccessful as his former attempts had been. The adventures of this monarch from the time of his dethronement are quite a romance:—on his release from imprisonment in Cashmere, he accompanied Runjeet Sing's Dewân to Lahore, where he had the happiness of rejoining his family; but he had not been many days in the Sikh capital, when his host began to act a very unworthy part towards him. Shoojah had preserved some valuable jewels, among which was the "Koh-e Noor," or the "mountain of light," a diamond of immense value, taken from Mohummud Shah by Shah Nadir, when he invaded Hindostân, and which at the death of the Persian monarch came into the possession of Ahmud Shah Doorraunee. This rare stone Runjeet demanded, in a manner which showed that he would not be refused. Shoojah was naturally unwilling to part with a gem of such value, especially when his adverse fortune rendered it probable that he might need it, and it was not until his unfortunate guest had suffered every indignity, that the possessor of millions was able to extort the jewel from him.

The Maharajah's rapacity was not even satisfied with the possession of "the mountain of light," for he used many unworthy means to obtain the jewels which yet remained to the royal exiles; so that seeing the terms upon which they were to remain guests at Lahore, they resolved to seek refuge in the British provinces.

A Puthan horse-dealer, named Arab Ali Khan, was the person who assisted the ladies of the harem to escape; providing horses upon which they made a forced march to the Sutlej. The following account of their flight was written by a native then resident at the court of Lahore, who had means of ascertaining the facts.

The princesses and their female attendants dressed themselves as women of the country, leaving the palace which had been allotted to them as a residence, repaired in the evening to the house of a banker in the city, from whence they went to the residences of two other persons, in order to elude pursuit. Their departure from the palace, and their disguise, had been noticed, and it was judged necessary to acquaint the Maharajah with the circumstances, but the King had drunk wine and was asleep, and the Jemadar Khooshaul Sing dreaded to intrude upon his privacy; however, as the case was urgent, he sought the advice of Fakeer (or Hakeem) Azizoodeen, a sort of Oliver Dain, barber-physician and minister, who, possessing the entire confidence of his master, scrupled not to rouse him: the monarch, therefore, being awakened, and told of the necessity, immediately gave orders to secure the fugitives, and they were taken before they had set out from the city. But notwithstanding this failure, they immediately after contrived to elude the vigilance of the palace-guards, and, through the assistance of the Puthan horse-merchant mentioned, safely effected their escape across the Sutlej into the British territory. On the 2nd December, 1814, it was anounced to the political agent at Loodeeana, that Wuffa Begum, and the females of Shah Shoojaa's harem, had arrived in the town of that place. Embarrassing as was the circumstance of their arrival, considering our political relations with the king they had fled from, there could be no doubt what course to pursue; the British agent therefore sent to assure the royal fugitives of the protection of his government, and to welcome them with the courtesy due to their sex and misfortunes.

Shah Shoojah, being more closely watched, was detected in an attempt which he made to escape at the same time with his family. When Runjeet heard that the latter had reached the British provinces, he closely imprisoned Shoojah, and treated him with much rigour; placing sentries in his very apartment, in the fear lest he also should escape across the Sutlej; for the Sikh monarch had not at that time learned sufficiently to appreciate the honour and good faith of the British government, and having from the first been jealous of our alliance with the Affghauns, he appears to have been filled with vague apprehensions that we might concert with, or assist, the ex-king to his prejudice.

All his precautions, however, to keep his royal guest a captive, proved ineffectual: in the month of April, in the ensuing year, Shoojah, in the most enterprising and wonderful manner, escaped from Lahore; climbing over the walls of several courts, and creeping through a drain to outside the city wall, and then continuing his flight to Kishtewaur, the Mohummudan Rajah of which country received him in the kindest manner, and not only welcomed him as a guest, but gave him money, with which he raised troops, and marched in the hope of being able to take Cashmere. Again fortune played this unlucky monarch false: on his march through the hills he was overtaken by so heavy a snow-storm, that some of his followers perished in it, and the rest were dispersed: it seemed as though he was but warring against his fate, therefore instead of returning to his generous friend, he disguised himself, and set out upon a hazardous journey over the mountains; after experiencing hardships such as fall to the lot of few men, he reached the British post of Subbathoo, and then proceeded to join his family at Loodeeana, where he has since lived, as a grateful pensioner of that government, whose embassy he had a few years before received when seated on the throne of Caubul.

The occasion of Futteh Khan's being called to

Heraut to check the Persians, in the spring of 1818, has been related. His departure left the Doorraunees east of the Indus to their own resources, and Runjeet Sing, ever prompt to seize an advantage, only waited till the Affghaun army had marched from Peshower, to send his disciplined troops and a battering train, to lay siege to the city of Mooltaun, against which he had made more than one vain attempt.

Nawaub Mozuffer Khan, who commanded at the latter place, held out obstinately against the Sikhs, his religious pride inducing him to scorn their proffered terms; but his garrrison was weak, and in valour only a match for the besiegers: he made one or two sharp sallies, and repelled some partial assaults during a long siege, but while he thus weakened his own force, he did not make any serious impression upon his enemies. On the 31st of May, the Sikhs mustering their whole force for the attack, made an assault upon several parts of the defences, and, after a desperate contest, succeeded in possessing themselves of the ramparts. The battle did not end here, for the deadliest hatred urged both parties to continue it; the remnant of the Affghauns fell back upon the town, and, till they were nearly all slain, maintained an unequal strife with the Sikhs, who pouring in over the no longer defended walls, fought their way from house to house, giving no quarter, and committing cruel outrages upon the defenceless inhabitants. The Nawaub Mozuffer Khan, with two sons, fell gallantly in the storm, and more than a thousand Affghauns are said to have died with him. The town was completely sacked, and when order was in some degree restored, the inhabitants were set to repair the breaches; a strong Sikh garrison filled the city, and all authority was taken out of the hands of Mohummudans; the cow was declared sacred, the cry of the Muezzin forbidden, and the idolatrous followers of Gooro-Govind tore down the crescent of Islâm.

Possessed of Attock and Mooltaun, Runjeet saw himself master of the Punjaub, and he soon ceased to apprehend any attempt on the part of the Affghauns to recover the country he had driven them from, for in the same year fell the long-tottering Doorraunee monarchy, and the rulers of the petty states which were established upon its ruins, even if they had not been engrossed with the care of securing their newly-usurped possessions, were not separately in a condition to make head against him.

The complete disunion of his long formidable enemies opened to Runjeet Sing an unbounded prospect of empire. His position at Mooltaun enabled him to overawe the Mohummudan chief of Buhawalpore, till then a subject of the King of Affghaunistaun; and further south, following the course of the Indus, the rich province of Sinde remained in a state weak enough to tempt his arms. The Ameers of the latter country took early measures to free themselves from the yoke of the rebel Sirdars of Candahar, still the Maharajah could not but contemplate the period when his superior force might cause the large tribute which they had paid to the King of Caubul, to flow into his own coffers. Runjeet's greatest efforts against the highlands of Cashmere, had hitherto been foiled by the firmness of the Affghauns, but when, in consequence of the murder of Vuzeer Futteh Khan, his brother Mohummud Azeem Khan marched to head his rebel kinsmen at Caubul, leaving the valley but imperfectly garrisoned by a small force under his half-brother Jubbar Khan, the Maharajah at once saw his opportunity, and putting himself at the head of his best troops, he marched with such speed north, that he was at the mountain passes before his enemies well knew that he had left Lahore. The hasty arrangements for defence which Jubbar Khan then made, availed little against the vigorous attack of the Sikhs, who, flushed by their recent successes, pressed on eagerly, and drove the Affghaun garrison from barrier to barrier, till, losing all heart, they retreated into the valley, and then, following the example of their leader, fled by the western pass through the mountains to Peshower. On the 5th of July, 1819, Runjeet Sing marched his victorious army into the capital of Cashmere; nor did his successes end here, for anxious to strike a blow which should convince the Affghauns of their inability to cope with him on any ground, he left his general in command of an efficient force in the valley of Cashmere and proceeding with the residue of his troops to Attock, he forded the Indus, in defiance of the enemy who occupied its western bank, and driving them before him to the city of Peshower, received the submission of the inhabitants of that place, after which he returned to Lahore.

Humiliated as the Affghauns felt at their entire defeat by an idolatrous enemy whom they had so long despised, the state of anarchy into which their country had been thrown by the revolution, prevented their making any strong effort to recover their character. The rebel Sirdars of Caubul, who were the most concerned in the aggressions of the Sikhs, feared at first to leave Caubul, but after four years, seeing that the ex-king and his son remained quietly at Heraut, they gained confidence, and in the spring of 1823, Mohummud Azeem Khan, learning that the Sikhs were again about to cross the Indus into his territory, marched at the head of all his troops to oppose them.

In the month of March was fought the last great battle between the Affghauns and the Sikhs. The latter crossed the Indus, and Mohummud Azeem Khan advanced from Peshower to meet them. Against the advice of his brother Dost Mohummud Khan, who commanded his vanguard, he made a fatiguing march from Peshower to a spot called Huzzaroo, where he was to be joined by his half-brother, Summud Khan, who had been sent on to raise the Khuttucks and Eusofzyes. On reaching the ground, he found himself close to the Sikhs, but separated from them, and from his allies, by a deep stream: he lost some men in a vain attempt to cross this water, and was compelled to remain an inactive witness of an engagement between Summud Khan's men and the Sikhs, in which the superior numbers and the discipline of the latter prevailed, and his countrymen, after an obstinate defence, fled to the hills in their rear.

Could Mohummud Azeem Khan have taken part in the engagement, it is probable that the Sikhs might have lost the day; for only after a long and bloody contest did they succeed in defeating the wild mountaineers who met them. The latter, urged on by the bitterest feelings of national and religious antipathy, fought like madmen; lads of twelve and fifteen years (it was related) though armed only with long knives, throwing themselves upon the Sikh battalions, and endeavouring to stab the soldiers behind their bayonets. In the rear of the highlanders were two hillocks, to which, as often as they were repulsed, they retreated, but only to rally and charge again upon their invaders; and with such undiminished vigour did they return to the combat, that the Sikhs began almost to despair of conquering them, and at one time were seen to waver, upon which Runjeet, the "Napoléon de l'Orient" (as a late French traveller aptly named him), who had watched the conflict from a height in the rear of his troops, seized the standard of his body-guard, and led into the thickest of the fight.

This restored the spirit of the Sikhs, and eventually their discipline prevailed. "The last stand was made near sunset, by two hundred of the Eusofzyes, who, forming upon the hillock in their rear, with loud shouts of "ULLAH!" charged bravely upon the infidels; but the kaufirs (said the narrator of this engagement) met them with their *Nizam*,* and their swords could not tell against it: some fell, as men should, blade in hand, and with their faces to the enemy; the rest did not attempt to rally again, but made for the hills, and as night was coming on, the exhausted Sikhs did not attempt to pursue them.

Mohummud Azeem Khan did not wait the night where he was, for recollecting that he had left his treasure on the road behind him, he began to fear lest his fugitive allies, the Khuttuks, should direct their course to it, and so marched hastily back to secure it, abandoning his guns and tents. These Dost Mohummud Khan, who had encamped apart with the vanguard, brought off the next day, defended from the Sikhs by the same obstacle which had prevented his taking part in the engagement: he overtook his brother near Peshower, and returned with him to Caubul; but Azeem Khan never recovered the shame of his reverse: he and Summud Khan both fell sick; the latter died in a few days, and shortly afterwards, Azeem Khan, feeling that he should not survive, collected his great wealth, and

* Discipline.

gave it to his son Abiboollah Khan, charging him to wipe off the stain from his memory, by raising troops and fighting the Sikhs.

On Mohummud Azeem Khan's decease, Abiboollah Khan was anxious to comply with his father's last injunctions, but when he would have assumed the seat of government, he was resisted by Dost Mohummud Khan, who declared that although he had respected his brother's seniority, yet that the Sidarship of Caubul was his by right of original conquest, and he raised a party to support his claim.

For some days Caubul was the scene of skirmishes between the troops of Abiboollah Khan and his uncle: as the former could afford to pay his followers well, he soon had the largest army, but fortune, which seemed to play into the hands of Dost Mohummud Khan, assisted him by a stratagem of his brother Sheerdil Khan, who, to sound the chance of getting Caubul for himself, wrote from Candahar to Abiboollah Khan, offering to assist him in ejecting Dost Mohummud Khan. Deceived by his professions Abiboollah Khan invited Sheerdil Khan to Caubul; when the latter chief arrived, he found that singly he could not hope to dispossess his nephew, therefore he privately made party with his brother: arguing with Abiboollah Khan upon the scandal of a quarrel between such near relations, and assuring him that Dost Mohummud Khan was willing to agree to a fair compromise, he persuaded him to come to a conference, and there seizing him, caused him to be imprisoned, after which he himself assumed the government at Caubul.

Dost Mohummud Khan did not dispute the rule with his elder brother, but as a recompence for his share in the plot, he demanded a large portion of Abiboollah Khan's confiscated wealth. Sheerdil Khan refused to part with his ill-gotten treasure, upon which the brothers were at issue, and fought morning and noon regularly for several days, when four others of the family, coming from Peshower, made the following terms between them. Sheerdil was to retire to Candahar with all his wealth, and to cede Caubul and its revenue to Dost Mohummud Khan. Sheerdil accordingly returned to Candahar, and Dost Momummud Khan assumed the government at Caubul, where he has ever since ruled in undisputed authority.

Now to return to the royal family.—Shah Mahmood, on his arrival at Heraut, resigned all exercise of authority to Kamraun, and endeavoured to lose the sense of his misfortunes in intoxication. A year after, Shahpussund Khan proposed to raise by subscription a force with which to march and take Candahar from the rebels; Kamraun to give fifty thousand, he ten thousand rupees, and the other Sirdars, the merchants, &c. according to their ability. Kamraun liked all parts of the scheme but the first, having, he protested, no money, and on this point he quarrelled with his adviser. Next representing to his father that Shahpussund Khan was the chief cause of their misfortune, Kamraun proposed to punish the intriguer, and in part indemnify themselves, by taking his wealth. Mahmood offered no objection, and Shahpussund was accordingly sent as a captive to Kullah Laush, a strong hill-fort on the border of Seestaun, which together with a place called "Juwaine," was his family inheritance. After Kamraun had extorted all the money that he could from his prisoner, he deprived him of the fort of Laush, but permitted him to retire to Juwaine with his family.

Shahpussund Khan now wrote to Hadjee Ferooz at Meshed, that if he would come to Juwaine, he would raise a force and take Furrah for him. Hadjee Ferooz was too badly off not to obey the summons, and Mohummud Khan Nahee, of Kauin, assisting them with some troops, they were able to take Furrah from Kamraun's Hâkim. The prince marched from Heraut to recover this fortress, and drove the allies within its walls. Shahpussund Khan being hard pressed, made a capitulation, the terms of which were—that he was to remain at Furrah as Kamraun's Hâkim, and that Hadjee Ferooz was to be sent about his business. The latter returned to Meshed, and Shahpussund Khan, not feeling sure of Kamraun, went to Killich Khan Timooree at Khaff, whom, with Ibrahim Khan Jemsheddee, he associated in a fresh plot in favour of Hadjee Ferooz, which that unlucky prince engaged in, preferring all hazards to living in actual poverty.

Kamraun applied to Booneard Beg Hazaureh for assistance, and his troops so worsted the rebels, that

Killich Khan was left on the field, and Ferooz with his other assistants, had they not fled early, would have been taken. They rode northward, but unluckily meeting on the way, troops which Mohummud Khan of Toorbut had sent co-operate with Booneard Beg's men, they took to a hill and fought. Ibrahim Khan was shot, Shahpussund Khan escaped, and went to Toorbut-Hyderah, where he made a fast friendship with the master of the troops he had fled from, but poor Hadjee Ferooz was made prisoner, and sent with the head of Ibrahim Khan to Heraut, where he was imprisoned in the citadel.

A few months after, Kamraun resolved to march upon Candahar. He left Mustapha Khan Zooree (Eimauk), in charge of the citadel, and desired one Manawullee Khan to follow him, when he had got what money he could from Mohummud Hossein Khan, a cousin of his own. The relative of the prince naturally took umbrage at a man who was continually dunning him, so repairing to Mahmood (who had gradually become jealous of the authority which he had resigned into his son's hands), he represented Manawullee Khan as a meddling fellow in Kamraun's interests, whom it would be well to confine, and getting so much leave from the Shah, he, in excess of it, put the man to death on his own account. He then made friends with Mustapha Khan; they brought Booneard Beg Hazaureh into council, and deeming themselves strong, seized Mahmood, and confining him in the citadel, released Hadjee Ferooz, whom they proclaimed King.

This farce lasted eighteen days; then Mustapha Khan, on condition of being made Lord executive, promised Mahmood to restore him. He brought the Shah down to the town with a party, when King Ferooz and his allies fled one after another. At this juncture arrived Kamraun from Candahar, and found the gates closed against him. This was the work of Mustapha Khan, who fearing Kamraun's vengeance, persuaded Mahmood that his authority would be at an end the moment he allowed his son to enter the town. Kamraun, enraged at such a reception, was for beseiging his father, but he fled hastily on the approach of an unlooked for enemy.

The Candahar brothers, hearing of the quarrels in the royal family, thought that good opportunity offered itself for completing their revenge, and, following Kamraun to Heraut, they partially invested the city.

Mahmood was now reduced to beg assistance from Shahpussund Khan, to whom he wrote requesting him to induce Mohummud Khan of Toorbut to move to the relief of Heraut. His application was effectual, and Mohummud Khan marched to Ghourian; but finding that the city was invested, he wrote to the rebel brothers that he had come to side with them, upon which, Sheerdil Khan rode to Ghourian to welcome him. They marched back together to near the city, when Mohummud Khan, greatly to the relief of the besieged, who had watched his party from the ramparts, turned off and was admitted within the walls. Upon this the brothers raised the siege and returned to Candahar.

Mohummud Khan received lands for his service, and he presented Shahpussund Khan, as an injured, still devoted, servant; Mahmood therefore restored him to favour and confidence. But this arrangement did not suit Mustapha Khan, who, conscious that there was not room both for himself and Shahpussund, imagined that the policy of the latter would be to bring in Kamraun, who would kill him. "You entertain jealousy against me," said he;—Shahpussund denied it. "Then come and give me your hand* upon the Korân that you do not." When Shahpussund went to the citadel, he was seized and imprisoned; Mahmood, apprehending fresh violence to his own person, fled from his city, and Mustapha Khan remained lord of it.

Mahmood stayed his flight at Subzaur. Doorraunees, however sundered, have common causes which unite them, and they flocked round their king in a case which involved their nationality.† Kamraun

* 2 Kings x. 15.—Jehu meeting Jehonadab, salutes him, and asks —"Is thine heart right, as my heart is with thy heart? And Jehonadab answered, It is.—If it be, give me thine hand." &c.

† Mustapha Khan was not even an Affghaun, though it is probable that to make Heraut his own never entered his imagination till Mahmood's flight put him in possession of it.

came from Furrah with a force, jealousies were forgotten, and they made one cause against the usurper. Meer Sâdik Khan, Berdoorraunee, wrote from within Heraut that he would open the gates on their approach. Kamraun pressing on, was admitted into the town, and immediately besieged the citadel: he sprung a mine under a bastion, and Mustapha was glad to resign his brief authority on promise that his life should be spared; but Kamraun foully broke his oath; for he had not been many days in Heraut, when he put Mustapha Khan to death—(in the winter of 1824).

Affairs fell into the old train, and Shahpussund Khan, and the other lords about Mahmood, seeing themselves without interest, moved him anew to take the supreme power into his own hands. Those about Kamraun played the part that suited their interests, and working on the fears of Mahmood by hinting that his son wished to seize him, caused him to retire to Gauzer-Gau, a village four miles from the city, where is entombed the famous Soonnee Saint Khojeh Abdoollah Ansàrree. There he resided for six months, when getting a fresh fright, he fled over the Moorghaub. The Wallee of Meimunna persuaded Derveish Khan Jemsheddee to assist him with three thousand troops, and with these he retraced his steps. Kamraun sent his Sirdar and his son Jehanguire with two thousand men to keep the road from Meimunna, but the Shah was in correspondence with a man of this camp, Sumunder Khan Baumizye, and having information of their position, he came circuitously upon them in the grey of the morning, when, by help of Sumunder Khan's treacherous flight, he routed them; but wanting resolution to follow up his advantage by attacking the city, he went and intrenched himself outside it in the Baugh-e-Shah. Kamraun, reinforced by troops from Furrah under his general Yar Mohummud Khan, attacked his father's allies, and had not beaten them out of their advanced intrenchment, when Mahmood mounted and fled over the Moorghaub again.

The Persian prince Hussan Ali Meerza, had marched from Meshed to help Kamraun, who had made friends with him after the battle of Kahreese, but finding that the enemy had fled, he returned home, leaving his son Arghoon Meerza at Heraut, with three thousand horse. This young prince, joined by Kamraun's Sirdar, pursued Mahmood; after some skirmishing with the Hazaurehs, a treaty was made, the chief article of which was, that no assistance was to be rendered by them to Mahmood. He was accordingly told to seek refuge elsewhere, and this unfortunate, now old man, was again a wanderer. He retired to Laush, where he remained a year in a pitiable state, wanting every thing: Kamraun, at last, struck with remorse, sent two sons with presents and a dutiful message; they brought him with a show of honour to Heraut, but he closed his eventful life after a year, and Kamraun was legally king.

Though it is impossible not to compassionate a man so severely visited in his old age, yet there was little in the character of Shah Mahmood to render him worthy of commiseration. His first act was rebellion against his king and brother, Shah Zemaun, and no feeling of gratitude for the forbearance which had been shown him, interfered to prevent his dethroning Shah Shoojah, to make himself a second time king. He appears ever to have been more studious to indulge his sensuality than to promote the good of his people, and as he did not gain the throne by any merit of his own, so he was unable to sustain himself at the height to which fortune had raised him: short-sighted as ungrateful, he murdered the man to whom he owed every thing, and deprived of his support, fell through his own weakness.

The character of Kamraun has been described in the journal: for the bad qualities which mark it, we could wish to find apology in the circumstances under which he was educated, but nothing can excuse his cruel ingratitude to Futteh Khan, or his unnatural conduct towards his own parent. His bad conduct as a ruler may in some measure be extenuated, when it is remembered that, having lived almost without a friend, he has often suffered from the treachery of those to whom he trusted: now driven to a corner of his dominions by rebel enemies, he has thought it expedient to fill his coffers, in order to be prepared for a still greater reverse, or, haply, for an opportunity of recovering the throne of his father.

OVERLAND INVASION OF INDIA.

OVERLAND INVASION OF INDIA.

My journey having afforded me peculiar opportunities of judging parts of this oft-discussed but ever-interesting question, I venture to exhibit the result of some reflections formed upon it during my travels. I will not attempt to embrace within the limits of this sketch, the arguments belonging to all parts of so extended a subject, but rather confine myself to such as are connected with the politics of Asia.—*Calcutta*, 1831.

Twenty-three years ago, France threatened our possessions in Hindoostân, and the British Government deemed it expedient to send ambassadors to the Shahs of Persia and Affghaunistaun, to secure their friendship, and so provide against the danger. We need not now busy ourselves in debating whether or no the French could have carried their great threats into execution, for the events of late years have entirely altered our political relations with France and Persia, and reduced the arguments upon this question within a much more tangible compass. Instead of fearing our near European neighbours, we hope that for the future their interests will be allied with ours; but, in our endeavours to crush the power of Napoleon, we gave strength to Russia, who now *commands* from her adjoining frontier, the influence over Persia for which France *intrigued* from a distance; and so far has the new power thrown forward her boundary of late years, and so marked a contrast does she present to the nations on her east, that we may now speculate upon the probable as well as the possible effects of her politics upon the countries of Central Asia.

The views upon our Eastern possessions which the Russians may have entertained, have necessarily been distant and indefinite. Perhaps it is speaking most accurately to say, that the Russians have long been anxious to have it in their power to attack us in India, in case of a quarrel rendering such a measure expedient;—and whether they now can, or hereafter will be able to do this, is the point for discussion.

It is with this question as with most others; few will take a medium view of its merits. One party will insist upon drawing a parallel between the light troops of former Asiatic armies, and those of Europe in the present day, and argue that because Timour Lung, Mahmood of Ghuzni, the Emperor Bauber, and Nadir Shah, all rode to Hindoostân, the Russians can make a dash through the countries which separate our frontiers, and turn us out of India before we have time to prepare for defence: while the opposite class treat the whole question as chimerical, and dispose of it by a few general remarks upon the great difficulties of the march, — the national poverty of the Russians, and the instability of their government,—the many political eras that must elapse before they can mature their plans,—and the great control that we have over their commerce. I will endeavour to hold a moderate course between these two extreme opinions.

Some years must elapse before the Russians can themselves advance, or extend their influence, to points whence they can make a fair start for the invasion of India; but distant and uncertain though the danger may be, it certainly is one that the British government should provide against, since the Russians can still extend their power eastward, and since it is their policy to do so, in order to the increase of their military and commercial ambition.

There are two great routes, and I conceive only two, by which the Russians can invade India. They will either make Khiva their base, and thence going up the Oxus to Bulkh, will proceed over the Baumeeaun mountains, *viâ* Caubul and Peshower, to the Indus; or, taking the Persian frontier for a base, they will follow the great roads through central Affghaunistaun.*

The mere distance that they would have to march either way, is less a matter for consideration than the natural facilities and difficulties of the countries through which the route would lie, their political state, and the degree of assistance, or otherwise, that their inhabitants could, or probably would, render to foreign invaders. We possess nothing like the information, either geographical or statistical, that we ought to have of these intermediate countries, but with what has from time to time been gleaned, we may make a fair guess at their actual conditions, as well as at their relative means; while our large experience of Eastern character, enables us pretty confidently to predict how the rulers of such states would act, if they were called on to choose between the interests of two rival European powers.

In reviewing our journey into the Caspian desert,† I offered some suggestions upon the policy of the Russians in Toorkestaun, and drew the conclusions that, directly or indirectly, they could establish

* Many persons have speculated upon our being invaded from the south of Persia, by troops shipped in the gulf, or by an army marched along the coast, and supplied with provisions from the sea, in improvement upon the march of Alexander the Great; but this is almost supposing us to have no ships on the ocean.

† See from pages 142 to 162, vol. i.

their authority in Kharazm, if not in Bokhara also. It is plain, I think, that the Russians cannot well invade us through the countries as they now stand between the Oural and the Indus; but if they can establish their influence so firmly at Khiva, as to be able to base their operations upon that place, the invasion of India, though still a difficult, would be by no means an impracticable undertaking.

Speculating particularly, in a later chapter,* upon the extension of Russian trade by Toorkestaun, I supposed that our rivals' earliest endeavour on gaining footing at Khiva, would be to throw open the Oxus. Every thing then said with regard to increased facility for the conveyance of merchandise, applies to the transport of military stores and troops, and of course, the more commerce enriches, increases, and settles, the people of the naturally fertile country round the marts which must grow on and beyond this new great channel of trade, the greater will be the sources whence invaders may draw supplies.

I may here repeat, that the Oxus would easily lead the Russians to Bulkh, which would probably become a large and rich commercial place. The route hence to Caubul would lie through the passes of the Hindoo Koosh mountains, which are practicable during six months of the year. This, though not a very long, would be an extremely laborious

* See page 234, vol. ii.

journey, and provisions must be carried all the way. From Caubul, the road goes through a mountainous, but very passable, and well-watered country, *viâ* Jellallabad and Peshower, to Attock, where the invaders would cross into the Punjaub, unless they passed the river higher up, for the purpose of occupying the strong country of Cashmere.*

At Attock, then, I will suppose the Russians arrived, and there leave them, to take a view of the second route by which they may advance to India;—a route concerning which my information is more certain, and which, whether we regard the political or the natural condition of the countries through which it lies, offers surer and more immediate means for such an undertaking.

Whatever the Russians may do in Toorkestaun, many years will be requisite to bring their plans to maturity there. Possibly, circumstances may delay hostility between us until such time as they are able to invade India from both the suggested bases; but it is through central Affghaunistaun that the attack will be chiefly conducted, if ever it is made, because it is in this direction that the Russians can most easily push on the Persians, and increase the resources of the country, by substituting a settled for a pastoral people.

* There are passes above Attock into Cashmere, which were often used by the Affghauns when they had possession of the latter country. My accounts state that the roads are not practicable for artillery.

Overawing the Persians from their own southern border, the Russians can command a road through their neighbours' empire, wherever it may extend to, either for advance or retreat. The Persian frontier, I assume, would be the line from which the Russians would make their last start for India, and it is probable that this frontier will soon be thrown considerably more eastward. Affghaunistaun, in its present disunited state, offers every temptation to the encroachment of the Persians, and Heraut, which I have shown they claim as the ancient capital of Khorassaun, will, there is little doubt, ere long fall into their hands. I will not here enter into speculations regarding the further extension of their empire in the direction of India, but remark merely, that settled at Heraut, their influence would extend at least to Candahar.

The roads from the present Russian frontier on the Arras, to Heraut, are practicable for an European army. Troops might also be transported across the Caspian to Astrabad, thence marched, by the roads shown in the journal, to Meshed, and on from the Holy City, by the two described routes, to Heraut: or be marched from Astrabad across the mountains to Neshapoor (where they could as well be supplied with provisions as at Meshed), and thence proceed to Heraut by either, or by both, of the onward routes through Meshed and Toorshish.

Heraut could be made a place of considerable

strength: nothing can well exceed the plenty and excellence of the supplies from the valley, and an army might be garrisoned there for years, with every necessary immediately within its reach.

The country between Heraut and Candahar, though hilly, would offer little obstacle to the march of an unopposed European army; water is in sufficiency, and partial supplies might be procured on the way. The neighbourhood of Candahar could furnish abundant supplies, and an army would be comfortably situated there, if the people were well-disposed towards it.

The situation of the latter capital marks it for a pivot upon which the operations of the expedition would turn; for there the invaders must establish themselves firmly, make dispositions for their advance towards India, and provide for their retreat from it.

From Candahar they would either go *viâ* Ghuzni up to Caubul, and thence on through the before-described country to Attock; or, through the mostly barren and difficult country *viâ* Pisheen, Quetta, Dauder, and Baugh, they would march south to the Indus about Shikarpore.

The first is not a difficult road during nine months of the year, but it is next to impassable in winter, by reason of the heavy snow that falls, and the extreme rigour of the climate, in the neighbourhood of Ghuzni especially. "The country," says Foster, "has generally a barren aspect, with a scanty supply of wood and water." Supplies of food are not to be looked for in great quantities from the pastoral people who border the road, and Ghuzni is no longer a town of any consequence.

With regard to the second route from Candahar; partial supplies of provisions might be obtained in the valley of Pisheen, and at the towns of Quetta, Dauder, and Baugh, and a sufficiency of such as the country produces at Shikarpore. The want both of water and wood would be often experienced on this road, and I can say no more regarding it, than that it could be taken by a befriended army, during the favourable season of the year. At the best time, the train of an European army would suffer much injury from the roughness of the passes between Quetta and Dauder, and during summer this tract of country is impassable.

As far as only the difficulty of roads,* or the capability of the country to yield common supplies, is concerned, I do not doubt that a Russian army could march through Persia and Affghaunistaun to India; but there remains much to be considered after this admission.

The distance between the Russian frontier and the Indus could not be marched in less than two

* When I say that roads are not difficult, I mean either that they are at present practicable for an European army and its train, or that they might be made so by pioneers without extraordinary labour.

campaigns,—say the first would bring the invaders to Candahar,* —and, with every assistance, the Russians would incur incalculable expense in such an enterprise. The undertaking I say is feasible, as far as regards the natural obstacles of the countries through which the march would lie, and the capabilities of those countries to furnish sufficient supplies at certain commissariat points; but these points are far distant from each other, and supplies for consumption on the marches between them, must be carried with the army, while many mess and hospital stores which are necessary in quantities for the European soldier, must be brought, with all proper articles of modern military equipment, from the starting-point. This would require very many beasts of burden:—camels, horses, mules, and galloways, are easily and cheaply to be obtained throughout these countries, but so large a demand for them would greatly raise their price, and they must carry every sort of food for themselves as well; for hardly any where on the line of march, would be found sufficient grass for the cattle of the smallest army, and to supply the deficiency, the invaders must carry chopped straw, which the

* I have here in view an army strong enough to hope for success against us in India, attended by its requisite train. I mean not to assert that a small army of Russian troops might not march at once to the Indus, if it were favoured by all the people on the road;—supposing that promises of strong support were held out by disaffected parties in India, to induce such an undertaking.

people of these countries store as provender for their cattle.

Fuel is a very scarce and dear article throughout Central Persia and Affghaunistaun, and sometimes an absolute want of it is experienced even by the travellers of kafilahs.

Water is not generally found in such abundance, at the different stages on the roads through these countries, as to admit of many cattle halting at the same place on the same day; a large army must therefore divide its columns, and submit to much delay in marching from one great point to another; and frequently very fatiguing marches must be made, in order to procure a sufficiency of this grand necessary for the smallest division of such a force, unless a supply were carried with it when necessary. The last remedy brings an increase to the evil of an immense train of baggage cattle.

In speculating upon the chances of an overland invasion, we generally flatter ourselves that half our enemies would die of hard labour, bad diet, change of climate, and inclement weather, before they reached the Indus: some very prejudicial changes of air, food, and water, must truly be encountered on such an expedition, and unless the Russians do considerably ameliorate the condition both of their commissariat and medical staff, we may reasonably calculate upon a great mortality among them before they exchange shots with us. I do not lay so much stress upon their exposure to bad weather, because the climate of Khorassaun is regular, and if the Russians could afford time to come, they might choose their seasons; but what serious obstacles do not the different seasons oppose to the co-operation, to the very communication almost, of troops separated in some parts of Affghaunistaun itself, or in Affghaunistaun and India! During winter, troops at Caubul and Candahar could not march the one to the other; during summer and early autumn, the road south through the mountains to Quetta is closed; so that not only could not troops concert a simultaneous enterprise by the two routes to the Indus, but an army pushed on by the southern road, would run the risk of being cut off from its reserve in Khorassaun.

As it is uncertain under what circumstances the Russians would come, it is scarcely possible to calculate all the difficulties that they would have to encounter; but it is to be observed, that all the preceding observations set the undertaking in its easiest light, for they suppose our enemies to be assisted by the people of Affghaunistaun as well as by the Persians.

Now the Affghauns have little to gain, but much to fear, from letting the Russians enter their country; they are natural enemies to the nations by whom the Russians must in the first instance be assisted, whether Oosbeg or Persian, and they moreover cherish a strong fanatical antipathy against the latter people. The Affghauns have little reason to fear us, and they derive benefit from their commercial intercourse with our Indian provinces: we should therefore look upon them as our natural allies.

If the Affghauns, as a nation, were determined to resist Russian invasion of India, the difficulties of the march would be rendered wellnigh insurmountable; for though Affghaunistaun is a country through which an unopposed European army could without great difficulty move, its natural advantages are so many, that the resolute people occupying its fastnesses could greatly check, if not altogether prevent, the advance of an enemy into it; while they could greatly straiten, or altogether withhold, the supplies for which these invaders would otherwise look to them. It may safely be assumed, that however desirous the Russians might be to invade British India, they would not attempt to *force* their way to it, either from the north or west, through Affghaunistaun. They would hardly attempt to push through, and leave in their rear, a warlike nation of adverse highlanders, even if these stood alone in their hostility; but in the crisis supposed, we should join heart and hand with the Affghauns, and give them such aid as would almost certainly enable them to repel, on their very frontiers, the forces of any league that might be formed against ours.

At the period when we apprehended invasion from the French, Mr. Elphinstone, who was sent as British ambassador to the court of Caubul, succeeded in establishing very friendly relations with the Doorraunee monarch. These were interrupted by a revolution, from the effects of which our neighbours have never recovered; but were they reunited and settled under one government, we might renew our connexion with them, and reasonably calculate upon their cordial assistance against the Russians as a common enemy: it may however be doubted whether, if certain evident schemes are allowed to take their course in Central Asia, the Affghauns will not either cease to be a nation, or lose the power fully to serve us; for the Doorraunee monarchy is virtually dead, and in their present distracted state, the Affghauns cannot offer effectual opposition to the Persians, who will be quietly used by our rivals, as an instrument to destroy the strongest barrier that could be established to protect India from invasion on the west.

Different opinions have been held regarding our fittest policy towards this people. Affghaunistaun, some have argued, in its pastoral and distracted state, is probably a better defence to our eastern possessions than it would be were it settled under one government; for in the latter case, there would be a greater extension of the fixed population, and the resources of the country would be more generally brought into action; therefore by using our influence to restore it to order, we should perhaps but be making provision for an invading enemy: and, it has been added, it might be impolitic in us to aid the re-establishment of one ruler, instead of the many chiefs of opposed interests with whom the Russians would have to treat for the means of advancing to the Indus, because none of these would be disposed to admit foreigners into their states, or to assist them in any way, unless they were influenced by motives of interest or alarm; for the favour of such chiefs as were to be bribed, we could bid as high as our enemies, and by sending a few of our disciplined troops into the country of these brave mountaineers, to assist them in making the most of their natural defences, we could enable them to set all invaders at naught.

The last proceeding would be expedient in either case, and there is some plausibility in the first arguments, but in objection to them recurs the danger that the different Affghaun parties will be subjected by the Persians; if not entirely, at least to such an extent as to incapacitate them from being very useful to us hereafter. But even if we could feel satisfied that the Persians would not encroach upon our neighbours, and that the latter would remain the disunited inhabitants of a generally barren, because pastoral, country, it is questionable whether it would be wise in us to leave them thus.

The rulers of petty Affghaun states, cannot have the motives to oppose foreign invasion of India that would be felt by a monarch whose dignity and interests would in many ways be associated with ours; neither would they feel the same reasons for remaining steadfast in alliances that might be made with them by the distant British Government; and there would probably be as much difficulty in managing their conflicting interests, as in opposing the enemy. Singly, the chief of a small state could not offer effectual opposition to an European invader, and it would be easy to gain him by encouraging his ambition against his rivals at home, or doubly to profit by it, by directing it on India.

It would require great inducements to tempt a reigning king, from a sure and profitable alliance with us (his protecting power), into an undertaking which, at best doubtful, would entail ruin upon him if it failed; and it is difficult to believe that the intrigues of our enemies could so deaden the jealousy of an Affghaun sovereign, and so totally supersede our influence at his court, as to induce him to let the Russians establish themselves throughout his dominions; which they must do in order to the regular invasion of India. The Russians could offer an Affghaun sovereign nothing but promises, the fulfilment of which would depend on their success; but supposing always that they could hold out expectations sufficiently dazzling to seduce a mónarch in instance, from honourable certain empire, to the unworthy chance of greater, and that he should prove venal, with the hold that we should have upon him, we should be able to bribe up to our enemies' price, in case it were worth while to do so: at worst, after some years' friendly communication with this nation, we should not be without friends among them, and early as it would be necessary for their king to manifest his intentions, if they proved treacherous, we should have time enough to excite a revolution and make a party for ourselves, or forcibly to occupy some passes leading from this mountainous country, so as to keep the war out of our own as long as possible.

Moreover, with regard to the notion of our deriving security from the existence of many parties in Affghaunistaun, it is to be remarked, that at present the country is not shared by many chiefs of opposed interests, but unequally divided between two families, —rebel and ex-royalist: there may be jealousies between the different members of the rebel house, but so long as the Suddozyes retain a portion of the country, the Baurickzye Sirdars must keep together for the sake of their common cause.

Supposing these two families to preserve their relative positions till the anticipated day of invasion, the Russians would find a ready ally in the exroyalists: with this aid they would hardly be a match for us and the other party, if we coalesced, since we should be in possession of the greatest portion of a strong country, through which their route must lie. But this assumes, what is doubtful, that all the Affghaun people subject to the Baurickzye Sirdars would make party with them; for, not to reason upon their desiring change from the oppression of these petty despots, the right of the Suddozye family to the supreme government has hitherto been considered sacred by the Doorraunees, and there would always be a strong feeling in their favour if they put themselves forward. Even though the Baurickzyes should entirely deprive the Suddozye family of rule in Affghaunistaun, for some years to come the name of the latter would serve invaders as a war-cry to raise as many adherents as they would pay for; but I conceive that I am putting unlikely cases, and that the Persians assuredly will advance, and settle the rival claims—by destroying both.

Could the Shah of Irân content himself with driving out the Suddozyes from the ancient capital of Khorassaun, the remainder of the once great Doorraunnee empire would probably remain in the hands of the Baurickzye Sirdars. These might bequeath their states to their descendants, or themselves be supplanted by other upstarts; or possibly, a chief, such as the present ruler of Caubul, would form the different states into one, which, if left to itself, we might expect to see undergo a series of petty revolutions, similar to those which destroyed the monarchy: but to recur to the grand danger; if the Persian monarch takes Heraut, he will not be disposed to rest long on his arms there, and he will march farther eastward, if the Baurickzye Sirdars do not submit to retain their states under the bond of allegiance to his crown:—in either of which cases, the road to India would be greatly opened for the Russians.

The preceding speculations* are built upon the belief that Russia has established a paramount influence over Persia. In order to show reasons for this opinion, I must refer to the circumstances of our political connexion with the latter country in 1800.

The continually threatened invasion of India by Zemaun Shah, Doorraunee, induced Lord Wellesley to form a defensive alliance against this restless monarch with Futteh Ali Shah, Cujjer, who readily came into the Governor-General's views, as he had recently failed in two invasions of Khorassaun. In January, 1801, Captain, afterwards Sir John Mal-

* This chapter was first printed in the Calcutta Courier, 2nd and 3rd of July, 1831. My English Editor deeming it too long for entire republication with the journal, cut off the latter portion, which I now restore, as it contains some arguments that (justified, like the foregoing anticipations, by recent events) closely bear upon the existing politics of Persia and Affghaunistaun.—Note to Second Edition.

colm, concluded a treaty with the Court of Tehraun, the leading article of which stipulated that the Shah should attack the Affghauns on their west, whenever they advanced east to invade Hindoostân, and that his majesty should make no peace with them, unless they promised to refrain from aggressing us. For this the English government engaged to give the Cujjer king every necessary assistance, in the event of his being attacked by the Affghauns.

The same year relieved us from fear of invasion by the latter people; for Zemaun Shah, while intent upon his favourite scheme of foreign conquest, was deposed and blinded by his brother Mahmood,—the extent of whose ambition was to have the means of indulging in idle sensuality at home. But the first article of our treaty with the king of Persia, led to a more important one; Zemaun Shah's menaced attack being but a link in the great chain of dangers which at this time surrounded our empire in the East.

Zemaun Shah projected the invasion of India on his accession to the throne of Caubul in 1793, about which time he received a secret embassy from Tippoo Sahib, who proposed to attack the infidel foreigners by concert from the north and south, so as to destroy them from off the face of Hindoostân.*

From the time of his signing the treaty of Serin-

* Vide Sultaun Tippoo's secret correspondence with Zemaun Shah —As. An. Reg. 1799.

gapatam, Tippoo had devoted himself with increased passion to intrigues with every eastern power, foreign or domestic, whom he could possibly hope to excite against the British, and he had especially endeavoured to form a close offensive alliance with our declared enemy the French, who were now in Egypt, professing to have gained the first step towards the destruction of British empire in India.

The sedulously prosecuted intrigues of the French in Hindoostân, had led to the growth of other strong factions in their favour there, and their now undisguised and desperate exertions to ruin our power through our commerce, made it expedient for the British Government, by every means, to prevent the extension of their influence in Asia. Our ambassador at Tehraun was able, apparently, to show the Shah a common danger, for the second article of the aforesaid treaty bound the English and Persian nations in close alliance against the French.

By this article it was agreed, that in the event of French troops attempting to form a settlement on any island or shore of Persia, the two allied powers should co-operate for their extirpation. It was engaged, moreover, that no individual Frenchman even should be permitted to reside in Persia; and the Shah's 'firmaun' authorized the governors of his provinces to disgrace or slay any person of this nation who attempted to pass their boundaries, or to obtain footing in any place.

The exaggerated tone of the Persian monarch's

professions was a true index to their value: not clearly understanding his position with regard to two nations of Europe, who addressed him from different parts of the East, and ignorant of their comparative power to serve or injure him, Futteh Ali Shah made friends with those who seemed nearest,—the splendour of whose embassy, while it evidenced their greatness, was flattering to his vanity,—but probably without being able to discern much community of interest in an alliance with either party. He might with some reason have repented of the ignoble temper displayed in the latter part of his treaty with us against the French, but it was not necessary for him to send a mission to Buonaparte in 1806,* nor was he in any way justified when, two years afterwards, he welcomed the French General Gardanne, who arrived at his court "with the declared intention of establishing a connexion which might facilitate Napoleon's views of attacking the English in India."

The danger which at this period menaced our eastern possessions, appeared so alarming to the authorities both at home and in India, that they simultaneously despatched ambassadors to the court of Persia, to counteract the designs of the French there; but such a change had been wrought in the Shah's disposition, that when General Malcolm arrived at Bushire, on an embassy from the Governor-General, Lord Minto, he was refused permission to

* Meerza Reza, the ambassador on this occasion, concluded a treaty with Napoleon at Finkinstein.

come to the capital as before, and directed to treat with the viceroy of Shiraz. To this indignity he would not submit, but memorializing against it to no purpose, he returned in anger to Calcutta, when the Governor-General gave orders to prepare an expedition to sail to the Persian Gulf.

However, Sir Harford Jones, who shortly after arrived at Bushire as plenipotentiary direct from the English crown, encountered not the obstacles that had been thrown in the way of the Governor-General's envoy, and taking a different view of the matter, he proceeded to join the Persian court at Tehraun, and entered into a negotiation for a fresh treaty.

Futteh Ali Shah had by this time been made aware of his inability to resist the *Russians*, who in the last ten years had advanced their frontier four hundred miles,—"from the north of the Caucasus to the banks of the Arraxes,"—and his majesty's fears inclined him to prefer the alliance of those who promised him the best assistance against this colossal enemy. Napoleon's professed object in sending General Gardanne to the Shah was, in order to concert with him an invasion of Russia's eastern provinces; though the principal cause of the mission is declared to have been "the emperor's wish to strike England in the heart of her Asiatic possessions."* The Persian monarch, however, was too

* Vide de Bourrienne's Memoirs.—"Gardanne's embassy," says this writer, "was at first conceived on a much grander scale than that on

wise to discard the English until he could be sure that the French would better assist him against the Russians; and as his ministers and the French envoy were mutually employed in endeavours to sound and circumvent each other, it is not surprising that their negotiations came to nothing. During their stay, the officers attached to the imperial mission assisted to discipline a Persian corps, and the Shah's favour towards General Gardanne went to the unprecedented extent of creating an order of knighthood for him; but after a while, seeing reason to doubt whether Napoleon could fulfil either his promises or designs, perhaps alarmed at the report of hostile preparations in India, and, above all, irresistibly tempted by a high bribe of English gold, he (to use political language) returned to his first friendship, and dismissed the French mission from his court, with less ceremony than was courteous.

Events in Europe had now added the Russians to the number of our enemies; therefore we were able to extend our engagements with the Persian Government, so as to suit the policy of both contracting parties. In a treaty concluded by Sir Harford Jones, in March, 1809, it was engaged that the

which it was executed. Napoleon had resolved to send to the Shah of Persia four thousand infantry, commanded by chosen and experienced officers, ten thousand muskets, and fifty pieces of cannon; and I also know that orders were given for the execution of this design." * * * * "Circumstances," adds he, "did not permit the emperor to give the mission all the importance he desired."—Alluding, it is presumed to Napoleon's engagements at the treaty of Tilsit.

English Government should subsidize* the Persians as long as they were at war with the Russians, on condition of their aiding to repel any attempt of the French; or in other words, as Sir John Malcolm justly observes, "for the fulfilment of the engagements which they had contracted ten years before."

Upon the settlement of this treaty, Futteh Ali Shah sent Meerza Abool Hussan Khan, as his friendly ambassador, to the throne of England.† The Governor-General's envoy again repaired to the presence at Tehraun, to efface all unpleasant impressions, and the Shah condescended to extreme graciousness, in order to atone for his late "hauteur" and insincerity.

The war in Spain at this period drew Napoleon's attention from the East, and he found no subsequent opportunity to renew his intrigues in Persia, so that Futteh Ali Shah's second promises were not put to the test; but our experience of the character of a Persian court is quite sufficient to warn us against placing much trust in its professions. Friendship indeed

* The subsidy was settled to be 120,000 tomauns (about 100,000*l.*) per annum; a supply of 16,000 stand of arms; 20 field pieces complete; and such numbers as could be spared of artillery-men and officers to instruct the Persian army.—*Malcolm's Pol. India*, vol. i. chap. 6.

† On his return to Persia, in 1810, Meerza Abool Hussan Khan was accompanied by Sir Gore Ouseley, Bart., K. L. S, Envoy Extraordinary from the King of England, who towards the end of 1813, mediated a treaty between Persia and Russia. Sir Gore Ouseley returned to England *viá* Russia in 1814.

between states is a mere name; and though the Shah's conduct must be borne in mind, the chief question for us to consider is, what it is most for his interest to do henceforward.

Since we destroyed French influence in Persia, English soldiers have fought against Russia under the Persian banner, and England having felt particularly interested in checking the growing power of the northern emperor since Napoleon fell, the ministers of Britain and Irân have held very friendly counsel together. It might not be altogether foreign to the present question to inquire, whether by drawing close to Persia, and displaying her jealousy of Russia, England has not added a great spur to the Czar's ambition against his eastern neighbours,—and whether by our half measures of support to the latter people, we have not made them an easier, because a more confident and tangible prey; but this consideration apart, whatever we may have done for the Persians, we have not prevented them from being completely conquered by the Muscovites; the most vigorous assistance that we could now give the Shah, would hardly enable him to drive the Russians so far back as to secure Persia against their future encroachments,—and nothing else would serve him. The time is past when Georgia would have put herself under Persian rule! Russia's best energies will be employed to improve the resources of the fine country last acquired south of the Caucasus, and her special care will be, to fill it with good troops that she can pour across the Arraxes at a day's warning.

I humbly conceive that in the existing conditions of Russia and Persia, we can form no compact with the latter people that will contain what must be the essence of every effectual bond between nations—common interest. While there was hope that the Russians could be kept back, this feeling existed; but having regularly forced their way to a commanding frontier, the Russians have so manifested their superiority, as to reverse the policy of Persia, and oblige her to be friends with a nation who, having proved themselves irresistible as enemies, may now be very serviceable as allies.

The Persians must be aware that they cannot of themselves withstand the Russians; and even supposing (England and Russia being at war) that they should desire to commence a fresh struggle, with our hearty co-operation, a glance at Irân, and at the relative positions of Russia, England, and British India, will show the advantages that our rivals would still have in such a contest. It is about 450 miles from the Russian frontier on the Arras,* by the high-road *viâ* Tabreez, to Tehraun. The nearest point to the capital at which we could land troops is Bushire,† distant more than 700 miles, and our

* From the Russian frontier below the Arras, in Talish, where troops might be collected for war without positive breach of peace, it is but 326 miles to Tehraun, *viâ* the port of Reshdt.

† It is more than twice as far from *Bunder Abbas* to Shiraz, but the road is much easier, and by taking it, from 450 to 500 miles of sea voyage would be saved.

nearest point to it is Bombay; so that it is impossible to say what the Russians might not do before English help could reach the Persians. Whatever forces we could send from a great distance, the Russians could out-number from their adjoining frontier; and to meet them we must march up to the capital, for they would have no object in coming south of it. Thus the expense of our share in the war would be very great: nor would our portion of risk be inconsiderable; for if our Persian allies wavered (and they are neither the most resolute nor constant people in the world), we should have many miles to retreat to our shipping; and our defeat in Persia would produce a very injurious effect upon popular opinion in the countries beyond;—in India itself.

I am not unaware of the effectual check that we might oppose to the advance of the Russians on India, if we raised and sustained all Persia against them, but question whether the end of a war waged in the latter country, for such purpose, would repay the vast means necessary to prosecute it there: from Russia's strong position too in regard to her neighbour,—commanding, as she does, entrance into the Shah's finest provinces south of the Arras, and those which lie at the base of the Caspian sea,—there would be continual danger that she might obtain such advantages as would induce the Persian government to patch up a peace at our expense.

Little as the Persians in general may like their neighbours, the reflecting among them must see the advantages to be derived from friendly contact with their late foes. The Russians can impart to the Persians, on a reasonable scale, and with good effect, systems which we have for some years been importing in parcels, to little purpose: in particular, they can lend the Shah a sufficient number of cheaply paid officers, to discipline an army which will protect and keep in order his present dominions, and enable him to take much valuable country both east and west,* in lieu of the provinces ceded to them: and though

* By merely permitting a few thousands of his disciplined soldiers to desert, the emperor can add such force to the Shah's ranks as will ensure them victory over any eastern army opposed to them. Allusion has been made in the journal to the number of Russian deserters in the Persian service: to these might be added many who would gladly escape to the easy service of the Shah. In my observation about Russian *officers* being lent to drill the Shah's army, I may seem to have forgotten the advice which always has been, and still is, pressed upon the British Government—to send a sufficient number of its officers upon this duty. It is without doubt advisable to encourage to the utmost the introduction of Englishmen into the Persian army, but there are difficulties in the plan of sending many British covenanted servants. The pay of one English officer will suffice for many Russian subalterns;—a great consideration for the Shah, if he is to pay them, and a great consideration for us, if we are to send many; (and many are required.) A case might occur, like that of the last war, when, however much we might wish the discomfiture of the Russians, we could not, consistently with our friendly relations with their sovereign, permit men of our own army to direct hostile operations against them; and it would not exactly suit the Shah to have soldiers who would choose in what quarrel to fight. Russia desires to discipline the Persians, in order to push them as conquerors into countries through which she may require a road to India. England wishes to make the Persians strong, in case she should need their aid against a power of which she is naturally jealous. Between her two wooers, Persia should get a good army at a small expense, but she will be sometimes puzzled which to favour, for though the Shah would naturally rather trust his army to Englishmen than to his late conquerors, still should he be intent upon extending his empire towards the *Indus*, he might fancy that Englishmen would not be very cordial in that service.

they will do this for the sake of their own policy, it cannot be denied that Persia has no better course than to let her interests be so advanced, since she is of herself unable to forward them.

The Persians, doubtless, will not in any case readily submit their councils to Russian guidance, for they must long be distrustful of their conquerors, —"et dona ferentes." The Shah may be dazzled with the prospect of widely extending his empire through the assistance of his brother the Czar, but as he must ever feel the yoke of so forcible a friendship, it may be questioned how far he would be willing to break with the only nation who might possibly assist to emancipate him from its trammels. We may work upon this feeling so as to delay Russo-Persian schemes, but we cannot altogether prevent them, for Persia's natural ambition, as well as her obvious policy, will direct her arms to the vast field that invites her sway, and it would be difficult to say by what arguments we should prevail on our friends not to seize valuable countries which are within their grasp, merely because we anticipate danger to our eastern colonies from the extension of their empire in that direction. The Russians will be ever prompting and assisting the Shah's ambition, and whatever professions they may make to us in this respect, they can easily violate them with an innocent face.

Seeing then, that for the present at least, it is rather Persia's interest to be friends with Russia than with England, and that her policy has a tendency, however distantly, to endanger our eastern possessions, we should make ourselves as independent of the Shah as possible, and as far as we safely can, thwart his ambitious views in the direction of Hindoostân. The first great means of effecting this that offers itself for consideration is, our interfering to restore the monarchy of the Affghauns, and giving this people strength to resist the encroachments of their enemies, so as to establish them as a solid barrier on our west. It appears that this nation's political interests are in a great measure connected with ours, and that the extension of our trade beyond the Indus must chiefly depend upon their restoration to order. I do not myself doubt that the British Government might effect this, by lending itself heartily to such a measure; but those who are better qualified for so important a task must decide, whether the prospect of Persia's extending her empire upon the ruins of the Doorraunee monarchy be so near as to make our immediate interference necessary, and whether or no the embarrassments with which we might surround ourselves by such a policy, would outweigh the advantages to be expected from it.

The greatest objection, perhaps, to our directly interfering to build up the Affghauns, and supporting them as a nation, is the danger of our being thereby embroiled in a quarrel with Persia;—an event in every way to be deprecated, which our rivals would of course do their best to promote. If, in the present posture of affairs, the last-suggested plan should be deemed injudicious, it at least behoves the British Government to pay the most watchful attention to the politics of all the countries between the Oural, Arras, and Indus rivers, and, I would humbly suggest, be prepared to seize the first good opportunity of taking part in those of Affghaunistáun; for until it does, the anticipated intrigues of Russia can neither be well known, nor effectually counteracted. The effect indeed of her influence upon Persia may be in a great measure watched by those who are at the court of the latter country, but concerning the progress of her schemes to the northward, we now cannot have any certain information. When Russian influence begins to work in *Toorkestaun*, it will be necessary that we have footing there also; but that we obviously cannot obtain until we have secured the friendship of the intermediate people.

It is possible that the Suddozye tribe may themselves be able to restore the royal government in Affghaunistaun; in which case, we could enter into such political and commercial relations with them as might be convenient; binding ourselves to no particular line of conduct, but quietly doing our best to strengthen our neighbours, or regulating our future policy according to our increased knowledge of their resources, and experience of their character. Again, if the now rebel Sirdars should succeed in altogether ejecting the royal family, or if, in consequence of the Persians taking Heraut, the Baurickzye chiefs should be left in possession of the rest of the country, we might form such connexions with them as best suited the politics of the times. In the latter case, it should be the especial object of the British Government to form an alliance with the chief ruling at Caubul; this post being one to which we can have easy access, which is sufficiently near our possessions to warrant our insisting upon its not falling into the hands of those who may be made a means of aggressing us, and which in a military point of view is of the greatest importance, inasmuch as that, situated at a convenient distance from our frontier, and in the midst of a naturally strong country, it commands two of the three routes by which an European army must march to invade Hindoostân.

What might be the precise object, or the effect, of such an attempt on the part of Russia, it is not the design of the present treatise to inquire. My endeavour has been to show, that the Russians, having of late years gained a vast increase of political influence in Central Asia, are pursuing a system calculated still further to extend it, and that if certain of their schemes succeed, they will so lessen the difficulties now opposed to such an undertaking as the invasion of India, as to make it very probable that they would attempt it in the event of their going to war with us. Their plans would be formed according to the success of their intrigues, but hostile nations are seldom deterred by the greatest risks and difficulties from attempting to hurt each other, and it is probable that Russia when at war with England, would be so checked in Europe, that she would redouble her exertions to injure us in Asia. I am far from apprehending that Russia's utmost efforts could subvert our eastern empire; and I believe, with the generality of those who reason upon the extent of our means in India, that by judiciously using the same, we should be able (Deo favente) to give any invading army a very good beating. But this is not a point to be decided by any number of persons' opinions, nor is it possible for the wisest to determine what would be the result of such a collision. It is not doubted, that the mere circumstance of the Russians being in a situation enabling them at any time seriously to *threaten* an attack upon India, would be a cause of constant great anxiety and expense to the British Government; and therefore perhaps it will be conceded, that the more barriers we can oppose to such a danger, and the further we can keep it from us, the better.

In the preceding paragraphs, I have ventured to urge the speedy adoption of precautionary measures against this growing danger *abroad;* in conclusion, however, I would remark, that whatever may be our foreign policy, it is above every thing requisite that we trust mainly to our own resources in India;

timely and skilfully appropriating to the purpose, the abundant means that this country possesses of defending itself. The great natural strength of western and northern India, is so clearly seen on glancing the eye up the Indus, from the sea to the parallel of Cashmere, and down again from this natural fortress of Hindoostân, through the Punjaub to the Hyphasis, still southward through the great sandy desert to the *Runn* of Cutch, that it is needless to particularize it; nor is it great boasting to say, that sincerely assisted by the native chiefs whose states lie between the British frontier and the Indus, we might hope to "burn the fathers of all the Russians" who could be sent to invade us.

As yet we have not interfered to strengthen the assailable side of Hindoostân by means of the noble river by which it is bounded:—the line on which, it is presumed, an invading enemy would be met, and on which therefore we should repose in established strength; feeling ourselves at home in the position, and commanding there supplies of every sort, in full, unforced quantities. Concerning the advantages of this river as an advanced line of defence against invasion from the westward, it will be sufficient to remark that troops and stores might be conveyed to it directly from England,—so from any of our foreign possessions, or from either of the three Presidencies of British India itself,—and that from the sea up to Attock, if not also through the tributary streams that divide the Punjaub, communication might be carried on by means of steam-boats during nearly the whole year.* The military reader may be startled at the recommendation of so extended a line of defence, but it must be remembered that we know where to collect our strength on it; since whichever way the Russians might march overland to invade India, they could only débouche from the mountains of Affghaunistaun by two routes, so that we might expect them at Attock, or at some spot near the island fort Bukkar:†—in case of threatened invasion, our troops would of course strongly occupy the hill country west of Cashmere, and an army would also be collected at Bombay, or some other convenient part on the western coast; thus even if the invaders succeeded in forcing our first line near either of the above points, they would march on under increased risks, since retiring upon our reserves through the strong country yet intervening either way to the British provinces, we should ever present a front to our enemies, while an army might be sent either from the hills, or from the sea-coast, to take them in the rear.

However it is not my wish to detail a plan of

* The season when it would be most difficult to beat up these rivers (the rains) is one during which no army could keep the field.

† There is indeed a road, through the mountains, from Candahar to Dera Ghazee Khan, which we know to have been marched by Asiatic troops; but according to the best information that I could obtain, it is hardly practicable for an European army. However my informants were merchants, who do not travel the latter road for fear of the lawless tribes through whose mountains it passes, and perhaps they magnified its difficulties.

defensive operations in India, but to press the expediency of our employing the present time of peace, in assuming situations which would enable us promptly to use the fullest means of defence against any foreign attack; and I humbly conceive it to be very necessary that we should now obtain the entire navigation of the Indus, as well as free communication from the interior provinces, to certain well-chosen spots on its bank, at which to establish entrepôts for our trade;—objects which are surely to be obtained by friendly negotiation with the rulers of Sinde and the Punjaub, and which, as they must ultimately tend to the great benefit of these princes, are the means best calculated to cement our friendship. The long scrupulously forbearing conduct of the British government towards the independent native chiefs of western and northern India, has dispelled much of the jealousy that they naturally entertained against its rapidly extended power, and while it has stood aloof, their political circumstances have thrown them all within the sphere of its control, so that it would appear that we have but to step forward to secure the objects necessary to our commercial and political welfare. We only need to bring ourselves into friendly contact with these princes, to convince them how true is the policy we profess, and how greatly their interests are connected with ours, and when satisfied of their cordial friendship, we might with more reason than at present set at nought the designs of our rivals. In this way, a system of defence will be quietly organized by the lucrative extension of our trade, and our political influence will go hand in hand with our commerce into the countries beyond. In a word, with reference to all the preceding remarks it may be said, that when we have freely opened the Indus to our trade, and secured the friendship of the neighbouring people beyond, Russia may float her commodities up the Oxus, but we will undersell her:—she may float armies up instead of manufactures, and we shall be prepared to meet them.

THE END.

APPENDIX A.

WHEN I travelled through Affghaunistaun in 1830, none of the native merchants whom we consulted, seemed to think that *wool* could be profitably exported from their country. Since that period, however, Colonel Pottinger has effectually opened the Indus, and given to the Affghauns, as well as to the Beloches, means of easily reaching a near great market, where they may exchange as much of this raw material as they can produce, for the manufactured goods into which we will work it up.

A decided trade in the wool of "sheep pastured in those parts of India bordering on the Indus," commenced at Bombay in 1833, when 69,944 lbs. were exported. It has since increased at an extraordinary rate, no less than 2,444,091 lbs. having been exported from Bombay in the official year of 1837.

The European demand for this article being unlimited, how earnestly should we endeavour to facilitate the means of its transport by the Indus, so as to enable even the far Nomade tribes to send their fleeces, at some profit, to a market from which they will take our various manufactures in return. It must be British vigour that will really keep this fine river open, and if private enterprise is not strong enough to make a good beginning, the British Government should encourage it.—I may here note a remarkable fact, to show how much we and the Affghauns are mutually interested in making the Indus a cheap channel of trade. Syud Keramut Ali, in 1834, got from merchants with whom he was intimate, musters of all the manufactured "Russian goods" imported *viâ* Bokhara, that were then selling at the usual good profit in the Caubul bazâr. I lately gave a set of these to a gentleman interested in our trade with the East, when he ascertained from an experienced merchant to whom they were forwarded, that more than two-thirds of them were of Glasgow and Manchester make. This corroborates a statement made by Mr. Masson, in his valuable "Report upon the Trade of Caubul," which was published by order of the Government of India.*

* See a small pamphlet which was compiled, I think, under the direction of Macgregor Laird, Esq., when it was proposed to form a British Company for the navigation of the Indus.